WAKEY WAKE-UP RISE & SHINE

An inspirational guidebook using true events along with the insights and lessons that presented themselves along the way

By

Linda Jane W

Originally Self-published via Amazon KDP March 2020

Second Edition April 2022.

ISBN 9798804567430

Preface

I always knew I had a book in me and my life has been so filled with drama, excitement, fun, tragedy, insights, love, loss, growth and bouncing back with 'Tiggeresque' vigour after every single thing, that I thought it would make a great read. I even had the name picked out 'Never A Dull Moment'.

What I didn't realise is that at a very young and highly energetic fifty-two years old my life would give me the reason, time, space and subject matter, to actually get on with it.

Because of my vast energy reserves I wondered if I burned myself out, hence my heart almost gave up on me. However, the truth is that my overenthusiasm, blinded me to what was going on around me and I missed the messages, the lessons, the signs and signals, because I was determined that nothing and no-one was going to take me down. I kept bouncing back up regardless of what life threw at me and I was so proud of that, and my mother is in constant amazement at my resilience. Little did I know that I was naively sending out messages to The Universe that I was this was acceptable to me, and so The Universe (my soul) kept sending me more of the same.

Indeed, at some point during this quest my curiosity was sparked about Carl Jung's twelve "Archetypal Identities" which are mentioned in card 6 of The Balance Procedure, when we're asked to consider which of the twelve we can relate to. Given my unflinching resilience, I realised that I could relate to the "hero" archetype

But that was way out of balance, hence I was attracting incident after incident to triumph over and then tale tells of daring do in true Beowulf fashion.

If only I'd slowed down enough to even see the signs instead of making like that Bat Out of Hell and not seeing the signs ahead until it was way too late! Maybe that's part of me because in Chinese astrology I was born in the year of the Fire Horse and apparently Chinese people do what they can to avoid having a child in that year as we're crazy and too much trouble! Stop Linda! This resilience is signalling "bring it on, I can take it" – when instead, all I had to do, was ask myself "why is this coming my way again? What did I miss here?"

I've been guided through so many lifetimes within this lifetime and so I have a fairly wise head on my shoulders, although I have to say that I've wondered throughout my life how an intelligent, quick witted, businesswoman can be such an airhead at times! It has been fun having both sides as it surprises people constantly. My first ex-husband recently told me that I'd always been wild. I hadn't seen myself like that, just as fun and adventurous. With that, unfortunately, came ungrounded as I didn't have the awareness. Instead I grabbed life by the horns and rode it with plenty of "yee-ha's" and "whoohoo's" but, wow what fun.

A writer friend of mine recently returned from a Writing Workshop where she learned that you cannot write a Memoir until something life changing and significant has happened to you - well it did, it was and it totally changed my life from the party girl that never missed a night out or an excuse to have fun; to a non-smoker, non-drinker, clean living – but far from party pooper girl. However, I really had to work hard to survive let alone thrive. Everything changed from point break but the upside is that I got to write this Teaching Memoir and in this revamped edition I've removed much of the drama and steered more towards it being a guidebook as my aim is to inspire change and so it's important that you relate your own circumstances and make your own decisions, using my experiences as a benchmark for change.

Indeed, it's well known in healing circles that the reason that we become Healers in the first place is because we need healing ourselves and so are naturally drawn to healing modalities which always start with ourselves. We then graduate to others as we experience the benefits first hand and being the Healer types that we are, we want to share this with others to help and empower them. As we begin to see the world and energies differently because we're working with this newfound skill and witnessing the power of alternatives, so begins our journey in earnest.

As a result of my life to-date, I've grown into a strong and successful woman, I was a 'YUPPIE' in London for thirteen years in Telecommunications sales. I love the finer things in life – I am a Leo after all – I've been to most of the Caribbean islands, I've owned several houses, I own a stretch of riverbank and I bought a modest house in Spain and project managed the refurbishment. However, my life is quite simple these days, gaining pleasures from birds singing and peace in my heart and soul. In my London days it was well known that I didn't take any nonsense from anyone and I said it how it was – very eloquently I might add! We're not talking Little Britain's Vicki Pollard here darlings, we're talking Boudica or Cleopatra, so you'll find no sob stories in this guidebook! That is still an integral part of me but as I've mellowed and wised-up and recognised what I can and cannot tolerate in my life, I rarely have to bring my fierce side out of the attic – although when I do, I do. Indeed, Igor's favourite expression when I verbally pounced on someone who had pushed my patience too far and overstepped the mark, was "They picked on the wrong hippie there didn't they!"

Whilst healing myself from my memoire-provoking, life changing moment, I pretty much declined medical intervention and took myself off medication with the exception of blood thinners and a medication to maintain elasticity of my blood vessels whilst my heart repaired as I realised that even stubbornness had its limits and there was balance to be found if I was to live to inspire and guide others along their own path to wherever they wanted to go!

I originally started to write this book five-and-a-half months after my heart failed, with a functionality of just 17%, because the voyage of discovery was incredulous and I knew straight away that I needed to share it. Unless you've been through it personally, you have no idea of the far reaching ramifications that come with any comparable event. The medics didn't expect me to survive the night, my friends were preparing for the worst – but so soon afterwards I felt so full of life, energy and motivation – all because, as a Holistic Practitioner and Tutor, I decided to put my money where my mouth was and strut my stuff. I first published ten months down the line from my awakening and as I revamp and relaunch, nearly three years in total have passed since my world changed forever – for the better!

What I continued to realise over the coming three years was that, just when I thought I was back to normal, I'd have a breakthrough which would up-level me. I'd be alarmed at the thought that I hadn't been back to me after all, but hoped that maybe I was now?

The more this happened, the more it slowly dawned on me, just how close a call I'd had and just how much had been stripped from the life that I'd taken for granted every day. Even having the energy to dance (rather than just move about a bit) or to sing a whole song without getting breathless became a real achievement. I'd have occasional "wow" moments when I'd feel an energy shift, as if my energy had lifted onto a different plain. One memorable occasion, on the acupuncture table, such an energy shift happened as this new energy swept through my body I felt level, regular and calm and on a higher dimension. It was almost like levitating whilst remaining fully grounded.

It was moments like this, as more time passed, made me realise that I was actually growing beyond who I had been and I was surpassing the original me. Because I'd decided to stay in this lifetime and go through a "dark night of the soul" to act upon my "Wake-up call" in order to achieve an "awakening", I was shedding more of what was no longer required, I was looking at things in a different way, evolving, having setbacks (emotional, physical and spiritual) and coming back even stronger from them.

I've developed a crazy sense of humour over the years and so hope to bring light to the darker times of my recovery mentioned herein – so enjoy the ride, be inspired and be aware that in drawing inspiration from whatever you read and take from this guidebook, the entire concept of what you're about to read, is that you must take responsibility for yourself and it is bloomin' hard work to do that, but I promise you, it is totally worth it, and if you're going through a medical drama then what greater way to spend your recuperation time – it's got to be better that sitting on your derrière watching daytime television for sure.

It's also worth a mention here, that at this moment in history, we are two years into the Coronavirus pandemic. In July 2019, I knew that I was preparing for something big and I'd written in my journal App to that effect. Little did I know!

Indeed, during late 2020, a BBC radio news report stated that in the UK alone from March-July 2020, 800 younger people had died of heart disease that should not have died. They apparently went undiagnosed because lockdown reduced their ability to see a medic; or the fear of going out kept them at home and they did not call for help. As the pandemic gathered momentum, waiting lists for medics increased massively, suicide rates apparently increased by 200%, depression and physical ailments are being exacerbated due to the isolation and my dear friend Dougie has passed which the pandemic was instrumental in in so very many ways. His story is not, unfortunately, unique, so I feel that it is more important than ever, to use holistic practices daily to maintain our health by listening to our intuition and learning the skills to maintain our mind and body.

Regardless of your political views, i personally feel that we need to take responsibility for our own wellbeing, get in touch with ourselves, our bodies, our minds and make best friends with our intuition because these are our truest guides to empower us along the journey of life and become the best version of ourselves – i.e. who we were born to be. Our body speaks to us through ailments, accidents and wellbeing so we need to learn to listen to what our body is telling us, and to act on it. Indeed, the clues are all around us in so many ways, ways that most people are oblivious to and this is what I will share with you within these pages. We can then integrate every bit of help that is sent our way rather than wait on a list to be saved.

On chatting with Tanya my Yoga Instructor one day, we agreed that there's no replacement for taking responsibility for our own health. We can go to the Doctor, Hospital, Holistic Therapist for them to use their skills to rebalance us and set the healing process going, but the actual healing has to come from us as an individual. It's our body that does the work, we just need a nudge sometimes as we can get too engrossed in the story of the happenings, whether they be medical, spiritual or emotional.

We can get our energy centres (chakras) rebalanced but we have to learn how to do it for ourselves.

We can go for Reiki but we have to take steps to keep yourself healthy, including listening to and actioning the intuits that come our way in the following days.

I feel as Healers we can empower people's mind, body and spirit to heal, but we have to show everyone how to do it for themselves rather than us take responsibility for their welfare, which in itself, is overwhelming.

It took me five years to build a holistic practice in UK but as much as I valued and appreciated them, I became overwhelmed by the sense of responsibility for my regular clients. I intuitively felt that I wanted to take them to the next level and I wanted them to learn how to heal and balance themselves through Reiki, The Balance

Procedure, mindfulness, etc (and more recently, acupressure) rather than rely on me for that. These last two years have demonstrated how important this is, I feel, and I also feel that this will be the case for quite a long time yet

As we chatted, we agreed that clients can leave the therapy room in a beautiful and blissful state but be knocked off balance emotionally in an instant with a phone call, an incident, a message. I had experienced this myself a few months ago when I'd left Jeremiah and Janet's all relaxed and calm and received a weird message - and the magic was gone, my heart went crazy and out of rhythm and that was that for another week!

After this I took it upon myself to manage the triggers differently, to learn how to bring my heart back into rhythm with acupressure, breathing exercises, Rescue Remedy, visualisations, mindfulness ... We must take our health into our own hands and that is the object of this guidebook. To inspire and empower you to do exactly that.

Acknowledgements

All of my tribe need a huge thank you for being there for me - I believe that you'll come to understand why more and more. They are my besties without a doubt, and I love them dearly. My friend Dougie asked me if I didn't live here at the time of point break, do I think that I would have survived because the friendship and sense of community here is exceptional. This mountain seems to draw Adventurers to its peak and so we agreed that everyone here already had a connection before we'd even met. This friendship, support and love made me fight to survive for sure and I most certainly wasn't ready to throw the towel in as there was still too much living to do.

As I've learned during my holistic rehabilitation, anything that could be perceived as negative occurrences were simply life's way of showing me what I needed to address that within myself in order to heighten my vibration and enjoy life all the more for it. I believe that everyone around us is a supporting actor in our own life movie and without whom the film would lose its drama and drive. Regardless of how it might have appeared at any given time, a HUGE thank you to you all for being my guiding light.

A particularly huge thank you to Pauline and to Pedro who got me down from our mountain village to the hospital pronto and without whom I'd have surely have perished and been found half eaten by my cats – all nine of them. The crazy cat lady jokes I used to crack about being eaten by my cats don't seem that funny anymore as I realised that this could very easily have become a reality at point break! Having said that, when they were kittens the previous autumn, I noticed that when one of them was unwell, someone in the litter was always with them, cuddling up and washing them for days until they were well again. Weeks after I arrived back from hospital post-heart hissyfit, I realised that one of them was always with me. They were taking turns in watching over me – I was one of the clouder, the pounce, the pillow; I was one of them – and so my thanks goes to my feline angels too.

A big thank you to Grace who gave me the confirmation that I needed whilst doing a reading for me completely unaware of my recent events and told me that I would be writing a very successful Guidebook. Ta Daaaa!

Thank you to Holly who raised the alarm to Pauline on my behalf and for her friendship, support and encouragement in bringing this book to life.

Thank you to Gary and Hayley Browne who did my photoshoot for the cover – at dawn in the Cemetery at the top of our village! I couldn't help but laugh at the irony of Gary's proposed location as I was almost a resident there in that fateful May, but his insight produced the most beautiful result for Wakey Wake-Up Rise & Shine. www.thestudiounderthewall.com

Thank you to James Redfield, Author of The Celestine Prophecy for his kind permission in allowing me to quote from his wonderful book which turbo charged me along my spiritual path over a decade ago when it found me.

Thank you to Jenny and Alan Cox for The Balance Procedure which remains a fundamental part of creating and maintaining my life and for their permission to quote from The Balance Procedure.

Thank you to Esther & Jerry Hicks and their team for their kind permissions in quoting their amazing work within Wakey Wake-Up Rise & Shine. It's well worth investigating their work further online and in their books, seminars, etc.

My Acupuncturist Jeremiah is very experienced and has a wealth of both science based and spiritual knowledge and wisdom. He's something of a guru around here and I was, and continue to be, completely blessed to have him and his wife Janet who is an amazing Herbalist, working with me, my body and my energies and I can honestly say that they are largely responsible for me still being here to tell my tale with their care, expertise and encouragement. My body was very fragile when I first rocked up and I must have been a daunting case to take on and for that I am eternally grateful.

Susan and Phil who came to visit two months after point break. Sue is an incredibly gifted Psychic Medium, Clairvoyant and Healer and whilst we were sat chatting she held my hand and I could feel her directing the healing energy my way – within 24-hours my heart was back in rhythm.

In order to protect identities, some of the names have been changed.

Contents

Section 2

Ole Ole Land

Having set the scene and tone of this book and why I was so driven to share my wisdoms with you, I'll now set the scene on how I ended up going into heart failure in the middle of an olive grove, 2400' feet up a mountain, on my own in southern Spain.

Well, I am a Leo and we do like drama. If it happened in urban UK, I honestly don't believe that I would have had the opportunity to soul search so profoundly, nor have been nurtured by the raw energy of Magic Mountain here in Andalusia.

Setting the scene is as much about the emotional rollercoaster as it is about the logistics. It's the emotional rollercoaster that led to my heart failing, not in a slushy heartbreak romcom movie way, but in a quagmire of raw, anger, resentment, fear, overenthusiasm for life and by being so bloomin' resilient that I bounced back time and again instead of throwing the towel in. We can be too forgiving and understanding and I wished I'd learned a lot of lessons sooner - two decades ago to be precise! Since becoming an Astrology student during my holistic rehabilitation, I've become aware that the comet Chiron is responsible for this aspect of my personality and that astrology can help us to understand ourselves. Indeed, these were all my own lessons – the people "misbehaving" were simply showing me what I needed to address in myself – it was written in the stars at the time of my birth - I hope you're intrigued by that! Read on ...

Briefly, to set the scene, I met Igor Parker in a bar in Essex, England where he was gigging. This very cheeky musician bounced off the stage and straight up to me and a quick-fire round of a chat up went as follows:

"Hi, I'm Igor, who are you here with?"

"I'm here on my own"

"Where's your boyfriend?"

"I haven't got one"

"You married?"

"No"

"You single?"

"Yes"

"You got kids?"

"No, I'm more of an animal lover to be honest"

"I can be a bit of an animal!"

"Yeah, I'll bet you can!"

"Do you fancy going out next week?"

"Yes, OK"

When I told my closest friend, she said "GO!" I protested that I didn't know anything about him, and she replied "Linda, someone has been brave enough to ask you out. GO!" So I did. Our relationship developed into a six-and-a-half-year long roller coaster ride which had me squealing with delight or standing tall, hands on hips spouting forth my family's historic moto "who dares meddle wi' me?!" (which I have since had tattoo'd around my forearm as a reminder!) During this time we became aware that it was likely that he was bipolar, the upside of which was a very exciting time with fabulous adventures and he really was a genius coming up with solutions to everything that life sent his way - and mine - and we had a lot of fun working on projects on his boat and my smallholding.

The downside was his depression and when his sparkly green eyes would become devoid of emotion and turn battleship grey as he stared blankly at me. The highs outweighed the lows for years, as we used my holistic practices to bring balance to us as individuals and as a couple. He managed his diet and reduced his coffee and alcohol intake really successfully until one day he announced that he liked being crazy as his magic came from chaos. I understood but it was a question of brace for impact and it did indeed become too much too often as meteor showers of chaos slammed into Planet Linda again and again. My bubble of joy was burst frequently, my patience tried, my heart broken every few months and I lived between fear of when it was going to happen again and undying optimism that it wouldn't — but it always did. It happened repeatedly in the UK, in Morocco, in Spain, in public and in private, each time leaving me bewildered and to fend for myself where I was out of my comfort zone and sometimes in a very vulnerable situation.

Every time, I was left wondering when he'd find himself again and return, all charm and smiles, his harsh words swept under the carpet as if they had never been said — but the bump under the carpet was always there. He would go AWOL, hiding in his van somewhere that he knew he wouldn't be found for a week. I would be frantic, fearing the worst. It was a nightmare, I could barely function for fear of what he might do to himself. This happened every few months and sucked the joy out of my heart, which was still reeling from the grief of divorce and exhausted from fifteen years of melodrama.

On the flip side of the coin, his wild and non-conformist ways set me free spiritually. I felt liberated mentally from the materialistic and corporate world and the conditioning of the 9-5 workplace mentality. I am eternally grateful to Igor for loosening these shackles so that I could fly high. As I did so, my energies also gathered momentum and I couldn't help but focus on my healing and holistic practices. I started to do more courses to add different therapies to my repertoire and to promote my own holistic business which became delightfully successful over the years. Our life living on the narrowboat together was pretty basic and definitely not for the faint hearted as we were completely powered by solar and a wind turbine and we often ran very low on power early into the winter evenings but we were cosy with the wood burner and watched movies that we'd downloaded and went through several laptop batteries throughout the film. Our time together was often quite magical.

Igor had some land in Spain, and we set about building a log cabin on it. Due to work commitments we could only be there for long weekends or sometimes we'd take two or three weeks to really break the back of a building phase. It was to take us four years.

Just as Spain was embracing me, Igor was becoming distant, and one day I asked "Igor, why do you talk to me like I'm an inconvenience?", he replied with full bipolar blankness "that's because you are. I don't love you, I don't even like you, you cramp my style and I don't want you here". Despite knowing that it was just another biopolar hissyfit which would pass, this time it was the straw that broke this camel's back.

Although this was far from the first time that he'd been so rude, I decided in that moment that this was not my life, not my future and I no longer consented to being spoken to like that and my energies would no longer be used on his projects, on living in fear of a verbal onslaught or worry about what I'd do, where I'd go and would anyone actually like me because I'd been told for a long time that they wouldn't.

And so, this is how I ended up having heart failure in southern Spain!

Still smarting from Igor's verbal onslaught, I used The Balance Procedure (TBP) to rebalance my energies and bring myself out of fight or flight; and into a relaxed state so that I could literally hear myself think and decide what to do, where to go and how to rebuild my life solo. This situation had knocked me way off kilter but within a few minutes I tuned into my intuition so that I could then confidently make whatever the hell the right decision was, without a Scooby Doo YIKES in sight. (Chapter on The Balance Procedure is in Section 2 of this book).

In this case, at this moment, it was decision time. I needed to know what to do next. I chose card 3 for Clarity and held the cards to my chest with this one on top and asked myself "should I stay or should I go now?" (we know a song about that don't we boys and girls!) As the cards focus our attention our body dowses the answer and as my energy came back into balance, I swayed forward and the word "stay" dropped into my mind. "OK I will! Whoohoo, adventure time!" I'd completely fallen in love with the typical but also exceptional Spanish town and with the mountain that is was atop. There is some kind of magic in this Andalusian mountain range and over the coming months I realised that it seemed to promote realisation of dreams for all who landed here. Our tribe includes Artists of different genres, Photographers, Healers, Yogis, Authors, Musicians – the list is endless – all with the sense of liberation and the energy to fulfil our passion in life.

I'd been using TBP for several years and I have become a Teacher as well as a Practitioner. We teach that using this system heightens our connection, gives us the tools to tap into our intuition and rebalance our energies quickly and simply. When we balance our energies we come out of the "fight or flight" state and into a "relaxed" state. When our mind is relaxed, we are perfectly placed to make the right decision for ourselves because our mind is peaceful and so we can hear what our intuition has to say to us. When we are not using energy on panicking, we can then use our energy to manifest what we want and TBP teaches us how to do this very effectively.

And so, with the decision made that I should indeed stay in Spain, the next item on my list of things to do was to find my own house to rent. I used card 8 of TBP which has the affirmation on it "I am an alchemist", in other words, I can transform myself and make things happen! Because I had used TBP to bring myself into a relaxed state with the intention of manifesting, I was able to quickly and methodically set about doing just that.

I made my wish list for my future home:

As I'd fallen in love with this Spanish mountain range in Málaga province and I'd made a real connection with the few people that I'd come to know, I decided here was the place to be, in between the two villages where my friends lived and the bars, where there was the most fantastic and surprising social scene 2400ft above sea level. I wanted neighbours but not too close and so I asked for secluded but not so remote that it was scary (Igor's land was extremely remote and when I found myself alone there from time to time over the years, I realised why the women in the spaghetti westerns that I was brought up watching, emerged from the house toting a shotgun when they saw the dust trail of a stranger approaching their smallholding). My home should be approached by a decent road but far enough away from the actual road to keep my cat safe from traffic. The track to my house should be in a decent condition (tracks are frequently washed out by landslides with the heavy winter rains). My house should be affordable. My house should be surrounded by nature and have a fabulous view. My house should be up the mountain rather than down. There should be somewhere for me to practice and teach my holistic therapies. My house should be available now. My house should be secure. The owner should be fine about my cat living there too.

My list completed within the hour and I set off up the rough, unmade track in my 4x4 to the local bar where I knew a couple of Estate Agents hung out sometimes. Damn it! They weren't there. I bumped into a local Spanish man called Pedro who spoke the most fantastic English and whom I'd met just a night or two before. I explained I was looking to rent a house and then with the emotion of it all, I got a bit drunk! At 11.30 that night Pedro telephoned me and said he'd found me a house. He saved my life bless him - little did I know that he would *literally* save my life a couple of years later.

Pedro had called around and one of his neighbours was apparently just getting a house ready to rent out. I am not exaggerating when I tell you that it ticked every single box on my wish list! The landladies were so incredibly generous that they allowed me to move in almost immediately and brought the contract round a couple of weeks later. Ah, the contract! I had hoped for a short-term agreement – maybe three months – but The Universe had other ideas and I was obliged to commit to an eleven-month rental agreement. I was terrified! Igor had dented my confidence over the years with his tactless comments and whilst we'd laughed "Un-PC Parker reporting for duty" when someone else was on the receiving end of them, when combined with bipolar resentment, it had me honestly believing that I was an unlikeable person. What if I signed a contract for eleven months and he was right, and no-one liked me?! I balanced with card 2 of TBP which is for life being full of joy and getting on well with people and embarked on a life of flying solo in Spain.

The roller coaster had amazing highs too. Our nights out were often so very much fun and we were perfect partners in crime dancing, getting up to mischief, singing together, playing music and going to festivals. We'd talk for hours, scheme our next adventures or projects and have great fun getting everything together to make them happen. When things were good, we were inseparable and spooned all night and had incredibly passionate times. I learned how to build a log cabin, all about solar panels and wind turbines, alternative living, I lived a charming life on his narrowboat and I bought a 400ft stretch of Norfolk riverbank on which to moor it.

It balanced out the lows but self-preservation has to kick in at some point and it did. Following that final insulting outburst, the straw broke this camel's back and when he tried to rekindle our relationship a few weeks later I politely declined and he severed all contact.

I had a few dalliances in the couple of years that followed and a lot of fun going to music gigs, dancing, partying and enjoying something of a dalliance with a very handsome, much younger Englishman who'd been brought up in a neighbouring Spanish village. I shall call him Beau for that is what he was – beautiful and my beau. Our dalliance was to last over a year and during that time we would talk for hours and hours until dawn, we'd drink wine, smoke joints, dance naked out in the garden, laugh and philosophise, talk about mystical things and our pasts and had a very cool time. Despite the twenty-three years age difference we had an amazing connection and both felt that we'd met in a previous lifetime.

When we were in each other's company we both found that our psychic gifts and clairvoyant abilities heightened tremendously so it was a very exciting time all round. If one of us pushed the boundaries playfully we'd both fall about laughing as instant karma bit the other one on the arse within seconds by tripping us over or spilling our drink everywhere or something equally silly and entertaining that spontaneously happened without either of us lifting a finger or so much as a wiggle of our nose.

Our time together could be quite magical to the point that we never wanted it to stop and so we would often stay up all night enjoying moment after moment just because we could. We would often be asked "what's the deal with you two?" when we were out in public because of our obvious chemistry and hopefully not so obvious age difference (hmm, who am I trying to kid?!) and we'd just look at each other waiting for the other to answer and when neither of us did, we'd laugh, shrug and say "we don't know!" and carry on having fun and confusing people as we totally rocked the dancefloor with our moves which locked our energies together into a very hypnotic groove. Beau does look very mature for his years especially when he grows his gorgeous designer stubble and he is tall, dark and handsome "Mamma Mia, here I go again …..!"

Unfortunately, at this point in his life he was fighting his own demons which would cause him to have sudden mood swings after a few drinks and rant, so his behaviour could be horribly unpredictable and dangerous. Hew would become verbally abusive and once or twice, physically abusive. I sent him packing time and again, but months later he'd be in dire straits and contact me in need of help. By that time the memories had diluted and I was willing to help him. I hadn't realised that I had reverted back into my old behaviour patterns of wanting to save and be a hero. Exposing myself to triggers and negative energies only served to suck the joy out of my heart – as I would soon learn.

My friends could never understand why. I saw the potential in him and genuinely wanted to empower him to succeed in life. This was a repeating pattern in my love life. I could see the good and the potential and ended up tolerating very questionable behaviours rather than throw the towel in.

(A couple of years down the line, as I developed an interest in astrology, I realised that this and other aspects of my personality was literally written in the stars. It answered a lot of questions I had about me being too lenient, too understanding, too sensitive (all according to others' judgements of my character), and I replaced the word "too" with "very" and suddenly I wasn't so bad actually. It isn't just our zodiac sun sign which generates our personalities, it's the position of all of the other planets in the solar system at the time of our birth that influence us. When we look into our natal chart, as I describe in the Astrology Chapter in Section 2 of this book, we get lots of information about who we are and this in itself, gives us a clue as to what we need to work on during our lifetime. Accepting ourselves, shadow side and all, maybe creating boundaries, maybe learning to back away and let others learn what they need to learn. It's all there. I work through these aspects with my clients as part of my Shine-On Course which you can find out more about on my website: www.LindaJaneW.me)

However, for every time I helped him, he would relapse very quickly into his old behaviour patterns – just as I had (mirror mirror) and my fragile heart would be put under more stress, more anxiety, put in physical danger, until the day I realised, that by "saving" him from his self-inflicted dramas time and again, I was actually stopping him from learning his life lessons. His lessons were coming back around time and time again, and I was saving him time and time again – just as I had picked up the pieces from Brad's alcoholic chaos and Igor's biopolar chaos.

Oh My God!! The cartoon lightbulb went on over my head: If we remove a person from our life before we have learned the lesson that they are there to teach us, they unwittingly pass the spiritual baton to the next player in our game of life. That new player will continue to try to teach us the lesson until we get it, but if we then remove that person from our life before we've learned the lesson, they will pass it onto the next person, and so on it goes. If we want to move up the board we have to learn the lesson which means working out how to respond differently.

For twenty years, I had rescued and cleared up the chaos caused by one love after another. Once I finally stopped saving Beau, he disappeared from my life – because "I" had learned my lesson – it took a while, but much reduced from the 15-years with Brad and the 6 ½ years with Igor (I was getting it quicker). Then one day I swear I heard my Guardian Angel exclaim: "By George I think she's got it!"

I had been sent another dalliance a few months down the line from the last (The Universe obviously knows that to get and hold my attention is through interesting and fun fellas). This time, as soon as the warning light went on about chaos, my awareness pricked up and I kept a comfortable emotional distance as I started to observe the situations rather than jump in feet first. It took several months for events to unfold and we did have some interesting times but wow, once you see it, you can't unsee it and I now recognised that this was not a situation that I wanted to tolerate. I'd tried to throw them a rope, but they hadn't grabbed it and I knew that they didn't want to be saved.

I also became aware that my soul knows me well enough to know that in this lifetime, it can grab my attention by presenting me with a handsome face, some fun and diverse adventures and something that I haven't experienced before. That's how my lessons come to me.

I have to be grateful for my soul's ingenuity even though my love life had become a standing joke and had been stressful for decades – albeit a lot of fun at times; but my friends volunteered to vet any potential dalliances for me as I was clearly pants at it myself! I thought this was really funny and played up to it until one day when, in working with the archetypal identities within The Balance Procedure, I realised that my archetype "The Jester, the Fool, the Comedian, the Joker" was out of balance and rather than me being "entertaining", I was "the entertainment". Upon realising this, the joke fell flat and I vowed never to put myself into that position again. Quite simply, I balanced on it with card 6 and the shift happened within the day. I caught myself a couple of times that week as I began to say to someone "oh my God, you'll never guess what, you're going to love this ...." and then I stopped myself and my own jaw fell open as I realised the extent that I had been playing The Fool, especially where love life was concerned.

I love making people laugh and smile. BUT, in establishing myself as the Joker for my love life, that meant that I was attracting more of the same and so I would not find a serious, long-term relationship, just another mismatch with a humorous tale to entertain.

The Approaching Storm

My great friend and mentor Adrienne Green who introduced me to The Balance Procedure (TBP), described to me once that when you see the storm coming it's heading your way and you're being shown what's coming so that you can take evasive action. We also learn with TBP to try to avoid "the story" as we'll get so engrossed with it, that we'll miss the point of what is actually going on. I'll explain more of the meaning behind this as we go throughout this book.

However, I would like to tell the tale of the approaching storm, because I do feel that we can all relate to it in our own way, with our own experiences; and no matter how tragic, dreadful or close a call we experience, there is a way through it and out the other side.

During that spring I had noticed that I wasn't quite able to dance all night like I had been doing all of my life, and that I was getting a bit hot especially at night

I found that I was getting tired and my muscles were tiring easily. I've always been a horsey bird, strong as an ox and take no nonsense and loved being around these big strong beasties, so this was a weird experience for me.

I purple rash had grown on the backs of both of my legs which was completely symptomless. I'd tried many natural approaches including Apple Cider Vinegar, Aloe Vera, Coconut oil, Lavender essential oil, Tea Tree essential oil, I took activated charcoal, I applied homemade oat milk. *Nada*! Nothing worked and food allergy testing drew a blank. I had blood tests which showed that I was severely vitamin B12 deficient (a side-effect of me being vegan for several years, despite the fact that I'd been taking a B12 supplement for months. My level was 151 ng/ml and the normal was between 211 and 911 ng/ml. At that point my dad piped up "your Great Grandmother died of Pernicious Anaemia" (that's when the body can't process and absorb Vitamin B12, you end up anaemic and die). Eureka, I thought! An answer. I started on 2000% RDA Vitamin B12 tablets and my energy returned, my uncontrollable body temperature controlled itself and many of the symptoms disappeared …. apart from the rash! Damn it!

My breathlessness was explained away by it being a particularly bad spring for olive pollen. Even those born locally up here in the Andalusian mountains were suffering terribly and having to wear face masks but still their eyes were streaming, and they were having difficulty breathing. I'd also been on antibiotics for a couple of weeks for a bad tooth infection and the side-effects included breathlessness so all in all, there was a viable explanation for it. The last thing I thought was that it was heart failure looming.

I also noticed that when I was talking, I'd run out of air and my voice would start to fade midsentence. I'd have to stop and have a sharp intake of air to continue. At one point I realised that I sounded just like my Nana did when she was alive. I didn't know at this stage that she had had a heart condition.

My storm was gathering energy and the thunder was beginning to sound but at this stage in my life I was too busy to connect the dots. Even when, during the couple of weeks running up to point break, I'd woken up on several occasions in the middle of the night to find that I was breathing very rapidly and had to sit up in bed to calm myself down; still no alarm bells went off.

Add into the mix, a tremendous pain deep in my right shoulder blade – that I explained away as occasionally get a right shoulder ache if I've overdone things due to a horse-riding accident at the age of 14-years. I was also really confused as the night before I kept burping and it was really embarrassing as it was guttural and felt like my whole gut was opening up and releasing air from my stomach. They were really loud and not very feminine and hardly the impression I wanted to make on the chap who was cooking dinner for me!

I've quizzed my Acupuncturist Jeremiah, about this and wondered if this is a particular symptom. The abdominal aorta is a major blood vessel in the 'V' where your ribs meet. When things are going wrong with your heart and your circulation, this becomes distended – unbeknown to me, mine was rock hard. This is the centre of your body's own energy and if ever you want to burp, try pressing there and it releases it. In addition, this is the "Conception meridian" and is known to become energetically blocked with heart issues (see Acupressure Chapter in Section 2).

This was my body's final warning that things were about to go seriously wrong. It would seem that heart attack symptoms can be very different in women from men. A friend tells me that this is a little-known fact because most of the research was carried out on men and so us ladies are looking out for pain in the jaw, pain down the left arm and chest tightness none of which I had experienced.

The Wake-Up Call

When the storm broke on Sunday night, I'd not long retired for the night, having locked the front door as usual and left the key in there as a precaution - my Dad is so security conscious that I was brought up to secure doors and windows but to leave the key where it's accessible. Spanish doors are designed so that if you close them with the key in the lock - as I just had - you cannot get in from the outside even with a key. Crazy but there must be a rationale there somewhere.

I laid down but after a very short while I sat bolt upright before even being awake. I couldn't breathe. There was an elephant on my chest. A tight band stretching across from armpit to armpit across my chest. I was panting out of control and my breathing was so rapid it was ridiculous. I did my best to control the rate at which I was breathing – my body wouldn't listen. I couldn't do anything about it. Yikes! "What is going on?" My dad has had asthma in his life so "I'm having an asthma attack" I thought. I wasn't. My mum has suffered with heart problems for years so "I'm having an angina attack" I thought. I wasn't. "It'll pass" I thought. It didn't! I wondered about calling one of my friends for help, but it was late and being a Sunday night most of them would have had a few drinkies during the day, it was dark, and I thought I'd be fine soon enough. As the rapid breathing carried on into the early hours I thought about calling an ambulance but because it isn't easy to describe where I live to my friends who know the area well, the chances of me being able to describe it to the Emergency Services with my limited Spanish were next to none.

Throughout the night I was sitting propped up in my bed as I couldn't breathe at all if I lay down and reflexively sat up in a panic if I tried to and I was in and out of consciousness. During one of my waking moments, I remembered that the front door was locked with the key in and so no one would be able to get in unless I got out of bed and took the key out. I thought about it and a voice in my head said in no uncertain terms 'DO NOT MOVE. DO NOT GET OUT OF BED.' It was such a strong knowing that I didn't move but I also got the inkling that this was now very serious. The beauty of learning to listen to your intuition is that, the more you listen, the more it will speak to you, the more you will trust it and it will look after you like nothing and no-one else.

I've been a Reiki Master since 2007 so for twelve years at point break. During the night I drew in Reiki healing energy to keep me calm and to do what was necessary for my own greatest and highest good. There is a chapter on Reiki in Section 2 of this Guidebook. I teach Reiki in-person and via video-calls. For now, I will say that I strongly recommend that everyone learns this self-healing method because I truly believe that it was fundamental in keeping me alive. Basically, it induces a deep state of relaxation and you literally draw in the energy from around yourself so that your body can use it to heal itself. It helps you to listen to your intuition so when I felt "Do not move, do not get out of bed", I listened! Since then, in chatting with others who have experienced heart attacks, everyone agreed that they too had an inner knowing: "Panic and you're a gonner!"

At this point I realised that I was alone, 2400 feet up a mountain in southern Spain in the middle of an olive grove, the doors locked and no one could get in without taking bars off the windows or breaking down the reinforced metal door with a five level mortice deadlock on and any way you looked at it, it would be epic!

My intuition was speaking very firmly to me to stay calm and I knew that I had to pay attention beyond a shadow of a doubt otherwise that would be it, game-over and my cats, now increased to nine, would probably eat this Mad Cat Woman at breakfast time – nope, still not funny!

Eight hours later, at 8am on Monday morning I was exhausted, but all had calmed down and I called my friend Pauline because I knew she was going to the doctor that morning. She came and got me, and I saw the GP. I still thought I'd had a reaction to the pollen, and it'd triggered an asthma attack.

The lovely Spanish GP who speaks really great English listened to my lungs with his stethoscope and prescribed strong antihistamines and an inhaler. He apparently tested my blood oxygen levels which was high – an indication of a breathing problem and checked my pulse which was normal. I don't have any recollection of this which is odd as I generally have the memory of an elephant. I'm not really sure if they helped or not. I went about my business for the next few days and spoke with my parents about their personal experiences with asthma and with angina and I came to the conclusion that it was indeed an asthma attack presumably brought on by the pollen.

Then on Thursday evening Pauline said she wanted to come over with her stethoscope and have a listen. Strange I thought, but ok. So, we sat having a chat and a glass of vino and she listened to my heart and was alarmed at how fast it was going. I felt fine. I was having a groovy evening with her so, almost to my peril I refused her and Holly's advice of going to hospital. I'm fine I said. I thought I was. Once again, I ignored the warning shots and my angels.

Friday morning arrived and as I got out of bed I could hardly walk, my body felt like lead and I couldn't breathe. I knew I was in trouble so I phoned around several of my friends but unfortunately they were all out and about. Then I managed to get hold of Pauline and her husband Dougie who said they'd meet me at the small Accident & Emergency in the local hospital which is twenty to thirty minutes away down the winding Spanish mountain roads. She suggested that our friend Pedro come and talk to the ambulance as his English is superb and being local, he could explain to them how to get to me and said she'd call him. She messaged me five minutes later to say that Pedro would be with me in about fifteen minutes.

By then my memory had gone and I had no recollection of what was going on or why Pedro coming over and what was this inhaler doing in my handbag? I was compos-mentis enough to sit still and keep very calm until Pedro got to me. I knew that if I freaked out it could have massive consequences. I did venture to a mirror to see if I was having a stroke. Thankfully not. Once again, I invoked Reiki to help me with whatever the hell was going on and to see me through it. The Reiki most certainly kept me calm and so alive because as I've just mentioned, panic and your body simply won't be able to cope with the additional stress, given the incident that it is already going through.

Pedro got me to the hospital where we met up with Pauline and Dougie and the Medics hooked me up to the heart monitor. My heart rate was 186 beats per minute. Normal is about 60. My heart was beating so fast that my blood had become very thick and so I think that there was insufficient oxygen going through my system to enable my brain to function.

My friends could see what was going on and had to keep leaving the room as they couldn't bear to watch and thought I was going to die at any moment. I was oblivious and wasn't capable of doing anything more. I handed myself over to the Medics but nothing they tried brought my heart rate down so they stretchered me into the ambulance and blue lighted me to the regional hospital in Velez Málaga – another twenty to thirty minutes away.

Here, I objected to them telling me I was staying in overnight – I honestly did not know how serious the situation was and I wanted to go home. When I needed a pee, they said that it was too dangerous for me to get out of bed, so I had to use a bedpan. Yuk! My awareness of the severity of my situation had slipped away I assumed that they meant that if I got out of bed, I might knock over the machines and break them. It wasn't until one of my follow-up appointments several weeks later, that I realised that it was me that was in danger – of quite literally dropping down dead. I lifted myself into yoga bridge pose to get myself on and off the bedpan but every time I did, alarms on the heart monitor went off and nurses came running. So, you see, even the slightest effort set my heart into overload as I was in a critical condition I guess. I remember feeling confused. Why was that beeping going on when I was only doing bridge pose? I do a whole yoga class without problems. How strange! This is how quickly life can change.

During the night I was in and out of consciousness but being a Holistic Therapist and Reiki Teacher I continued to invoke Reiki and was drawing in Universal Life Force energy – more on that in Section 2. At one point I felt fingers close around my right hand, one finger at a time, and hold my hand tight. I opened my eyes but there was no one there even though I could still feel a hand holding mine. I just knew it was my grandfather Peter who had died before I was born. I could feel the love. He held my hand for a long time over night. This was confirmed to me during a Ouija board session the following November which I was delighted about.

Pauline had been told by the Medics that she couldn't stay and so had to leave. Bless her heart, she was in a dreadful state. When she returned later that evening, the Doctor did his rounds and told me that tests had shown that I had indeed had a heart attack at some point over the last week. It was still a while before I realised that was what had happened on the Sunday night, and even longer before I realised the Thursday before that was probably the first one! It was weeks and weeks before I even knew that I'd had heart failure. I've no idea if that was down to a language barrier or that I wasn't capable to retaining any information.

Your intuition will always look out for you as it has your best interests at heart, so when you become aware of repeating thoughts like this, know that it is your intuition calling you to action. I'd had a craving for steak for months – if I'd listened, maybe my body would have received the nourishment that it needed. Eighteen months later, I kept thinking that I should get a dog. I dismissed it a few times before I realised "ah, hello Intuition, I'm receiving you loud and clear. OK, I'm not a dog person but there's obviously a good reason so I'll get a dog!" He's become my best friend and this Mad Cat Woman never expected that!

I was in hospital for six days and during this time I noticed how fearful most of the other patients were. I suppose by handing ourselves over to someone else, we have no control and so of course we will feel scared. By taking control of our thoughts, our energy and taking responsibility for our own well-being, it changes everything, and this is what I aim to inspire in you, safely. As I live alone, I decided to look at it as "Whoohoo, I don't need to cook, and I'll be fed and watered three times a day every day!" I was given sedatives and so slept a lot and I took whatever pills they told me to. However, I was also consciously drawing in Reiki healing energy almost constantly throughout my hospital stay and using the Reiki ideals as my mantra and so I was intentionally programming myself not to waste precious energy on worry and to count my many blessings (as you'll read in a moment). Once again, I felt my grandfather's hand close around mine one finger at a time and I managed to open my eyes to find no "body" there …. he was there in spirit and I was reassured that all would be well whichever direction it took. It was the most beautiful feeling of being watched over that you can imagine.

(Reiki works "for our own greatest and highest good" so it will work to send us off into the next dimension to rest in peace (RIP) or it will do what is best for us and heal or bring a different situation forward into our life. As a Reiki Master Practitioner and Teacher, I advocate that Reiki isn't just about healing or a way of potentially earning a living, it is a lifestyle choice. By reciting and believing in the Reiki ideals which I teach during a Reiki attunement, they become an affirmation. Affirmations work by repeating a statement regularly to yourself and in doing so, you're basically instructing yourself and the Universe around you, what you wish to become a reality. The more thought you give to something, the more energy it receives, until it has so much energy that it is actually able to happen.

In reciting the Reiki ideals daily, you are having a regular thought, which then becomes a regular mood, which then becomes a habit, which then becomes a personality trait and so becomes you as a person.

THE REIKI IDEALS *(Hatsurei-Ho)*
Just for today I won't be angry,
Just for today I won't worry,
Just for today I'll be kind to every living creature,
Just for today I'll do my day's work honestly,
Just for today I thank my parents, my teachers and my elders,
Just for today I count my many blessings.

During my hospital stay I was ambulanced to another hospital for an angiogram. When they told me, I was going to have this done, I drew down Reiki and sent it forward to the date of the investigation with the intention that there was no need for an operation and that all is well. Being so much of a medical drama fan, I was only too aware of the heart surgeries that are performed, and I didn't want that for myself. However, rather than give my energy to the worry of a worst-case scenario, I acknowledged that it was a possibility but then consciously set my intention for the best outcome and sent Reiki that way. I did this at every opportunity so that it had sufficient energy to become a reality.

What do I mean by "it had sufficient energy to become a reality"? In order to make anything happen, it needs energy. You want water to boil for your cup of tea, you need to give the water energy to heat up – a kettle does the trick with electric energy which gives it the energy to come into a reality. Thoughts are energy and so the more thought you give to something, the more energy it has to become a reality. If these are dark thoughts, that's what you'll get. Positive thoughts will also be delivered. Reiki turbo charges these thoughts - because you're working at a higher vibration, they have more power to become reality. More on this throughout the book – it's a learning curve and we're just at the outset of it so all will become more clear as you continue.

I also used one of the holistic practices that I teach – The Balance Procedure (details in Section 2 of this book) – to rebalance my energies, rebalance my chakras (energy centres within the body outlined in Section 2) and to create the result that I wanted from the angiogram. This investigation tells you the state of the heart and the vessels in and around the body. I used everything in my spiritual toolkit to manifest the reality of a simple, easily healed diagnosis without major long-term implications.

During my angiogram it showed an enlarged heart but thankfully my vessels were clear. I knew that I must be getting better when I was lusting after the good-looking ambulance driver and also I was beginning to question the medication that I was being given!

Being a Holistic Therapist and Teacher (and who has now evolved into a Holistic Mentor and Author) I've been a long-term sceptic about the morals of pharmaceutical companies and taking drugs to counteract the side-effects of drugs. Whilst I acknowledge that they did keep me alive, maybe it was too easy to dismiss me with an inhaler and antihistamines as these gave me tachycardia and nearly finished me off - so my conclusion is that there is indeed a balance to be found and to work with during the journey back to full health and then in maintaining that well-being. There are so many variants which are all very individual, and my choice was and continues to be as natural as possible which I aim to demonstrate. We're all so busy that we fail to spot the signs creeping up, we're all so busy getting messed up and messing others up that we don't spot the work that we have to do emotionally, in order to evolve up and out of this state of being, and raise our vibration, stop and smell the coffee, the roses and simply relax and enjoy the simple pleasures in life.

En route to and from the angiogram, I shared the ambulance transport with several other patients, and I remember thinking how down and how grey they all seemed. They seemed resigned to whatever fate had in store for them whereas I was determined that my body would be well and strong - I didn't make room for doubt in my head. The whole way there I unflinchingly focused my thoughts and directed Universal energies for a great outcome for me and my heart, which would be achieved easily and quickly. However, I looked around at the worried expressions on my fellow ambulance travellers' faces and realised that they had relinquished all control of their fate. They felt powerless in the outcomes, powerless in what action to take, they had handed over the responsibility for their wellbeing and their very lives to someone else.

I feel it's really important to point out here, that that "someone else" does not live with the consequences of action or inaction, nor do they have to live inside our body – we took on that responsibility when we were born. It's up to us to look after our body (and our mind and our spirit) and preserve our own very existence on this planet and to listen to what it's telling us through our emotional and ailments. What I aim to inspire within these pages, is how to start doing just that. Everything starts in our mind. Our thoughts create our reality and if we want to be healthy then we have to decide to be well, and to seek out and then to use different tools available to us to achieve it. That's why I teach my modular Shine On course and include modules for Reiki, The Balance Procedure, acupressure, mindfulness, astrology and more.

I had decided to stay in hospital until I didn't want to anymore and then when I felt that it was time to go home, I used The Balance Procedure and sent the energy of my intent that way and *created* my reality and sure enough, I was discharged home that very day without me having to say a word to anyone. I can remember feeling incredibly weak and lightheaded to the point of floaty and wondered "Jesus! What has happened to my strong body?" Although I was a tad nervous at being home alone, I gathered a bit more strength by just being in my own space, surrounded by nature in my beautiful mountain olive grove. I also needed to be on my own after being around people 24/7 for a week and settled down to quiet time. Ahhhhh bliss, just me and my cats! Although I have to say that I did not lock my front door and I consciously gave my cats *plenty* of food that night!

Still oblivious as to how seriously ill I was, I'd asked the Cardiologist if I could have a glass of red wine or two. I was told absolutely NOT. I was a bit taken aback as I'd been hearing for years how a glass or two of red wine was good for the heart. However, because my family history included my mother's unstable angina, my brother's heart attack and that my grandfather, James, had dropped dead pouring a cup of tea at my age (gosh, when did I become the same age as my grandfather?! I didn't see that creeping up on me), alcohol was a big fat NO. I was told that the cause of my heart attack was congestive heart failure due to arrhythmia – an irregular heartbeat. Stimulants such as coffee, alcohol and nicotine along with stress can cause this and given my family's background it would seem that I had a predisposition to heart problems. I refuse to use the word disease – well actually maybe I can - because what I have since chosen to do, is to find and release the "dis-ease" from my very being and to thrive. This is the point of this handbook – to inspire you to apply what I've learned, to your own life and just as I think the heart attack saved my life, I hope that you too will start to feel that your own life changing event has done just that.

Reality now started to hit home! This party animal was no longer able to drink if she wanted to live; nor continue being a social smoker nor relax and giggle courtesy of an occasional joint. No to all of the above. *Nada.* Nothing. Cold turkey here we come and no amount of cranberry sauce was going to sweeten it! Lifestyle change is here like it or not, The Universe has spoken! 'Life as we know it Jim' was no longer an option if I wanted to live - but I did hope that maybe when I saw the Private Cardiologist, she'd say that I could have a drinkies!

Earlier in the year I'd realised how off track I'd become on what I believed to be my life's purpose of being a Healer and spreading the word on holistic lifestyles, holistic healing and that we consciously create our own life – be it positive or negative – and coaching people on how to bring their wildest dreams into reality. It had often crossed my mind that if something happened to me which meant that I couldn't charge around being a party animal and all-round busy person, then I could write my book instead. Little did I know what I was manifesting eh?!

I was discharged with a long list of medication which I queried. Much to my amusement, one of the hospital's duty Translators who was standing behind my Cardiologist grinning broadly and giving me the thumbs up sign as I interrogated the Cardiologist about the necessity and action of each of the medications. When it came to the blood thinners, the Cardiologist told me that I was to take these and come back for Cardioversion in three weeks. She then moved onto another subject ….. "Whoa there horsey! What's Cardioversion? She told me that they would sedate me and put paddles on my chest and shock my heart back into rhythm. This is what you see the Medics do on television when people die, and they try to re-start the heart and the patient jolts off the bed as electricity blasts their soul back into their body. It has a very good success rate apparently, but I politely declined and said, "no thank you, I'll do it naturally". The Doctors were visibly irritated and almost ranted that 'naturally' was impossible and the only way to get my heart back into a normal rhythm was with Cardioversion. Again, I said this time more firmly "no thank you, I'll do it naturally" – "they don't know who they're dealing with here" I thought. I had no idea of the severity of my condition, nor the hard work that I was letting myself in for by making this choice, but by the time I was one-year down the line I knew 100% that it was the correct decision and I wouldn't have missed a single moment of my incredible journey back to health.

I decided to make use of the private health care that is obligatory to have when one becomes a Spanish resident and I made an appointment with a private Cardiologist. My friend Avra came to translate for me and her face dropped when she asked the Consultant why I couldn't I have the odd glass of red wine. I must have missed the fact that on the night of my admission they didn't expect me to live through the night and now even a single drink could stop my heart without further warning, and just like Grandpa James, I would drop down dead on the spot. No to drinking, no to smoking, no to caffeine, no to all stimulants and I interpreted that as no to fun!

I had a follow-up appointment with the hospital where I'd been an in-patient and following an ultrasound of my heart, I was told that my heart function had improved and was now 33% …. up from 17%! I was shocked rigid and as I realised just how close a call I'd had and that I wasn't out of the woods yet. No wonder I was so weak. I literally went home and laid on the sofa in a state of shock and I had to gather all of my strength and will power to stay positive and not collapse into a sobbing jelly. A week or two later I learned that even the fittest athletes' hearts function at about 75% so it wasn't *quite* as bad as I first thought … and that's the thought I worked with.

Positivity is crucial and we absolutely must stay focused on our goal and will ourselves into how we want to be. Whilst we can be aware of the not such good news, dismiss it to the archives of our mind and put all of our energies into manifesting wellness.

When I returned home, I was appalled at the number of boxes of prescription medication that I had to take – blood thinners, betablockers, diuretics, proton pump inhibitors, a vasodilator and statins. Not only did it go against my belief system of holistic practices, but it made me feel old and infirm and I wasn't about to accept that. In an effort to make myself feel vaguely more positive about it all, I found a beautiful silver shoebox in my wardrobe and threw the shoes out of it and instead, stored my meds in this "treasure chest" and crazy as it sounds, it did the trick – for the time being!

At some point I realised how weak I had become and that this was far from over. Unfortunately, it wasn't a case of "OK, I've had a heart attack, now back to my life", this was just the beginning of my dark night of the soul and I really had to actually work at getting fit and strong again. I knew that I needed to focus every ounce of my energy on me right now and focus on healing myself and figure out what on earth had gone wrong with my body, so that I could put it right. I was weak as a kitten and even hanging out the washing was a epic endurance. Overnight I'd lost my strength and stamina. I couldn't even sing along to a song on the radio without going dizzy and my chest muscles aching, let alone dance all night; and my mind was alarmingly numb and slow.

- and so began the journey of my awakening.

Rise & Shine

I resolved to use every one of my holistic practices and then some. In particular, I used The Balance Procedure to correct my heart and to get clarity and make my decisions in order to create the results that I wanted and I did so every day throughout the day.

The wake-up call wasn't just about the future as I'd expected, there was a whole lot of reflecting back into my past that I ended up doing. My hospitalisation was the result of many years of living my life and in my view, to prevent a recurrence, I had to start to do things differently – but until I recognised where I'd been going wrong thus far, I couldn't start that process. It isn't a sudden process, it's gradual and it's so enlightening – because let's face it, we all love talking about ourselves; it's utterly indulgent in that respect and we get into some really fascinating revelations. I'm sure you'll love it as you tread your own path.

They say in spiritual circles to teach by example, and so I use my own experiences herein, to demonstrate what I've learned and that involves a lot of casting my mind back. In doing so, I began to see things in a completely different light and in doing that, I was able to forgive, let go, be thankful and move forward much lighter and enlightened having ditched the baggage that was weighing me down. I truly hope that these help to put things into perspective and make more sense of it all for you on your own journey.

For the first few months there were moments along the way when I started writing this book, that my heart would become a bit erratic for a couple of days and once again I had to gather all of my strength and resolve to stop myself from getting down in the dumps and feeling like a complete hypocrite. This in itself has been yet another journey. I realised that it's not the curing one's self that is the aim of the book, it's the journey of awareness because we have had one hell of a wake-up call and to Wake Up, Rise & Shine, we need to keep doing it until our mind and our body get used to the fact that we're now listening and working as a whole – (w)holistically and we acknowledge that we're responsible for everything that comes our way, even down to how others treat us and behave around us.

I started learning and recognising the triggers – emotional and physical that pop my heart out of rhythm and I have learned how to bring my heart back into rhythm when stressed or when tiredness or upset cause it to go random on me – which is totally normal by the way – and so the aim of this book is to demonstrate to you how we can manage your mind, your body and your emotions and take control - whatever your situation is.

Since point break, I took on a nine-month long Way of Your Soul Course which I heard about through my good friend Adrienne, and this further empowered me and was crucial to my journey. During this time, I came to learn that such life changing, dark events are indeed an awakening and "the dark night of the soul". Now is the time to change your ways and your thoughts, learn and grow from the experience and pick yourself up and head in a new direction. It was fabulous to have my intuition validated and for me, everything that I was hearing reinforced my decision not to have cardioversion and to set my sights on coming off all pharmaceuticals as soon as it was safe for me to do so.

It scared the sh*t out of those around me, but thankfully, I found strength and support that I needed went around my circle of friends like a Mexican wave and so there was always someone who was able to back-up my decisions and spur me on during my holistic quest. During this time, I was encouraged to stop calling it "point break" and instead call it "my awakening" or my "wake-up call" which figures as let's face it, the clue was always in the name of this book "Wakey Wake-Up Rise & Shine". Henceforth, I shall be referring to it as my "wake-up call".

Despite not wanting to take any pharmaceuticals, I had to acknowledge their necessity (for now) but after several months my intuition told me to stop taking the Betablockers from which I was experiencing some side-effects - which bizarrely mimic the symptoms of a heart attack. That in itself was giving me anxiety – which is another side-effect. I personally think that it makes sense that side-effects are the body's way of objecting that we are not listening to what our body is trying to tell us. In taking the pharmaceuticals which are masking the symptoms, we generally choose not to make the changes that are necessary for good health. I'm not necessarily talking about diet and exercise, I'm talking about emotional changes, shifting our perceptions, accepting responsibility for what shows up in our life and looking at different ways of managing life in general.

Despite using all of my holistic practices I had some unwarranted moments of panic about a stroke, blood clot or relapsing and then what would become of me and of my book?! I thought about taking the tablets again but then I thought "NO! *Linds*, you have a message for people, a story to tell and to inspire – that's the reason you survived - and you will publish and inspire, so stick to your guns and put your money where your mouth is and get on with it!". I had asked my Acupuncturist and Herbalist if there was a herbal betablocker I could take and so he and his wife who is a Herbalist, advised Motherwort and I have never looked back. It is brilliant and get this, the Latin name for it is *Leonurus cardiaca* - It's like it was made for this Leo lady with a heart to heal!

When others ask me about coming off their medications, I emphasise that we can't just stop. If we're adamant that we don't want to take a tablet, we need to have a replacement in mind, whether it be herbal, homeopathic, diet, lifestyle. Not only that but we have to look at the effect that tablet has and work out how we can manage that aspect of our lives differently. With a betablocker, it helps to reduce the amount of adrenaline that is released, thus our heart is put under less pressure. Therefore, it follows that we need to work on our triggers so that our body doesn't get provoked into firing adrenaline into our systems. We might need to avoid situations or certain people, whilst simultaneously making the changes in our responses – including giving ourselves the option to simply walk away rather than engaging.

When reflecting on that episode in my journey I realised that when setting off along your path, it is of a huge benefit to have something to aim for, a goal to set your sights on, not just on any medical results or physical health side of things, but something that stimulates your passion for life. Mine was writing this book and spreading the word so I highly recommend starting or completing a project that you've always wanted to do. If you're in mid-health hiccup then The Universe has given you the time to do just that so make the best use of it because it makes rehabilitation a joy rather than a burden and is so much more rewarding that sitting on your derrière watching TV.

Once I had got my heart back into rhythm, on the very rare occasion it jittered a bit, I implemented all the holistic wisdom that I was accruing and got her back into rhythm extremely quickly. Everywhere I went and chatted about my wake-up call, people would tell me that they couldn't wait to read the book – this book – so the Universe kept nudging me, saying "get on with it, they're waiting for it" and so I did.

Just as the lessons started to happen when I quit my London job and I embarked on my Reiki journey, the decisions that I had made post-heart hospitalisation, signalled to The Universe that I wanted to go up to the next level of Spiritual School and as Anna-Louise had pointed out in The Way Of Your Soul course, this meant internalising lessons that came my way, rather than externalising. That means, I can no longer hold "The Universe" responsible for everything – I am responsible – well, "my soul" is. My soul is my universe and my teacher, mentor and guide is my soul, i.e. ME!

This was a fabulous turning point in my quest for a complete recovery as naturally as possible because if it was all down to me, then I could create my future which meant that I *would* achieve the natural recovery.

With my mind leaving no room for doubt now, the messages came spontaneously in rapid succession. I was watching so many videos on YouTube and Gaia channel to name but two sources, as well reading articles from so many different places which seemed to find me at the right moment and then lead me off on an enlightening tangent. The answers and information came so thick and fast and I didn't want to forget anything so I downloaded a journal app onto my smartphone and started noting the key points. As I did this the synchronicities grew stronger and more abundant.

> ➢ I'd encourage you now to start journaling your own journey because you will not want to miss your own insights and reflect back on them. Start with a new diary, notebook or journal app on your smartphone, tablet or device of choice and don't let anything slip by. As you read this book, you'll understand why more and more.

Trusting Our Intuition

In embracing my new life, I worked with The Balance Procedure (TBP) to realign my chakras (energy centres – see Section 2) as plenty would be knocking me off balance emotionally in the coming months and years as my journey progressed. I was entering new territory at 52-years old and I was now a complete novice which is not something I ever thought would be the case at this age. I had it all sussed and was thriving – ah, no, apparently not!!!

However, fear not! TBP is such an easy way of tapping into our intuition which makes it invaluable throughout life in general, but especially as I now had crucial decisions to make during my recovery. Every step of the way I used TBP to focus myself, my energies, my thoughts and decide what outcome I wanted. I then focused all my thoughts on that outcome. When I didn't know what on earth to do about anything then I used card 3 of TBP to bring clarity and be authentic, true to myself. The more you practice this, the more your intuition speaks to you and the more you trust it –

like any new friend. Your intuition always has *your* best interests at heart – pun intended – and so when mine spoke to me and said one word "Acupuncture", I knew that was the way forward. When the Cardiologist disputed my decision not to have Cardioversion, I told her that I was going to have acupuncture and she told me that it wouldn't work and could cause bleeding as I was on blood thinners and that she strongly advised me against it – my Acupuncturist, Jeremiah, and I proved her wrong – although I am eternally grateful to her and her team for saving my life.

One of the things that TBP shows us is that "balance" is essential and therefore flexibility is as powerful as passion and we must have the two in equal measure. To start with I was adamant about coming off the medication but over the weeks and months that followed I learned to appreciate balance with everything. If the scales are tipped too far one way, then we have a distorted viewpoint and will not be doing ourselves any favours. It is important that we see things from a helicopter view so that we can achieve that balance for ourselves.

Over the coming weeks several of my friends were adamant that I should have Cardioversion (CV) and gave me quite a hard time about my decision not to have it. They were worried for me and my prognosis without it. Every time I went out or saw them, they were lecturing me, reasoning with me, trying to persuade me, giving me information about it, suggesting that I think about it and keep an open mind about it. Such was the barrage of opinions that I didn't want to go out, didn't want their company and started to waiver on my decision and get a bit tearful about it all. I was tired and run-down anyway and defending my decision was using a lot of energy, but then in a burst of stubbornness I told them I didn't want to talk about it anymore and every time they tried to bring it up I batted it back with humour doing the Austin Powers' Dr Evil "shush"!!! And pre-emptive shushes!! I reminded them that I am a Holistic Practitioner and that I think and do things differently. This was part of the clarity that I felt from using TBP. I just knew my way forward.

One of my considerations was that I had had breast implants some eighteen years previously in my early thirties and they were doing just fine but on researching CV I had come across a case where a lady's implants had ruptured during this procedure and she'd had to have them both replaced. Apparently, the electric shock had put all her body's muscles into spasm as it does, including the capsules that had formed around her implants and her muscles contracted with such ferocity that it burst them both. The thought of the added complication of silicon leaking into my body and having one or two popped breasts and having to have an operation to replace them with a very weak heart was a no-brainer to me. It simply reinforced my gut feel that CV was not for me. This argument turned out to be a winner in keeping my caring friends at bay in their efforts to persuade me to have it. My Holistic Practitioner ethos alone didn't cut the mustard. I think they thought that I was worried about it, but I wasn't, I wanted to listen to what my body was telling me rather than bully it and my heart into submission.

I had no doubt that I had to hear what my intuition, my heart, my soul and my body were trying to tell me. There have been numerous influences on my beliefs throughout my holistic journey. My own experiences for my own wellbeing; incredible things that I've witnessed whilst working with healing energies on my clients, research, courses that I've done, knowledge comes from so many different directions once you're open to it.

We have to action our intuition otherwise it defeats the object of having it. Cut yourself some slack as you're learning to do this by proving yourself right. If you find that you're saying to yourself "I knew I should / shouldn't have done that", "I knew that was going to happen" or "I had a bad / good feeling about that", then your awareness will now spark up and you'll start to realise that this is your intuition ... Yay!

Louise Hay (08/10/1926 – 30/08/2017) who was an American motivational author and the founder of Hay House Publishing, had inspired me many years earlier. She authored several books, including You Can Heal Your Life, in which she describes how emotions are directly responsible for disease and to cure the disease, we have to work through the emotions that put it there in the first place – just as she did when diagnosed with cancer. She turned down surgery and searched her soul instead, turning to holistic practices.

I've also been a practicing Bach Flower Remedy Therapist for well over a decade. Dr Edward Bach (24/09/1886 – 27/11/1936) was an English Doctor, turned Homeopath but best known for developing the 100% organic Bach Flower Remedies. These address the 38 different emotional states, that, when out of balance, cause dis-ease, and so disease. See Chapter in Section 2.

My intuition told me beyond a shadow of a doubt that my heart issues were down to emotional dis-eases and if I didn't resolve these, I would surely continue to have "heart issues" regardless of treatment and medication. I'm also a believer that side-effects from drugs are the body's way of shouting at us "you're not listening to me, we have an emotional problem that we need to sort out and you're taking tablets to mask it, but the problem is still here". It's a tragic fact that some anti-depressants have suicide as a side-effect. I have to wonder if it's because the spirit is so frustrated at popping pills, rather than its host making the necessary changes to their life to bring joy and fulfilment.

Furthermore, as the acupuncture rebalanced my body's energy systems and I started to heal physically, it sparked my interest in acupressure and my intuition directed my to do so. I've since qualified and have a diploma in Acupressure and during this course, I was fascinated by the Traditional Chinese Medicine (TCM) belief system of the emotions which adversely affect each organ – e.g. joy is the emotion of the heart, anger is the emotion of the liver, overthinking the emotion associated with the spleen, etc. I cover this more fully in the Acupressure chapter in Section 2 of this book.

With all diseases, if we don't treat the root emotional cause, I believe they will return unless we treat the underlying emotional cause. How we do that is up to us as individuals because we have to take responsibility for our own health, life, body and mind. I don't think it's a coincidence that some medications actually give us the symptoms of the ailment that we're taking them for, by way of a side-effect. It's as if it's still happening but silently.

During my work as a Medical Secretary ten years ago, I'd experience clusters of behaviour patterns in patients with the same medical condition. Working for a Urologist who specialised in kidney stones, the patients were incredibly angry to the point of being vicious over the 'phone and one had me sobbing at his nastiness. I looked up kidney stones in Louise Hay's book and sure enough "chunks of unresolved anger". About this time, I met Igor and his anger could get biblical and yep you've guessed it, he'd had kidney stones! The Universe sends little bits of proof along the way in life – you just have to have a quiet enough mind to see and hear them.

So, what about hereditary conditions I hear you ask? If diseases are down to our own individual emotions why do, they run in the family?

My conclusion is that our families do not just teach us how to talk, walk, hold a knife and fork, etc; we are also taught how to respond to situations emotionally, and this is recorded in our ancestral DNA which is duly handed down through the generations like computer code. I am a product of my mother and my father for sure. In my mid-thirties I looked around and thought "actually, I don't want to respond that way anymore, I'd rather react in "x" way". I'd always questioned and disputed many things growing up, much to the amusement of my parents, but this was more of an ingrained characteristics side of things and so I changed the way I did things. I started to grow into myself. No doubt my mum had been taught by her parents – both of whom had heart problems too – and I'd been taught by her to be a delightfully open-hearted person. I often hear stories of how my grandfather was adored by everyone for his generosity – which infuriated my grandmother as he gave so much away! Coincidentally (or not), I was diagnosed by my Counsellor as having a "Fairy Godmother complex" – I just love waving my magic wand and granting wishes and desires it would seem.

However as if by magic, our astrological natal chart gives us even more insights into why we are the way that we are. It tells us our personality traits and what challenges we are likely to face during our lifetime. As my intuition drew me to learn more about Astrology, I've found this latest string to my bow absolutely fascinating as for the last few years, some of my new friends here on magic mountain have told me I'm "too sensitive". In looking at my natal chart (the location of all of the planets at the time I was born, not just the sun – i.e. our zodiac (sun) sign is just one aspect of our personality. Where Jupiter, Mars, Venus, the moon, etc, etc, were at that moment of our birth, are all insightful and significant. For example, I have 6 planets in water signs and my moon is in the water sign of Cancer – with all of that going on, I am majorly sensitive, psychic, emotional and an empath. So I, Linda, cannot help but be sensitive. I am not "too" sensitive. I am simply a far more sensitive being than someone with many of their planets in earth signs for example. See my Astrology Chapter in Section 2 and also the Module in my Shine On Course where we decipher who you were born to be – it's incredibly enlightening. Suddenly I felt empowered to be who I was actually happy being all along - but others had told me I was wrong and should change. How very rude LOL.

Acupuncture

As the word "acupuncture" kept dropping into my mind during my hospital stay, I intuitive knew that this was the way to go and in the past I had recruited the help of Jeremiah who lives locally to me and so I asked if he would be willing to be a part of my recovery regime.

Thankfully he and his wife agreed, although I must have been a rather daunting case as I was so weak but they said that they were honoured that I was happy to put my trust in them.

The forerunner to acupuncture is acupressure which is reported to have been a traditional Chinese medicine practice 2500 years before acupuncture and as it does not involve the use of needles anyone can safely practice it – with the usual precautions in pregnancy. There are over 300 energy points along the 14 meridians which can be stimulated to clear energy blockages and promote well-being for every organ and system in the body and boy do they work!

Upon examining my body on my first appointment Jeremiah felt that the lymph nodes throughout my entire body were enlarged and he strongly felt that I had a systemic infection which had made my blood thick (which is the body's natural response to a systemic infection apparently) and could well have been the root cause of the domino effect which led to the heart attack. (Isn't it interesting to note that natural antibiotics such as ginger, turmeric and garlic are also natural blood thinners! – Mother Nature sure does rock. The antibiotics clear the infection and the also thin the thickening blood to avoid complications.)

I initially went twice a week and despite me being in a precarious financial situation I had no doubt in my mind that this was money well spent especially as I live to the ideals of being a Reiki Practitioner which involves taking responsibility for our own health and well-being. We are taught that you must always receive something in exchange for your healing because it is essential that people recognise and appreciate what we are doing for them and they in turn take responsibility for their own healing – we simply empower them to heal themselves.

I was so fascinated by the acupuncture process because I could feel energy in parts of my body well away from the needles. The odd tingle or even a gentle whoosh as an energetic blockage was released. For this reason, I felt it important to quieten my mind during treatments because as I did so, clues and insights would start to pop into my mind as something was triggered or released. On one occasion, the gall bladder point reared its painful head at my ankle and as it did so, "Why don't you love me?" popped into my head. My previous relationships had placed an energetic block in this meridian and as these words released from my vibration, so the healing was taking effect. I had given my all to my romantic relationships and with my Fairy Godmother Complex, I had treated them like Kings and yet had not been appreciated as their Queen. Apparently Empaths and Healers are vulnerable to those who would take advantage of our good natures.

These instances would happen when I was doing my own acupressure practices at home. For instance, when I once used my fingertips to gently massage along the midline in in a circular motion, starting at my heart all the way down to my root chakra; where it felt tight or tender, I focused on drawing in healing energy with every in breath and releasing negative emotions with every out breath. I found that it generally took between half-an-hour and an hour and I'd do it lying down so my arms didn't ache. I noticed that every time I did this, thoughts pop into my head and initially I tried to dismiss them as I wanted to focus on the healing. Then I realised that these thoughts *were* the healing as they were the very reason that the acupressure points were tight in the first place. The reason that they were popping into my head is because I was actively releasing them with the massage. How incredible!

I started to combine my practices with deep meditation and I had so many insights including that I get my energy and my strength up here in the mountains so that I can then go to more populated areas e.g. therapy centres, holistic fayres, etc; so that I can practice and teach and to this end I would emerge from the meditation knowing that once I was fit to work again , it would be time to remember to have fun with it all. I started to get many insights into how the way I work is to change for the better. Essentially, it's time for me, for my healing work and it's time for me to have fun with as well as coaching people on how to reach a higher vibration level.

Each time I went for an acupuncture session, Jeremiah would pick up on one emotion or another through his needles and generally it was anger. This was incredibly insightful and that was when I started to realise that I had a lot of anger inside which I hadn't recognised. Both he and I were really surprised as outwardly I don't portray that at all and I hadn't acknowledged that myself. I had seen it in others around me but this was the whole point of my wake-up call – to start to understand the meaning of reflections from others, and indeed why horses are used in psychotherapy because they are emotionally honest and big enough that we take notice of their behaviours as they reflect ourselves back to us.

I continued with my acupressure homework and when watching a heart acupressure video and applying the techniques to my hand, I noted that one of the points is in the centre of our palms. At that very point I had an area of dry skin about the size of a penny. This had been coming and going for a long time but no matter what I applied to it – Aloe Vera, Lavender essential oil, Tea tree oil, etc, nothing had cured it. However, at some point, long after I'd given up and figured it was an abrasion from a broom or mop handle, it would just disappear of its own accord but this pattern always perplexed me.

When I explained this to Jeremiah, as it was directly over a heart acupressure point, we agreed that this was another warning sign that my heart was struggling and it shouldn't be ignored. Once I started my holistic heart regime the rash did indeed clear up without any lotion or potion being applied to it.

Jeremiah advised me as part of my homework, to carry out beating of my chest to the left, right and centre in order to stimulate muscle healing. I have to say that I was a bit nervous about pounding my chest in case it confused my heart as I was unsure of my heart at that point. However, I knew that Jeremiah was well read and had a wealth of wisdom in scientific and holistic practices and is a very intuitive Healer. So, I made like King Kong and beat my chest! The points to beat are on the breastbone in the centre of the chest. The left and right are just beneath your collarbone, just up from where your armpit joints your torso. If you look at pictures on the internet for "location of a pacemaker", it's where they put the metal pulse generator box (which surely can't be a coincidence?).

A few months down the line and Jeremiah noted a that all of my lymph nodes had gone down to the size of a pinhead from being pea sized when I first presented to him. He wondered if it was some sort of viral blood infection that started the whole .

(During a Cardiology consultation months later on 13th December I asked the Cardiologist what she thought had caused the whole thing. She shrugged and said maybe a viral infection! My thoughts immediate spun back to this day and Jeremiah's theory.)

The seed was sowed in my mind about acupressure training and was germinating!

Anger

Being a pretty patient person, I didn't realise how much anger was bottling up inside me as a result of the way some people behaved towards me because I'm different – I look different, I behave and think differently, my energy is different, I'm an individual for sure! Igor had said to me during our lovely phases "they didn't break the cast when they made you, you're hand crafted!" I loved that and it never ceased to make me purr and he enabled me to embrace my individuality.

In my mid-thirties, my alcoholic husband who I shall call Brad because he looked very like Brad Pitt (ay chihuahua!!) pushed the boundaries further than anyone else ever had. I started exploding at his lack of respect for me and his misogynist sneers at my attempts to run the pub as the business that it indeed was. I smashed every single glass in the pub one night as he vented his anger at me and I just broke. Boy did I love the sound of breaking glass in that moment (we know a song about that too don't we boys and girls!).

Brad was a six feet two inches tall with a great physique, rode a motorbike, played the guitar and sung like Elvis and he was the perfect person to partner with to rebel against the restrictions that my ex-husband had imposed upon me. We'd quaff champagne on a random evening in the local wine bar just because we could and our catch phrase when we were frequently asked "what's the occasion?" was "it's Thursday and we're still alive". We would take ourselves off on our motorbikes for adventures all over the place throughout the UK and down through France, sometimes I'd ride pillion and sometimes I'd be on my own Honda Hornet 600cc beautiful mean machine. Our friends cried when we split up for the first time because we were such an institution.

However, when we became the tenants of our local pub in a picturesque Essex village, that's when my emotional outbursts started to happen and were epic. Now at this stage I simply must point out that crucial things had just happened:

1. I'd resigned from my powerful London job and so my nose was no longer on that grindstone. I was actually seeing life for the first time outside of the professional confines of YUPPIEdom.
2. I learned Reiki and so I had signalled to The Universe that I was ready for personal growth and so it was time to go to Spiritual School – Unfortunately, I didn't realise that at the time. I thought it was about healing and I didn't know that I had *that* much to do! Let the lessons begin.
3. Little did I know, that Brad was my Teacher and he was about to show me what was alive inside of **me**. His anger was showing me that I had anger and resentment growing

within me. I wanted the pub, but it came at a price. It was very demanding, hard work, no privacy, I was indoors all day every day, I was drinking outside of my comfort zone, it was so much more than I'd bargained for and whilst I kept an eternal optimism head on my shoulders, Brad showed me what was actually alive inside of me by mirroring my inner thoughts right back at me.

At the time I didn't see that. What I saw was His drunken insensitivity and behaviour were so incredulous, and I hadn't encountered anything like it in my life before as for the last decade I'd been well and truly within my comfort zone, surrounded by London professionals and my ex-husband who was well brought up and a gentleman who'd whisked me off to Paris no less!

When Brad partially sobered up the next day he'd just shrug and say "I was drunk" and then the emphasis switched to me being the baddie for behaving like a crazed lunatic which drove me even crazier at the injustice of it or I'd skulk away in shame to hide and lick my wounds. My close friends didn't know what to make of it all as some of the happenings were morbidly hilarious and so definitely worthy of a black comedy.

I've always enjoyed a drink but before I knew what was happening, I'd got swept along with his addiction and I was drinking well outside of my comfort zone. I constantly pulled myself out of the whirlpool of alcohol, but he was determined to continue in his spiral of self-destruct, day in and day out. His words and behaviour showed me just how much he resented my willpower and it was heart-breaking that he would choose resentment over self-preservation. Indeed, my best efforts to "save him" only made things much worse. I was too deep in the situation to see it at the time. Instead, I felt rejected and confused beyond belief. Inevitably, when I consumed one too many vinos, my tongue would loosen and lash out like a serpent at the boundary fences around my own "well brought up" behaviour sending them crashing to the floor and scattering splinters of drama everywhere - Oops! Strangely he loved it and said it was like living with a tigress. I guess he was simply loving his job as my Spiritual Teacher! I on the other hand was not enjoying the process.

I kept trying to save him until years later I realised that he didn't want to be saved. He loved being an alcoholic – it defined him as a person. Of course, I didn't realise that he'd implemented his defence mechanism and was now gas-lighting me and my going crazy is exactly what is expected to happen. The term "gas-lighting" comes from the Academy award winning 1944 psychological thriller "Gaslight" which follows a woman whose husband slowly manipulates her into believing that she is descending into insanity.

So, with the benefit of hindsight and joining the dots across to my recent newfound knowledge of TCM, all became a bit clearer as to why my heart had stalled at 52-years old despite all my efforts to live a healthy and zen life. I had spent well over a decade living in fear of being provoked and losing control of myself (the emotion held in the kidneys). My kidneys didn't have sufficient energy to nurture my angry liver and they weren't up to the job of controlling my heart's output of joy – I was trying way too hard at bringing joy to someone that just didn't want joy. They preferred the darker side, but the tenacious me, kept on trying and sending it out there anyway.

As I've now learned, everything was down to me! Everything that happens around us, we create. We are here to learn and we are constantly creating experiences to teach us what we need to learn. It can get really deep, but essentially, over the last three years, my beautiful heart has a constant conference call going on with my spirit (Linda), my soul and my body and we have a multi-disciplinary team meeting daily and I'm told that if I am not being valued, it is because I am not valuing myself. If someone doesn't approve, it's because I'm not approving of an aspect of my life and I've got to change it − they are simply mirrors to me. If they are angry, they're showing me my inner anger; frustration, yup, emotionally unavailable − oh bloody hell!

Despite what was going on behind the scenes, front of house, the pub was a roaring success and we threw the best party in town almost every night and I adored our customers for bringing fun and light into my life. It was 2001 and we'd inherited a very successful pub from the previous tenants, and we took it even higher, increasing the turnover from £250,000 to £340,000 pa in six years. When we were riding high, we were fabulous and had so much fun with either live music or karaoke every week and when Brad was singing, I'd refuse to serve anyone saying "sorry, I'm swooning at the moment, you'll have to wait!". On these occasions the bar would be packed to the gills with joyful people of all ages, all of whom we counted as our friends such was the sense of community there.

On the much brighter side, at this time, I realised that something strange was happening and I was healing my pub customers' ailments. When I was squiffy I got obvious psychic insights and I just knew what was wrong with their shoulders, their back, etc and when I put my hands on a sore shoulder I blurted out "it's not your shoulder, it's your lower back – how do you sit at your desk?" I astounded them and myself although the reaction of some made me think I'd be burnt at the stake if I wasn't careful!

I was frazzled from thirteen years in a high-pressure sales environment, the challenging relationship and also from running the pub but one day I happened across a poster advertising a Reiki Workshop. I quizzed the shop-owner and said, "I think I'm doing that naturally, but I don't understand it". I signed up and that was the beginning of my Reiki and spiritual journey. I was eager to use my new found skill – some people were delighted, some were freaked out, some were both! I had the perfect partner to heal too – I had attracted that one into my 'Healer' archetype energy without a doubt.

My attempts "to save" Brad including when I tried to send him Reiki were met with fury, which was all the more confusing to me, "why wouldn't he want to be healed of his anger, his alcohol dependency, his depression?" I was too much of a Reiki rookie to spot the direct comparison with the story that we learn during Reiki training: The founder of Reiki, Mikao Usui, tried out his new healing ability on beggars in the streets and he did indeed successfully heal them. However, he discovered that despite their physical ailments being cured with Reiki, they were returning to beg in the streets within a few years as they were not ready to lead a responsible life and that they needed healing on a spiritual level too. We all pick up baggage along the journey of life, and some of it has deep roots and isn't something that we can just click our fingers and vanquish from existence.

Looking back, I was oblivious that The Universe was sending me the same message over and over again. Because I kept missing it, it kept sending it back to me but with increasing potency. It got harsher and harsher but being that Spaniel, I kept bouncing back for more, blindly ignoring the messages. I'm surprised that I didn't look in the mirror one morning to find "He's not ready yet!" scrawled on my forehead with a black marker pen by The Universe.

If I'd only learned that lesson, I could have saved myself a lot of heartache, moved on and progressed in my life so much more quickly. Instead, I literally held myself back for fifteen years as all of my energies were being spent trying to fix a toxic relationship that only one person wanted to fix and as we know, it takes two to tango! In the words of Dorothy from the Wizard of Oz "Oh my!" The worst thing is, that I did that to myself, I cannot blame anyone else. It was my lesson to learn, and I didn't pay attention and learn it soon enough.

The actual lightbulb didn't go on over my head until the latter stages of writing the first edition of this book when I happened across the phrase "gas-lighting" and on further research I found that Brad had used every one of the eleven gas-lighting techniques listed in an article (and probably completely subconsciously):

- Tell blatant lies.
- deny they said or did something even though you have proof
- attack what's important to you

- wear you down over time
- actions don't match their words
- positive reinforcement to confuse
- cause confusion to keep you off balance
- project what they're doing and accuse you of doing it
- set people against you
- tell you and others that you're crazy
- tell you that others are lying

I thought I'd got over it so many years later, but all of this remained in my vibration for over a decade and with different antics from different sources, one day my heart just couldn't cope anymore and physically broke – because I had still not learned my own lessons!

Brad was a classic example of chronic anger and he just would not let certain situations from his past go. He dwelled on them and they literally boiled out of his skin manifesting as boils and cysts on his face as he allowed the toxicity of his emotions to get the better of him. There was the physical evidence of his emotions being out of balance and him not doing the spiritual work necessary to release it. One of his classic expressions that he'd learned during his time in Alcoholics Anonymous was "poor me, poor me, pour me another drink".

He'd joke about 'stinking thinking' and yet he never worked his way out of that during our time together. I'll be going over forgiveness later on as this is oh so crucial to well-being and peace of mind. Great expression that isn't it "peace of mind", peace in your mind, a peaceful mind, peace, your mind has peace – and you can SmileInside. Because of my Reiki practices I was becoming increasingly enlightened and felt that I was evolving rapidly and that delighted me, but Brad resented me even for that and told me so directly. The more enlightened I became, the more sensitive to negative energy I was, and my situation was tortuous. We broke up many times over the last seven years of our relationship but he'd convince me he was doing things differently and so I went back, only to discovered that it was all talk and history would repeat itself. And guess what, I reacted the same way and so I hadn't learned either! Bugger! Until finally, one day, I learned and I never went back into that loop. All I had to do, was acknowledge that he did not want to change and accept that if I couldn't live in that loop, walk away, or put-up and shut-up. Within three months of stepping out of that circle, my life had moved on significantly.

Managing it all

So here's the tricky part. I recognised that I'd been gas-lit for many years, but now with a further two years of personal growth and awareness under my belt since that lightbulb moment, I now had to deal with a new way of working with such information. In the past, it was very neat and tidy to blame Brad, or Igor or Beau for their behaviours and me feel that I'd worked through the adversity of it all. Now, I had to recognise that I'd attracted it into my life through lack of self-worth maybe, as my measure of success could no longer be gauged by my sales targets and bank balance.

I could get oh so deep here but that wouldn't help to demonstrate ways of managing challenges in life. Instead, the way to manage situations such as being gas-lit, or indeed dealing with a narcissist for example, is simple: **We don't manage them, we manage ourselves**.

We cannot change other people, we can't save them from alcohol, their addictions, themselves, their past or the future that they create for themselves every day. We cannot release them from their triggers and we can't hide ourselves from them so that we don't trigger them into anger, resentment, upset, fight or flight. That is their journey and they could understandably resent us for interfering in their journey, because they are taking their life and their journey at their own pace, based on what their intuition and their soul and spirit is guiding them to do – or not as the case may be!

What we can do, is manage ourselves. If they want to take us as a shining example and follow suit, great, but we can't count on that. We have to take this as part of our own journey and say to ourselves "I do not consent to being treated like this", "spoken to like this", "this is not my life", "I want more respect", "I want peace and harmony", etc. Etc. And we can manifest this for ourselves by bringing our energies into balance, and it's easy with The Balance Procedure. The cards aren't magic, they simply give us focus. The system itself gives us the tools to recognise when we have been pushed or pulled out of whack and we need to get ourselves back on track for our Life path, our year and for who we were born to be, and the potential that we have within ourselves. We simply bring ourselves into balance energetically and the rest will happen naturally. We will stay, go, or our surroundings will morph to match our new and higher vibration and our inner joy starts to happen naturally. It's amazing and it works really really quickly. As with everything, we just have to want it to happen, and it will.

But, I repeat, we have to want this and do this for ourselves – not for anyone else.

If we are seeing someone else who is not reaching their full potential and we desperately want to pick them up, support them emotionally, heal them, support them financially - we have to ask ourselves, are we actually seeing ourselves right in front of our own eyes?

Are we not reaching our own true potential because we are engrossed in saving someone else? Are our own energies being used up by confusion and mopping up the chaos and mistakes created by others? Everyone makes mistakes so I'm not being judgemental here. Indeed, my mistake (again and again and again) was not learning that everyone has to mop up their own mistakes or they do not learn. By me saving them, I was hindering their learning. An analogy here is that we don't help someone to learn by doing their homework. They will never learn if we do that for them. I dearly wish that I'd learned that fifteen years ago!

(If we are feeling emotionally drained and unhappy by what is going on in our lives, maybe as a results of being a "victim" to a gas-lighter or a narcissist for example, we can simply use the emotional scale described in The Balance Procedure chapter in Section 2 of this book, to recognise that in the first place. Then all we have to do, is get out The Balance Procedure cards and rebalance our energies. If we are confused, bored, depressed, angry, pessimistic, resentful – anything below number 8 on that scale, we have to work on ourselves. We will naturally elevate ourselves out of that situation and we don't have to decide on how or get caught up in the finer details for now, we'll simply manifest a happier way of being without actually trying. Then, once we've gained a bit of confidence, we'll naturally get more creative with our own life and take ourselves into a new way of being.)

However, there was a good decade of Reiki personal growth before I happened across The Balance Procedure and that was a very profound time although there was an interesting conundrum that came with me learning Reiki. On one hand, I was calmer, less stressed and more at peace with myself. I felt and saw the beauty around me like never before and I will never forget the day that I was grooming my horse Penelope Pitstop (Penny-horse) and as I rested my hand on her muscular neck, I felt her life-force energy. It was the most beautiful feeling of warmth (physical and emotional), gentleness and strength, calm and yet ready to bolt. We would mosey around the countryside together in all weathers, soaking up the breath-taking scenery and delighting at the wildlife that we encountered. We would gallop and jump and squeal with delight. That big brown beastie totally saved my soul during my Pub Landlady days in particular.

The flip side of the enlightenment coin was that I became more sensitive to negativity. News was physically painful, arguments hurt, anger and resentment were absolutely offensive and I found rejection unbearable as love was so liberating and joyful, why would anyone push it away? .... and yet, I was being physically, emotionally and verbally pushed away constantly by my alcoholic husband. He'd physically sweep me to one side without a word and walk out rather than "talk it out". I'd use Reiki to maintain calm and to send to situations to resolve them peacefully and it worked pretty well. I was pretty confused when my heart literally broke years later but during an acupuncture session, as Jeremiah worked on a gallbladder point (anger), five words spontaneously popped into my head "why don't you love me?" I had given my all to my two marriages and the relationship with Igor and yet, well you know the rest.

After I divorced Brad and we split up for the final time, several months later I got together with Igor and he too began to push my boundaries as his undiagnosed and unconfirmed bipolar unfurled - I bet my Guardian Angel was banging her head against a brick wall crying "Noooo! Not again! Please not again, I can't take anymore!!" – but then again maybe she's responsible and played Cupid as I still had lessons to learn! Hmm! After several months, I started to have outbursts similar to those that I'd had with Brad and that I'd worked so hard to make a thing of the past - although they were nowhere near as profound as during my Brad years due to the work that I'd done on myself with my Reiki practices. So, when he stormed out of my house and reversed straight into the ditch, having peeked to check he was unhurt, I then left him to it. I was infuriated when he told a neighbour who enquired after his wellbeing (as he curled up in the van to block it all out) that we'd had a row - as we hadn't. He had been drunk and had stormed out in a hissy-fit entirely of his own making. I told him to own the responsibility for this himself and not drag me into his chaos. Oo, I bet my Guardian Angel was proud of that one! I continued to stand my ground over the years as he rained chaos over and again, but these occasions were still happening, presumably because I was still sending out the smoke signals that this was my version of love and so it was acceptable, hence that's what I attracted more of - but I was completely unaware of this notion at that time.

I think that The Universe / my Soul / my Guardian Angel was sending these relationships to me to teach me boundaries, i.e. what is acceptable and unacceptable behaviour and how to vocalise my feelings in a calm and considered fashion. I'd learned over the years that if I didn't listen to my inner voice, something always happened to say "told you so".

By now, unbeknown to me, I was slowly building the walls around my heart and would continue to do for good few more years yet, becoming emotionally unavailable in order to protect my romantically broken heart which ultimately then physically broke, from more angst.

It wasn't until relatively recently that a series of dalliances which had all ended the same way spurred me into connecting the dots - they were emotionally unavailable – and that resulted in my own "ah-ha" moment when I realised that I was being shown that I too was emotionally unavailable. That was a real shock to me but something that Beau had put in his own words a few times to give me those clues, saying "I can't reach you, you won't let me in". I obviously wasn't ready to hear and so I didn't.

Now that the cartoon lightbulb had gone on above my head, I set to work on remedying that situation. I felt that my heart was physically strong enough and that I had gathered enough research material to have the knowledge and the wisdom to manage whatever came my way. However, with this golden nugget of information, I was confident that I would be able to manifest someone to reflect my own emotional availability.

Since becoming aware of all of these aspects of my energetic smoke signals, I had to wonder how they formed in the first place. As I've learned, all we have to do is ask and our soul provides the answer in innovative ways: During a massage I had asked my Therapist to work on my stomach as my solar plexus which is of course the core of our being and our emotions, had felt really tight for over a week and which I figured was down to the emotions from writing this book. As she did so, out of the blue, I had two visions – one of a very young and confused me thinking "why aren't I welcome? What's the matter?" This vision brought me clarity and I was able to start to release the subconscious smoke signals I'd been sending out my entire life and which had popped up in many different guises. The other was "don't worry, you're safe now".

Boundaries

Within a week of me being home from hospital, Beau called. He was in dire straits again – homeless, penniless, fuel-less, with his dog in tow and not able to work that day for all of the above reasons. He wanted me to drive to Málaga with some money, but I explained that I simply wasn't strong enough, but that I was meeting friends at the beach and if he could make it there I'd give him some money to tide him over.

We agreed that in return for me helping him out, he would put his gardening talents to use and sort out the wreck of a flowerbed opposite my front door and create the Moon Garden that I've been hankering after for ages. It was quite poignant as since my return from hospital, every morning I stepped outside of my front door and faced the mess of a garden that I'd completely neglected and it reminded me that I'd done that to my body and it too was now a wreck. True to his word, Beau finished my Moon Garden. It took him two days to get rid of the metre-high weeds and transform my garden into a vision of beauty.

I was delighted for a few days until he had another mood swing, threw a tantrum and my heart's physical vulnerability was all too obvious at a time when I was doing everything that I could to heal and protect my heart holistically, and this fella was trampling all over my efforts. He had to go and so I sent him on his way.

(My friends were already dismayed at my benevolence but a couple of years down the line from that moment, during a meditation, I was given the awareness that my brother's mental illness had made me more sympathetic to lost souls. About the same time, I started a course in Astrology and I realised that it was written in the stars! I learned that the position in the sky of the asteroid / Chiron, at the precise time of our birth, tells us what our core wounds are and how we can overcome them. For example, Chiron was moving through the constellation of Pisces at the time that I was born. This means that I forgive readily as I take in people's history, and I make allowances rather than judgements.

The downside is that I held myself back by doing this because I went round in the same circles time after time. Had I prioritised myself and my own journey, I would have evolved much more rapidly and most certainly have achieved joy and a heightened sense of self. Instead, I was caught up in whirlpools of drama and repeated mistakes that didn't belong to me – but I myself repeated the mistake of rescuing them. In doing so, I stopped them from learning the life lesson that was intended from that drama, and so we mirrored each other repeatedly for years sometimes! If only I knew then, what I know now!

In the Astrology Chapter in Section 2 of this book, and also included in my Shine On course (see www.LindaJaneW.me for details), I explain why our whole natal chart is so important in understanding ourselves and why we react the way that we do in life. It's fascinating! The very reason that we were each born at that precise moment in time, under the energetic influence of the planets and the stars is because that shows us what aspects of our character we need to work on in this lifetime.)

As I've mentioned before, Beau's behaviour definitely led to fast-tracking me through my life lessons and before too long, we were friends once more and I had another to learn, still about boundaries.

Beau was having a lovely time in the evenings, smoking my weed – the weed that I could no longer smoke owing to that fateful night and this bloomin' awakening! Because of his track record, I'd set the condition from the outset that there was "no drinking alcohol" and he initially complied but then he started bringing beer back to my house and as I watched him lounging on my outdoor sofa smoking and drinking to his heart's content and getting sillier by the moment. He was breaching the boundaries that I'd set (probably because he wasn't use to me actually setting any).

Instead of sending him packing immediately, I carefully explained that there was no way I could have someone drinking and smoking around me in my home when I was struggling with not being able to do so myself any more. I said that he could stay for a couple of weeks but I reiterated that he wasn't to smoke or drink there. What I hadn't said, was that I felt vulnerable around drunk or high people as they were unpredictable and not in a good way. I didn't need to say it because straight away he unwittingly mirrored that sentiment and he mood swung straight into anger mode and had an absolute hissy fit again, ranting and shouting at me that "I should get over it!", that I was "milking it and feeling sorry for myself which wasn't attractive". Cheeky little f*cker! Such was the rant that he packed all of his stuff back into the van and wheel spun off.

Exhausted and upset with it all, my fragile body was shaking like a leaf and my heart pounding about all over the place so I had little choice but to stay at home that night although I had hoped to pop out for a while with my friends. However, interestingly, I had part 2 of that lesson to learn later that same night. I really didn't want to be around overly squiffy people at all, let alone after these episodes. Crazy how one found me anyway! ... Hmm, well manifested Linda!

(If we say "I don't want to be ....." then we're still giving energy to the potential of the negative and so The Universe doesn't hear the word "don't" and we manifest what we don't want! That's why it's really important to keep all affirmations and manifestations and thoughts in the positive context.)

Upset, I phoned a friend and he was really understanding and lovely and told me to relax and be kind to myself – but he added "what was I thinking letting Beau back in my house and my life after the heart attack?!" Yep, I really deserved that. What was I thinking?! I guess I didn't realise how fragile I actually was and was in denial.

Later I messaged my friend and told him that I was staying in and that I'd managed to calm myself and my heart down, that I was no longer shaking and that I was going to bed.

Unfortunately, maybe due to my mate's squiffiness he decided it was appropriate to send me a WhatsApp voice message at midnight and have a go at me about my poor judgement over allowing Beau back into my life and about keeping it a secret, and about how dangerous it was for my health, and about how dangerous he is, and that he's using me, and how he's manipulating me, and how he's trying to squeeze more money out of me, and how he's making a fool out of me.

I explained calmly that I'm different. I'm a Healer and an Empath and because of my late brother's mental illness (which was brought about by overdoing it on LCD in the 1970's) I have every sympathy for anyone with emotional issues and would continue to do what I could because that's who I am. I felt like I was living to my ideals and being kind and loving and forgiving and was happy with that response.

Then the anger kicked in! I tossed and turned for a couple of hours and then it hit me full in the face and I sent my mate a furious voice message saying that maybe he should protect me from Beau as I was the vulnerable one, rather than condemning my choices. I angrily told him that whilst "he" was DRUNK, I was stone cold sober and trying to sleep but I was now too angry and furthermore "I" could not have a drink to calm me down, nor could "I" have a joint or a cigarette to relieve the stress - I could do nothing to calm myself down and make myself feel better and I hoped he was pleased with himself because after I'd spent hours calming myself down after Beau's outburst I was now back to square one! Just what I needed after a heart attack – what was he thinking?! Obviously, he wasn't because "heeeee" was DRUNK!

I was livid and continued to be for days despite the betablockers. I told my mate to back off because he was drunk which was now a swear word to me – how quickly I'd jumped up onto my high horse!

However, the clever but harsh Universe had sent this situation to me for good reason. In defending the rationale behind me letting Beau back into my World, I realised myself that I'm a kind, generous, forgiving, loving person and I never will stop being that person, that is who I am. I actually felt proud of myself as it was something of a revelation to me that that's actually who I am. My mum had been saying that to me for years but the words never sunk in, maybe as past relationships had torn my playhouse down rather than appreciate my positives.

However, it was a real shocker to realise how stressed I had become, how fragile my emotions were and how vulnerable I'd felt, and whilst I'd finally accepted that I am a kind, loving, forgiving, generous person, here was a perfect demonstration of why boundaries had to be created and upheld.

I tried but I was a sucker for a good sob story until finally, a year or so of intermittent friendship / fallout episodes with Beau and after more boundary breaches, I finally said no more and realised that by "helping" Beau time and time again, I was actually stopping him from learning his own life lessons.

By constantly rescuing him, he was happily repeating the same mistakes over and over as I bailed him out. I was enabling him to go around in circles rather than simply letting him reflect on his words and actions and so make a conscious effort to take a different direction and thus learn and grow. That really was that.

With the insight of boundaries, came the awareness that despite the verbal beatings over the years, they were only important as the value that I allowed them to have.

Whilst Brad had actually said to me "you're too intelligent, you're too quick witted, you're too independent, you're too successful, you're more of a bloke than I am – you're just too f*cking much!" – that was a reflection of him not feeling good enough and actually nothing to do with me.

During his depressive episodes, Igor had told me what a horrid person I was for years and as I was learning my lessons courtesy of a subconscious collaboration between my mate and Beau, and I now recognised my worth.

Whilst another dalliance had told me as I was relegated to "being just good friends" because he'd met someone else "Linda, you're beautiful, fun, intelligent, sexy and I really love your company – but she's twenty years younger than you" – that was his insecurity aptly reflecting right at me. After my self-esteem had been dented by Igor and Brad I was a perfect reflection. The fabulous outcome from the latter episode was that he'd restored my faith in my body and absolutely reassured me that I had definitely not lost it (wink wink). Although that statement was then to give me a complex about my age which I hadn't felt before – deep joy! LOL! This bold Leo lioness has six planets in water signs let me remind you, and so the emotional cuts run deep – but as I'd resolved to take a holistic route, that just meant working on it!

And so I pondered on it and then it struck me.   I always had, and was always going to encounter people saying things that I didn't like or that I felt were insensitive, I just had build trust in myself by being authentic and true to myself, so that their words held no value to me – because the only value that they held, was the value that I allowed them to have. So what if they thought x, y or z – I don't care what they think any more! Oh My God, so powerful!

Lessons

When the time comes to choose to work on the aspects of our personality that have been "imposed" upon us over the years by others, it becomes a really fascinating process. Not only that, but by being authentic to our true selves, we live the path that we're meant to.

In the words of Anita Moorjani, if I allowed those parts of me that don't belong, the elements that are not mine, to fall away and reveal "me", then I could trust Linda more than anyone else. I started working on this philosophy. It took quite a lot of practice. It took quite a lot of standing up for myself. It took quite a lot to soul searching and being honest with myself at the risk of losing friends because I dared to be different and true to myself. I stopped asking people for their opinions on my decisions. I stopped asking what people thought because I realised that they held different values which did not match my own. No criticism or judgement here, just fact.

In doing this, I became aware of how much others were trying to intervene in my life and my decisions. How much they expected to be a part of what I did or didn't do. They would get quite animated and irritated if I didn't consult them on something as personal as me buying a car and if I didn't want to comply with their version of what I "should" do. I became more self-confident, didn't value their company as much, didn't value their opinions and I grew into myself. (It was a strange way of being and one I couldn't have done without my dog, my companion and my little angel - Vagabond! I bet he wouldn't eat me, and I reckon he'd stand guard to stop my cats tucking in! Hahaha!)

➤ I had happened across a video of a talk by Anita Moorjani when it was time for this lesson to begin. A friend had brought her into my awareness way before my own life changing event and so when her video popped up as a recommendation, I appreciated the synchronicity and settled down to watch it.

➤

➤ Anita had a near death experience but had a profound recovery once she agreed to come back into her body and continue on her life's mission. These are the points that resonated with me (I would like to thank Anita and her team for granting me permission to use her insights herein). I highly recommend further viewing and reading of Anita's messages as different aspects will resonate with you individually.

What have I taken on that's not mine?

Say no to things that don't feel right to you.

Let things go that are not you and set your heart and your soul free

Don't say yes when you want to say no

We already are what we were born to be

Don't work on who you want to be, let the parts that are not you fall away to reveal the real you ...

Focus on your light and don't allow others to pull you into their fears, their dramas or their darkness using guilt

Help others by holding onto your light

Fear stresses your immune system

We just have to chip away and let go of the stuff that isn't us, that doesn't fit, to reveal and to be ourselves.

This means being true to ourselves, speaking our truth, saying no or yes from the heart rather than what we think others want us to say. It means living the way that we want to, that nurtures our souls rather than puts us under stress, makes us anxious, angry or upset.

I know from my own work and beliefs that these emotions, whilst natural, are not meant to be the predominant emotions within our personality and if they are there too often or too strongly then we are on the wrong path and need to change our World to remove or de-sensitise ourselves to these triggers.

This tied in with a rune card that I drew a couple of days previous, which said don't follow others into the darkness. Let your light shine – so I did exactly that and let the parts of me that aren't me, fall away to reveal the true me and guess what - I really quite liked her. I started to feel focused, content, back on track for my life purpose, authentic for being true to myself and the lack of alcohol, caffeine, nicotine, etc means I'm being "real". Synchronicity eh?

******

Because I had been forced to take life at a slower pace now and I had consciously decided to investigate the reasons that The Universe had thrown my life into disarray, I started getting more thoughts and insights. For example, I started to wonder if I subconsciously created stress because I used to thrive on it and the adrenaline during my high flying days in London and so I had become an adrenaline junkie! Being pathologically late for everything fed my habit all the more as I charged around to get to appointments on time and so high adrenaline levels had become the normal in my body chemistry. Essentially, we are our hormones (chemicals). Think ingredients on a bottle of an energy drink – we are all our own recipe of chemicals – hopefully we're pretty organic but everything that we put into our body becomes part of the list of ingredients on the bottle that is you.

In addition, sometimes I'd become aware that my mind was going round in circles and that by holding onto those thoughts I was self-perpetuating stress instead of taking control to calm my mind.

I learned that stress related illnesses kill more people than anything else in the world including cancer.

Because of these insights I took action* mixing-up a Bach remedy including Walnut (to help with changes to my life and also to protect me from outside influences), White Chestnut (to calm and over-active mind), Star of Bethlehem (to soothe after trauma, tragedy and shock).

I've given a more detailed overview of the Bach Flower Remedies in Section 2 of this book as they are invaluable to manage emotions which are off kilter and causing problems in your world. They literally bring about peace of mind.

* In taking responsibility for your own wellbeing, we have to action the insights that come to us in order to actually make the difference in ourselves. This is the difference between "knowledge" and "wisdom" - i.e. knowledge is having the information; wisdom is acting on it.

Stress isn't just an issue generated by our minds, it's also a side-effect of what we put into our bodies. When we toxify it with substances, alcohol, nicotine, too much caffeine, foods that we're intolerant too or that require a lot of digesting and processing, we put our bodies into stress.

Our opinion of ourselves can cause stress and as the rice experiment later in these pages shows, feeling ourselves to be less than, is very damaging. I had been feeling rather down about my appearance as I dropped to a UK size 8 and I looked awful in just about everything in my wardrobe. I went to a market down on the coast and bought clothes that fit "whoohooo!" What a difference having a pair of shorts that fit and a fringed summer top to wear with them.

*****

At five feet eight inches I'd been a voluptuous eleven stone two pounds when I arrived in Spain. I'd never been that curvy before – it had crept up on me when I wasn't looking and I was bursting out of a size 14, with a muffin top which I wasn't chuffed about. However, as the rash appeared, the weight dropped off and when my friends raised concerns about my weight loss, I put it down to the fact that I was simply returning to my normal weight of 9st 8lb, probably with all of the dancing that I was doing. Following my awakening I dropped even more weight and was 8 stone 8 pounds. I thought I looked amazing but the photos said something different. I looked great from the front with a tiny waist, flat belly and cheek bones to die for (unfortunate pun there) but when I checked out my derrière in the mirror I was dismayed to see a saggy, shapeless bottom akin to a deflated balloon. That in itself was really upsetting and as soon as I'd noticed this, I attempted to tone myself up, but every time I tried to exercise, my chest muscles and diaphragm protested. I couldn't help but become breathless as the mechanical parts involved in breathing just weren't working effectively. It was alarming to say the least.

Therefore, given my low energy levels and my fragile disposition, it made sense to me to make the most of my time and soak up the information that would empower my mind, body and spirit back to health in a manageable way.

I had the luxury of a lot of thinking and processing time about past and present life events and things started to drop into my awareness and shuffle about in my mind to give me the benefit of hindsight. That in itself was quite an eye-opener and not all of it welcome. As I started to see how universal energies work and how we ultimately create everything around us, I had to start taking responsibility for some things which I'd conveniently blamed on someone else. My spiritual explanations and the terminology which my spiritual friends and I had been using for many years, started to feel novice level rather than intermediate or advanced. On one hand I was disappointed that I wasn't as evolved as I thought I was, on the other I was open to learning more. I had no idea just how much there was though!

I learned that barefoot grounding / earthing is scientifically proven to reduce inflammation, reduce pain and fatigue and bring about relaxation thus aiding better sleep. Simply walking and standing barefoot on grass, beach, the earth, etc (i.e. natural ground not concrete, tiles or carpet) "earths" the electrical circuits in our body so that it can heal itself. It goes into a scientific explanation about positive and negative ions but without getting technical, let's just kick off our shoes and get barefoot outside every day □□ and see what happens. I've always been a fan of barefoot, but with this actual knowledge I made sure that I spent fifteen-minutes every day outside, standing and sitting on the giant rocks that were scattered around the mountainside surrounding my house. When my friends and I headed to the beach, I also made sure that I spent a considerable amount of the time reaching down off the deck-bed into the sand and paddling in the sea. As the weather warmed, I noticed how incredible I felt after swimming and spending a day at the coast.

*****

I discovered that each chakra in the body has a different musical note associated with it and so listening to music is a great healer. I guess we've all been aware that certain music at certain times is a joy to listen to, but at other times it grates. It depends how our body is resonating at that time and what will benefit us, versus what will push our biorhythms further out of whack. I discovered chakra dancing and spent as long as I was able, dancing to the music that had been composed specifically to clear and rebalance each chakra in turn. I wasn't able to dance for long to start with and had to pause to catch my breath frequently, but the music's healing vibes was undeniable.

From here, I joined the dots from Jeremiah's chest beating advice, with the music, with another nugget of information that I happened across about generating those healing tones from within. Whilst I was beating my chest as part of my daily rehabilitation regime, I began to "ahhhh" and "oooooo" up and down through the music scale - Eat your heart out Tarzan!

I found that certain notes felt awful whilst others were soothing and I could really feel the benefit and so I keep going with those ones. This is another simple yet really effective way of learning to listen to our intuition and our body in order to turbo charge the healing process … how very groovy is that?! Rock 'n' Roll baby!

I learned that eating foods associated with individual chakras empowers wellbeing and I began to notice how I was being drawn to eating green foods (green being the colour of the heart chakra). In addition, whilst the colour red is associated with anger, to neutralise that emotion, eating green foods is recommended.

Colours greatly influence us consciously or unconsciously. The inside of my wardrobe looks like a rainbow as I need choice on a daily basis. I actually cannot wear a colour if it doesn't feel right such is the impact of that energy on me.

The impact of colour energy goes beyond clothes and food as we will find ourselves naturally drawn to aspects of nature that nurture the chakra associated with a particular emotion or medical condition for example

It might well be that you are drawn to trees and forests as I am – and of course the colour green is associated with the heart – need I say more? Sometimes the sky feels like it is drawing me in, in which case my throat chakra or lungs may be in need of nurturing or it may be that communications – written or verbal need supporting. When we bring colour into our homes, we are subconsciously providing ourselves with the therapeutic properties of the colours that we need more of.

Here are just a few pointers about each colour:

Red: Vitality, elevates the blood pressure, stimulates the appetite and can dispel depression. Use also for the skeleton and lower limbs. It is associated with anger so eat green foods to diffuse which is the complementary colour

Orange: Joy and happiness, warmth, free spirited and feeling well. Use for desires and the genito-urinary system of kidneys and the bladder and body fluids.

Yellow: Bright and sunny, detoxes the mind and body giving you clarity to situations. It balances emotions and overcomes lethargy. is great for the digestive system and skin.

Green: Balance and harmony. It soothes the mind and the body and symbolises growth and renewal. It is beneficial for the heart, lungs, immune system, circulatory and respiratory systems.

Blue: Peace and serenity. It lowers blood pressure and reduces rapid heart rate. Relaxing and used for the throat, thyroid, lungs, vocal cords and communication of all types.

Indigo: Promotes openness, respect for others and intuition. Sensory organs and senses, i.e. taste, smell, sight and hearing in addition to the sinuses.

Violet: Perception, the brain and central nervous system.

Pink: Caring and loving of yourself and others. Use for lack of self-esteem and where gentleness is required on yourself and others.

*****

As I began to come back into balance and to trust my intuition more and more, I reviewed my medication but asked a trusted friend for their input because I really felt left alone by the medical profession. I actually didn't mind that too much as they would only have wanted me to do things their way and I had my own ideas. Instead of doing nothing, I researched everything that I was taking and I decided what I was happy to continue with, what I was happier reducing to half the dose and what I didn't want to take anymore.

*****

I learned that it's OK to have a shadow side and that we have to embrace it rather than hide it. It's merely something to work our way through if we choose to.

When I was at the local bar for Open Mic one Friday night, everyone was getting squiffy and I was not used to this being a spectator sport which I was not allowed to play, so I thought "sod it, I need a treat!" and I ordered myself a triple chocolate mousse. The dessert was devilishly huge and so several spoons had been provided along with it, which several of my "drinking" buddies picked up with a view to diving in and sharing my sin. Without even thinking, I literally snarled at them "f*ck off!... You've got a gin & tonic, This is my treat!"

They were all shocked, as indeed was I, as it was a totally reflex reaction - and the spoons were cautiously put back on the table as they realised that this Leo lioness had pouted and roared and was deadly serious. I had no intention of sharing it! Everyone still laughs about it – thankfully! But I guess that anger had burst forth!

That same night one of my clairvoyant friends came up to me and told me that Spirit were looking after me and that I'll be fine. I thanked her and asked her that if ever they told her that my number was up, could she tip me the wink so that I could drink a bottle of champagne or two, get wildly drunk and have an orgy so that I could literally go out with a bang (or two, or three, or …. you get the drift)! (Bawdy ex-pub landlady strikes again!)

Oops, the expression on her face and the fact that visibly recoiled in disgust, told me that she was not amused and so I pulled myself together and thanked her from the bottom of my heart as I can honestly say that it was a huge and welcome relief to hear this from her, for whilst I was doing everything in my power to heal myself, one actually never know what's around the corner. Afterall, I hadn't seen the heart failure coming. One day I was bopping around in typical Linda 'Tiggeresque' fashion and the next I was hooked up to machines unable to go into get onto a bedpan without alarms going off and Nurses coming running. Wow! What a difference a day makes – We know a song about that don't we boys and girls.

It's really interesting reading this back 2 ½ years later as I was doing so well, and yet these incidences show me that I was actually suffering inside. Journalling is a great tool for reviewing your journey as hindsight is invaluable as when we're in the moment, much can be missed.

<u>Smoke Signals / Triggers</u>

During my intuitive research, the messages and insights kept coming and one in particular took the law of attraction to a chemical level. The law of attraction is generally described as us bringing things into our physical reality using the power of our mind and thoughts giving our desires so much energy that they cannot help to manifest. Some people use vision boards, others moon rituals, spells, and Esther & Jerry Hicks channelled the incredible book Ask and it is Given. The Secret is also a best seller in this way of thinking.

When we send out smoke signals into The Universe saying that we want this please (think Native American Indian smoke signals), The Universe sees these smoke signals and replies, delivering our request whether it be an unwittingly negative circumstance; or a delightfully positive one ... or an emotional one.

So now that we realise that we are also asking for emotions to be sent to us, we can make the hormonal connection as it is our hormones which deliver the emotional states: Endorphins for a mood lifting, love and peace, and everything is groovy state of mind; or Adrenaline for anger, stress, fight or flight, irritability or anxiety.

Each emotion has its own unique energy signature, which run through our bodies as electrical signals and we cannot help but self-perpetuate this as our body will start pumping out the mood-creating hormones as soon as it receives a known trigger.

A known trigger (such as being shouted at) will automatically set us off. This isn't just an emotional, verbal and behavioural reaction, but also a hormonal / chemical reaction occurs within our bodies which makes us to act that way – happy or sad, angry or euphoric.

Therefore, if we want to change our negative responses, it isn't just a question of saying to ourselves I'm not going to let that bother me, we actually have to un-programme our hormones too.

Because this is a physical response rather than the etheric emotion, if we want to change our behaviour, we need to consciously decide how we would rather react to a known trigger - BEFORE it happens.

In this way, the nanosecond that we're triggered we can say to ourselves "ah ha! I recognise that I'm being provoked so I'm going to call them out on it" or "I'm going to be calm and say I don't consent to that behaviour" or "I'm going to walk away and feel proud of myself for not rising to the bait". Preparation is key not just in the kitchen or the workplace, but in our minds and our bodies too!

After just a few times of reacting in our newly thought out, pre-determined way, we have reprogrammed our body's hormonal response and we will no longer be triggered because we have evolved our way of being!

Furthermore, and here comes the best bit, because we have changed our chemical signal and our electrical and emotional smoke signals, we attract more of the same i.e. calm, joy, optimism, respect, love, equality.

So now that we realise that there is an interconnected relationship between our emotions, our hormones and our moods - which then become personality traits as they become regular occurrences – we can ask ourselves "who am i?" and start to consciously create that person, bearing in mind any hormonal influences from food or pharmaceuticals. For example, my hormones had been messed about with from the age of 16 ½ years old when I was put on the pill, then through various hormonal fertility treatments as I dived straight into the menopause at 27-years old, then onto Hormone Replacement Therapy (HRT) from my early 30's until I was in my mid 40's. Given that we are our hormones, this new insight from Joe Dispenzer made me question if I'd actually been myself at all during my adult life?

Given that our emotions in the short-term create our mood I.e. angry, happy, resentful, silly. If these moods continue or return frequently then they become our personality traits. These personality traits are essentially who we are as a person, and so how we are known to be by others. A great example here is that when I was first learning to speak Spanish, I learnt the difference between "he is drunk" (el está borracho) and "he is a drunk" (el es un borracho).

Furthermore, because this is who you have become, you will attract more of the same to hold you in that vibration and keep you the same person with the same dramas, or looney happenings, or disrespectful people, etc. If that's all positive then fabulous, but if it's drama after drama, trauma after trauma, tragedy after tragedy then you have got to change your smoke signals.

*****

About nine days before I was hospitalised, I had a date with a chap whose dad had recently died after his cancer suddenly worsened. After my heart failed, he wanted to look after me and was so very thoughtful and generous but I'm such an independent person that I found this difficult and a bit suffocating. I intuitively felt that this chap was still carrying the vibration that he wanted to look after someone and since his father's death a week before he had a void to fill. However, I did not want to "need" looking after by anyone, nor be influenced by his energies. I instinctively felt that I should distance myself from him despite him being a really kind, genuine man and so over the next few weeks I politely declined invitations until we lost contact.

I enjoy joining the dots in life and I believe that if this chap was still sending out the same smoke signals, then he would attract the same situation, and if I wasn't mindful, I would get caught up in it.

Let's face it, my heart issues started to come to a head just after I started seeing him resulting in me being in the Emergency Room.

I know this might sound a bit superstitious to you, so I'd like to rewind about eight years to my early months with Igor and share something with you that happened. According to Igor, his ex-wife was an irrationally jealous woman and he was constantly on the receiving end of her accusations and behaviour. He was a nervous wreck when I first met him, not daring to look at another woman and I found this very odd as I'm just not a jealous person. However, within a very short time I started to feel really jealous and physically sick at the thought of him being with anyone else. I was in my mid-forties by now and had never experienced these range of emotions at all so they were very alien to me. I pondered on it for some time and whilst working to shift these bizarre thoughts, I realised that jealousy was still in "his" vibration and he was continuing to sending out those smoke signals.

I was subconsciously picking up on them and conjuring up the jealous thoughts that he was requesting from The Universe. Being clairsentient, I'm more suggestible than most to others' emotions. Once I realised what was going on, I used energetic protection and affirmations to counter these effects and thankfully returned to my usual liberal minded, happy-go-lucky self, but wow, I did not enjoy that experience at all. So do you see how we can be unwittingly influenced by others' thoughts and vibrations – and visa-versa?

> ➤ *Have you found yourself experiencing emotions that don't feel like yours?*
> ➤ *Moods or thoughts that are not normally in-keeping with your own character and beliefs?*
> ➤ *Do you feel that these emotions could be down to someone else's background rather than your own?*

NB It's very important to note here that there is no blame to be apportioned to anyone. This is all part of **our own** journey and we need to ask ourselves why these feelings have come forward at all? Have they been buried deep within us and so now is the time to address them? I found that using energetic protection was a great way to fend off the influence so that I could work through the jealousy without turning into a gargoyle in the process! In addition, the affirmations empower a change in our mindsets and so we can literally reprogram ourselves to a higher vibration and so inner peace whilst maintaining our core personality.

For example, to counter jealousy, we can use an affirmation such as "I am safe to trust my loyal partner", or "I intuitively know who to trust". As you'll read throughout Wakey Wake-Up Rise & Shine (WWRS), thoughts are incredibly powerful and in learning to control our thoughts, we start to empower ourselves into the person we want to be.

I very soon started to realise that my mum had always said to me of other's jealousy "we don't understand it because we're not like that are we". And so I had not acknowledged any green eyed monsters that had snuck into my subconscious but rather, I had buried them. I don't think it happened very much as I'm the kind of person who is genuinely happy for other's good fortune or their new outfit, but it was brought into my awareness to be addressed. Later in this chapter, I'll go into jealousy a little more and other ways to manage it.

*****

Five weeks down the line from my awakening moment, whilst I felt very well, I was still getting very tired. My diaphragm and chest muscles were so sore from being strained during the heart attack! I found myself having to work through lots of emotions as my life was upside-down. I could no longer escape with a drink, smoke or get stoned and my heart still had a lot of mending to do. I hadn't really grasped the journey to come or that this new life meant that I had to face the world, everything in it and my own emotions without an emotional crutch.

At various points along the road to recovery, I realised that I could no longer grab a coffee, an energy drink or pop a few drops of my famous home-made olive leaf tincture to give myself an energy boost when I wanted to go out and dance and socialise. I became very pouty that I had to succumb to being a mere mortal and allow myself to be tired. My friends had always expected me to be there and to party just as much as I had those expectations of myself.

In fact, for many years, I'd set those expectations. Brad would disappear from our bar, drunk without saying a word, leaving me to hold the fort on a crazy Saturday night; Igor would be operating on full throttle for weeks and I'd be keeping pace (he'd then burn out and go to ground for a week); Beau never wanted to sleep as long as there was alcohol in the building and demanded that I stay up too.

However, post-heart failure, my heart and my body were now saying "no". It was alien and I didn't like it. I couldn't please everyone all of the time any more – but one evening, after saying "no" because I was dog tired, I drifted off to sleep, really pleased with myself and saying over and over out loud "I choose me! I choose me! I choose me!" and the awareness came to me that it was an option to say that, mean it and be comfortable with it.

That was a radical concept to me and so the lessons that came my way started to sink in because I was giving myself the gift of time to process awareness'. Because I'd chosen a holistic path and to be awakened, I now had to have time to listen to what was going on around me to see it and deal with it. I had to make like one of the Seven Dwarfs, get my emotional pickaxe out and mine into the depths of my soul and my heart to uncover the raw emotional rocks that were hidden in my vibration and turn them into polished gems to honour and treasure and I wouldn't be able to do that if I was people pleasing. It would have been so much easier to go for the Cardioversion and take the pills forevermore but in being authentic to myself, I shook my leonine mane and said to myself "Brace yourself Linda, we're going in! Hi-ho, hi-ho, it's off to work we go!" and along came jealousy.

Jealousy

Since my awakening I wasn't having the fun that I used to have. I didn't have the energy nor the inclination to go out and party but my friends continuing to have that fun — and I sat at home and pouted "it's not fair!" The pangs of jealousy that I felt when I heard that my friends were going out and hadn't asked me and instead I was home alone. I loved my house and the peace and quiet was needed but it really didn't make it any easier to stomach.

The horrid thing is that I could literally feel jealousy turning me ugly. I could actually feel my face contorting into something akin to one of the Ugly Sisters in Cinderella although I felt more like Cinderella as I wasn't allowed to go to the ball. Thankfully I recognised it and consciously decided not to let jealousy take a hold. I decided that I had to do something about this weird emotion and I went online in search of answers and to understand what was going on in my head.

As a result of my research I learned that Jealousy is the fear of losing something that we have. Envy is wanting something that somebody else has.

If we feel jealous that's because we see ourselves in competition with the person that we share a given situation with .... so, we need to tell ourselves that we are not in a competition with that person. This made perfect sense to me as if I heard that someone was going out, I quite simply didn't want them to have more fun than me — how dare they?! I'm the local party girl! This was only since my hospital stay as I was no longer able to go out and drink and be the social butterfly who I was used to being. Instead I'd reverted back into a chrysalis, and social butterflies aren't supposed to do that! However, I was constantly tired and felt pretty fragile and so I had to cocoon myself in the safety and quiet of my house despite suffering from FOMO (Fear Of Missing Out). I can almost hear myself stamping my feet as I write this.

I had to think of a way of changing it in my mind so I could ditch the bitch in my jealous head and so I made a conscious decision to withdraw from the competition and so I told myself that because I was out of the competition at the moment, I had nothing to feel jealous about. Instead I decided to compare myself to an injured athlete, rehabilitating and that I'd come back even stronger and at some point in the future, I'd award myself a gold medal because it was not just my body that recovering, my mind was getting a software update too. I can honestly say that I had no idea that my spirit was also going to be enlightened and uplifted beyond recognition as part of the process!

From my research it would seem that jealousy is nothing more than messages from the brain telling us that we need to improve certain areas of our life and so it's totally okay to feel jealous. These are feelings which we're all entitled to. They are aspects of our shadow side and it's what we do with that emotion that makes the difference. We can consciously decide not to turn that emotion into a mood, that mood into a habit, that habit into your personality but instead act on it and make the necessary changes so that we have the peace in our mind to grow from.

Or we can act on that mood and become the green-eyed monster forever more because we're feeling insecure and lack confidence. It's not what happens to us that makes us the person that we are, it is how we deal with it.

So, when I felt jealous because I knew that people were having more fun than me, then I decided to take action to create my own fun but in a different way, one which was manageable for my then energy levels and needs capabilities. It worked and I eliminated the jealousy. In my head, my friends were out drinking and getting stoned and having a right giggle so my wonderful friend Alex started taking me out for lovely meals or down to the coast for a mega ice-cream sundae with sparkles on top, and that in turn brought back my sparkle. For his own reasons, Alex doesn't drink alcohol and so he was stable company and understood what I was going through.

I also learned not to feel guilty about feeling jealous. We are all conditioned that this is a bad emotion and how awful it is to be jealous - which is just what we don't need if we're already dealing with negative thoughts in our minds – an endless, self-perpetuating circle of guilt and jealousy giving us precious little space in our tormented minds to get a grip and start manifesting the groovy things we'd far rather have going on in our life.

Jealousy arises from the ego feeling a lack of something, separated and singled out and feeling like we're going to lose something like a friend or situation or the fun.

To re-dress the balance, we can make a list of what we do have to bring about the positivity of gratitude.

If we feel that we're not getting enough attention, think: What attention do I have? How can I get more positive attention?

Lack of social life... What social life do you have? What are you able to do in your present circumstances? .... get on with organising it!

Jealousy tells us what we need or want so if we use it to motivate ourselves rather than turn us into that green-eyed monster it is a very powerful tool to have as it gives us the direction for our goal. The trick is to recognise it rather than go into denial and pretend we're angels polishing our halos at every opportunity. Own it! Work with it and use it to make our worlds a better place for the energy that is us, to live this part of our wondrous lives. If we deny or disown jealousy it'll simply fester and make us ugly inside and out.

Whilst we might look in the mirror and see a beautiful face, the world will see our actions, hear our words, pick up on our energy and if it isn't a pretty picture only the shallow or insecure will want to be around us.

For a healthier way to be we must soothe ourselves and tell ourselves "hey, it's ok to feel this way". Now I've seen it, I'll work with it and make my World better."

If we find ourselves jealous because someone is fun, attractive, dresses well - maybe it's because we have a low self-esteem. There is so much that we can do to bring about change and confidence from simply carrying a piece of Rose Quartz our pocket or bra to full on self-help workshops. One thing is for sure is that we must start by loving ourselves as an individual.

We do not need anyone else to make us whole, that is co-dependency which becomes unhealthy and draining. We must become one, not half of one. This entire book is aimed at empowering that change with information and workshops available to stimulate personal growth.

Jealousy's best friend Shame also tells us that we're not on the right track with our thinking process and our energy. Remember that your energy is you. Your body is simply the shell that the energy that is you hangs out in. If we're ashamed we've usually done something we're not proud of.

A strange phenomenon is 'Comparison Thinking.' We compare the worst we know about ourselves, to the best we think we know about the other person to the point that if this was a competition, we'd put our money on the other person! However, we don't know their full situation, we just have a version of their perfect, and we would rather they didn't have it, or we did. How crazy is that?

Instead try being grateful and positive for what we have. I might not have long, thick, luscious locks or be fabulously wealthy or have a romantic partner who is perfect in every way but I'm thankful that I have high cheek bones, freedom, fun, intelligence, compassion, spirituality.

I've been so gratefully amazed since these jealousy insights and if I got a pang of jealousy about something, I actioned my learnings and was open and honest to myself and to others. Jealousy really does lose its power over you when you do so. Instead of scowling inwardly about someone's outfit, I'd say with a genuine smile on my face "wow, I love your outfit. I'm pea green with envy". I found that this switches jealousy into generosity to others as giving a compliment is a lovely thing to do and make someone else feel good about themselves and an instant karmic pat on the back is that it you immediately give yourself value to that person – and so yourself. Double whammy whoop whoop!

For extra help with managing jealousy, we can work with The Bach Flower Remedies to gently rebalance our emotions. There will be several, interconnecting and in need of bringing back into line. Whilst I can work intuitively with my clients, I tend to dowse when I'm creating my own bespoke Bach flower remedy as it uncovers the shocking truth which I may well be in denial about. Eek!

Section 2 of this book includes an overview of the thirty-eight different Bach Flower Remedies. However, in order to give some perspective because of events just described, let me share with you what I chose at that stage of my recovery (real time):

Holly: For anger and jealousy!

Now that my lifestyle has changed and I can no longer go out and party, I feel jealous of those who can. I never thought of myself as an angry or jealous person, but I have now recognised that that's exactly how I feel sometimes and it's the most bizarre thing. It might be the meds as side-effects include mood changes and anxiety. However, it might be the real me and I never realised because I was anaesthetised with alcohol when there was something to be jealous about! Or maybe because being squiffy was lovely I never got jealous or angry – or if I went beyond squiffy and got horrible I couldn't remember – Double Yikes! As I'm writing this up, several months down the line, I'm mortified that I was ever that person! The fact is, it really doesn't matter. Living in this present moment in time, I've recognised the emotion, it's out of balance and so I'm doing something about it without shame or guilt. I can't change the past, but I can change the present and the future and that's what matters.

Cherry Plum: Intense fear or losing control of yourself or your mind, doing something terrible to yourself or others.

This is a very calming remedy and as I'm doing my best to give my beautiful heart a rest from stress and anxiety, this remedy was called upon to ably assist in my treatment regime. As the meds give side-effects similar to a heart attack (seriously big Pharma?), it would be very easy to spin off into a panic and cause myself exactly that, when I experience chest tightness or breathlessness. It'd also be really easy to overthink and then panic about the fact that I live 2400 feet up a mountain on my own in the middle of an olive grove and if I have a problem again, I'm pretty stuffed! Cheery plum – hey what a great typo, that has to stay in – brings peace of mind and gives my heart a break ... of the right kind!

Walnut: Protection from outside influences and assistance with change.

My lifestyle has had a dramatic overhaul over the last month for sure! CHANGE doesn't get much bigger. The outside influences are so many fold. Everyone has opinions – and don't get me wrong, it can be helpful to hear all sides of a story, even when it's your own story yet to be written - and to get input can be invaluable. However, at the end of the day – which can feel very long at times – only YOU actually have to live in your body and to live full-time with the consequences of your decisions, actions and inaction. Protection is a very useful tool at this time. You can listen, take it all in and remain true to yourself and draw your own conclusions because as I say throughout this book, your intuition is the only one that looks out for you and only you.

Honeysuckle: Move away from living in the past and bring me into the present.

I have to face the fact that I must live my life in the present moment and if I want to keep hold of it - "life" that is – then I have to live the changes and do my utmost to ensure that I do indeed wake up tomorrow. There's no time for reminiscing ruefully about how much fun the past was and boo hoo the future just won't be the same. I have some positive thinking to do and some serious work in manifesting my good health, happiness, well-being and a most fabulous life going forward, that I will remain ever so excited to continue to enjoy year after year after year. To me there is no other option, but it won't come to me if I sit on my now skinny derrière thinking about the past. I must be in the now and in being so, be aware of every little thing that my body, my mind and my intuition are telling me so that I can act upon it.

Elm: Feeling overwhelmed.

It's very easy to feel overwhelmed at the moment, especially when I go out as I tend to be the focus of attention. People understandably want to know the gory details (I always do when it's someone else!) and whilst I am a Leo and we do love being the centre of attention, having to relive the dramatic events of my awakening and to explain what's going on now is tiring. Everyone wants to know how I'm feeling and what treatment I am / am not having which opens me myself and I up for discussion on my decisions.

As I'm a Holistic Practitioner I think very differently from other people so it's very difficult to have to explain to people why I'm not going with the mainstream for the recommended treatments and so I naturally open myself up to questioning on the subject, which leads me to second-guess myself on my decisions. My decisions are pretty radical I guess – but so am I! I am living on my own, I am independent, I am my own person and I know who I am and how I like to do things - I'm as stubborn as f*ck if I think I'm in the right - and to have people put a different and very valid viewpoint over which makes me second-guess myself is especially confusing as I don't have a long-term romantic partner I trust and who can be my sounding board.

Pine: Worrying about causing upset.

I've always felt guilty about saying no or upsetting people, even if it was justified because they'd stolen from me or trodden on my toes royally, basically about stuff I shouldn't feel guilty about. So often I said yes when I shouldn't have or later lived to regret the decision, then I felt guilty for not being true to myself or putting myself in a stupid situation when I knew better. I therefore figured that this might be part of the reason I'm in this situation in the first place - because I didn't listen to my heart and say no! My heart basically got fed up of not being listened to and had a hissy fit - i.e. a heart attack! Why should she get quite so upset about it all I wonder? Well I guess that's because I was living someone else's version of how I should live my life rather than my own. I'd got so far off track I wasn't living the very reason I was put here in the first place and so The Universe stepped in and sent a lightning bolt my way to wakey wake-up, rise and shine or game over!!!

White chestnut: Circling repetitive thoughts. An over-active mind – which is exhausting and confusing.

Sometimes my head just wouldn't stop thinking especially at night and especially about negative things – what if's, who said what, what did they mean? What shall I do? Am I doing the right thing? Is my heart OK? I don't want to take the meds – should I/shouldn't I? Enough! Be Quiet! I'm nearly there by practicing mindfulness and reprogramming and all of the stuff that I've been watching on Gaia but this is to make sure.

Chestnut bud: To learn from and stop repeating the same mistakes.

Quite simply let's not make the same mistakes again Linda! Because this *is* your second chance and despite being a big cat Leo lion, I've lost count of how many lives you've used up and it might be getting a bit too close to nine!

I have given a less personal outline of each of the thirty-eight different Bach Flower Remedies in Section 2 of this book as I am a firm believer in their efficacy. I have used them on myself, my animals, I have created bespoke remedies for clients and watched with satisfaction as their emotions have rebalanced and they have found peace in their mind and so their body.

*****

Beau continued to unwittingly deliver the life lessons to me, showing me that I had to trust my intuition and pay attention to the actions rather than the words. I'd get upset as he was putting me in physical danger but every time, there was a lesson to learn from the experience. The experiences came in many different guises and I blamed him for being young, drunk or irresponsible. However, each time it came back to me and reinforcing that I had to create boundaries and stick to them no matter what. These situations will continue to present themselves and push our buttons for as long as we continue to take the same action and allow them to happen. WE HAVE TO LEARN the lesson that is being taught to us. By being in my fragile state (albeit in denial about it), I was now on a steep learning curve and this time my soul was making sure that I was paying attention.

When people are high (or indeed in a manic phase) - which covers all sorts - drugs (prescription including anti-depressants, Valium, etc and social substances), alcohol, caffeine in excess - their perception of reality is altered not just for themselves but for those around them and so they probably don't understand what's actually happening. If someone else is anxious or upset, because the high person has purposely numbed themselves from their own reality, they have inadvertently made themselves blissfully unaware of anyone else's anxiety, upset or pain and are unfeeling. Strangely that helped me to reconcile my changing circumstances as I could understand that some had simply numbed themselves to my pain as well as their own. They're not being inconsiderate or selfish, they're literally devoid of sensation.

This is a really good lesson and despite my teacher, the Universe's methodology, reinforced by the line in the Reiki Mantra "just for today I give thanks to my Teachers, my parents and my elders".

*****

My financial situation was becoming more precarious because I was unable to do my healing work effectively as I didn't have the physical or emotional strength. Even doing my Medical Secretarial typing work was exhausting and physically painful as my chest muscles were very sore for months after the event. The hard work that I'd put into creating my Therapy room at home was all in vain and given that this was surely the reason I was on this planet, I was confused that the pause button had been pressed. Now, with the benefit of hindsight, I see that I had to go through more, in order to uplevel myself and become a stronger more proficient Healer with more experience and able to reach a deeper level with my clients – for their own greatest and highest good. I renamed my Therapy Room, my ZenDen and it became my space and my sanctuary where the energies were high and I could maximise my own healing. I drew the Reiki symbols on the walls, in felt-tip pen in each corner of the room to boost the energies and threw myself into the journey. It was essential to me that I got the most from this experience and as my Yoga Teacher, Tanya explained to me, "you can't give someone a present if you don't have it yourself" and so she inspired me that I had to become my Tiggeresque, healthy self again.

Anger has its place

I'd been working to remain calm in order to avoid putting extra strain on my damaged heart for the two months post-hospital stay, when one night I had an epic car breakdown.

Eve and I had a lovely day on the beach and then met our friend Alex in Torrox at a divinely expensive Chiringuito on the beach for dinner. When we left the restaurant about 11.30pm my car went into limp mode. I dropped Eve off about 1am and set off up the mountain to my home but the car just didn't have the power and cut out as the fuel pump had apparently expired. I called the tow truck (gruer) and despite my insurance being targeted at expats there was a big language barrier in trying to relay my location to them.

Realising that my heart was still very much in recovery I set the intention to remain calm and not give myself anxiety, stress or anger and I did really really well. Eve came out bless her but despite her advanced Spanish speaking skills even then there was a language barrier. We eventually managed to communicate my location by sending a drop-pin via WhatsApp, and was told that the tow truck would be 37 minutes. 40 minutes later they called and said another 2 hours. By now we're talking an ETA of 4am.

In order to encourage a much quicker ETA, I decided to play the "two women alone" card and the "in the middle of nowhere" card whilst still remaining calm … before the storm. When both of these failed my best intentions flew out of the window and my temper flew in. I had the most humungous hissy-fit which was really quite enjoyable as I really think I needed to let off some long overdue tension. I played the Ace card which I'd been saving for the grand finale if all else failed (which it had) and trying hard to keep myself in check, I said "I've recently had a heart attack, if you find me dead next to my car it's down to your company". I couldn't believe it when even that failed and I lost it completely and told them that their service was sh*t..... And hung up on them in a rage. It wasn't until reflecting on everything the next day it dawned on me that the Ace wasn't actually a dramatization, it was an actual possibility! YIKES! It took the re-write of this book to help me to realise that this situation had "triggered" me. I've become aware that one of my triggers is not being listened to / heard and hence I'd exploded. I've been working on it since then. Once we have the awareness we can acknowledge it and then work on it without any shame, blame or guilt.

Two minutes later the tow truck called and said he'd be there in twenty minutes – which he was! At that point I thought "right, my anger has done its job and now it's time for calm" and I set about calming myself and give my heart a rest from the adrenaline! I'd also been "heard" and so my anger had no need to hang around any more.

Along the research road, I read somewhere that 10 minutes of anger takes your immune system down for 6 hours and I didn't need an infection at this stage of my recovery. Too much anger literally damages your body. Increased heart rate can damage the heart muscle and send it out of rhythm causing all sorts of knock-on effects, high blood pressure – we all know that's a killer and anger will push that mercury right up on the reading. Adrenal glands can burn out causing you health problems and the age old saying that "stress is a killer" isn't wrong. Do you know that stress related ailments cause more deaths than cancer? Nope that was new to me too!

Anger is a natural emotion and it has its place in our lives, it's about using it only when necessary and then bringing yourself out of that state once it has served its purpose. That's self-control.

There were more dramas before I finally got home. Eve's car battery went flat so she couldn't go and guide the tow truck into our middle of nowhere location. Then when the tow truck arrived and carried my car up to the town carpark, Eve had to drop me home because there was no way a gruer could have turned around or manoeuvred these roads - and all with her fuel light on!!! It was 5am by this time.

No chance of a good rest to recuperate the following day as I had to organise and meet the tow truck again as unbeknown to me my mechanic was away. I had to get a lift from my friend Harley up to the car and my good friend Alex agreed to loan me one of his cars. I slept a lot for days!

My thoughts on it all - "The cosmos is having a f*cking laugh innit!!!"

However, it then provoked some thoughts on the matter and therefore some research on my part - which in turn brought me to ask "Anger... Is ok?" I still hadn't recognised myself as a particularly angry person - I felt indignant about certain things but I genuinely felt that I was within my rights to feel that way because of other people's behaviour or challenging situations. If I was provoked into anger, it never dawned on me that there was another way to respond as I felt I'd been pushed too far.

So I decided to do some research and, as I began to notice over the coming years, once you've made a decision to work on an aspect of yourself or that you need to understand something about a situation or someone, the information will flow to you. It's everywhere. It'll be delivered to you when you're out and about, maybe via a chance encounter at the market or socialising, even when you're home alone, you might get an insight from a TikTok video, a Facebook post, even when you're watching a movie, and of course actual research online or from a book. When you've tuned into wanting that information, you'll get it – if you notice!

The amazing thing about the internet is that it's pure energy and so I believe that it interacts with our consciousness which is equally pure energy; and will spontaneously present us with the messages and information that we need, at precisely the right time – ie when we've decided that is what we want and we're sending out those smoke signals in the form of energy waves into the universe. We just need to slow down and be present in each moment in time and space that that we actually notice it and get the full experience. For example, in walking past a beautiful rose, we only get a fraction of what it has to offer. However, If we literally stop and smell the roses, we're getting a whole lot more from that experience. The scent has therapeutic properties for a start. Rose essential oil relieves stress, fights anxiety and relaxes our muscles and our mind. It brings comfort and has anti-inflammatory properties – the oil is just the concentrated from of what you gain when you stop and actually smell the rose. We can take this metaphor into every situation – driving your car and instead of getting road rage at the slow car in front, are they saving you from getting a speeding ticket or being involved in an accident? Are you noticing what's around you that you'd miss if they weren't slowing you down? The examples are endless. Time isn't a luxury, we're entitled to every second and it's up to us how we value it.

If we spend our time on ourselves by allowing the process rather than being on fast-forward all of the time, you'll notice the information in a form that resonates with you personally, and it will empower you to sail through the drama, the emotion and the situation.

So, in answer to my own question about anger, it is a Red Alert signal to show you what in your life is out of balance and it gives you that information so that you can correct it. Yep, you can stop getting angry by listening to your anger, being aware of your triggers and then doing something about it. It's the most fabulous process.

We can allow anger to rear its ugly head if our boundaries being breached. It maybe that we are saying yes instead of no, no instead of yes, or nothing at all. If we lose our authenticity we start to lose our way and it's up to us to find it again. These pages empower us to remember who we are and what we want and how to go about that.

It's worth taking a little time out, to work out how we can politely say what we really mean. It might involve a few words behind the "no" or re-phrasing it to "I'm sorry, I'd rather not" and guess what? You don't necessarily have to explain yourself either! That's another entry in this guidebook! Why did I feel that I had to explain myself, my decisions, my outlook, my life, my choices? As someone who had had a lifetime of boundaries being breached this was incredibly empowering for me. It helped to shift anger and resentment that I didn't even know I had accumulating in there. If someone talks to me in a way that I don't like, I now find a way of letting them know as politely as possible. If I find myself having an angry rant it's my own fault for allowing my boundaries to be breached and not being true to myself. It's OK, we're all a work in progress and it takes practice and time to step into and own our power.

Anger comes along if you feel threatened. It's a safety mechanism to stimulate the adrenaline to get you out of a potentially dangerous situation but can apply to relationships – home and at work / school. You don't have to bop someone on the nose or get involved in fisty-cuffs. When something makes you feel threatened you can decide how to react but the trick is not to attract the situation in the first place.

Our root chakra is responsible for us feeling safe and secure and if it is out of balance then you may well be attracting threatening situations – or those that you perceive to be a threat, they might not actually be, it might be your perception of it, so that's worth clearing up – communication is key after all!

If you're naturally drawn to red that's a good clue that your root chakra is out of balance as your intuition is telling you it needs it to feel strong and safe again. The power of colour is absolutely astonishing. My wardrobe is full of colourful clothes as if I'm in a purple mood I literally cannot wear green or any other colour that day. It sends a shudder through me and I have to get it off immediately. Watch out for colours that you're drawn to as that's you telling you that you need a top-up! Equally, when using The Balance Procedure cards, if we're drawn to card 1, which has the red square as the symbol, this could be pointing us at these emotions being out of balance and it's really easy to bring ourselves back into a state of relaxation instead of fight or flight using this system.

The frustrating thing about life lessons, is that just when you think you've got that one covered, another angle appears that needs to be covered and so my Soul had decided that because I was such a good student, I was going to cover the next module in the Anger section and I had the most infuriating day – but I learned a lot. Here's what I learned.

I just watched a video about tyrants and it basically said that the people who constantly push our buttons are the ones who have kindly subconsciously volunteered to show us what we need to work on. (They've actually signed a Soul Contract with us before we arrived on Planet Earth but that's a whole other topic.)

The presenter also said that she loves "community" because when we are around people, we get the messages that we need to point us in the right direction. i.e. They who show us what we need to work on. This absolutely resonated with me at that moment in time because I'd found myself staying in rather than going out socially because drunk people were now rather irritating to me.

However, it would appear that these challenges and mistakes in life are our lessons and so we have to look into each situation and figure out what it is we're meant to work on or change in our lives. Why has it been sent our way?

This can often be misconstrued as a punishment "what have I done to deserve this?!", but may I suggest that you flip that over and change it into "giving you direction".

Well, I got yet more direction in the form of yet another row with Beau when he let me down at 7.30am on the morning he was supposed to be driving me to a hospital appointment and translating. I was furious at his attitude and lack of consideration and blah blah blah.

However, remember what I've said about clues being all around us. At the height of our exchange that morning, he said "it's not me making you like that, it's up to you how you react". At that time I was incensed by this comment. Of course it was him making me like that! Who wouldn't react like that? How does he expect me to react after letting me down? Angry is the only way that anyone could possibly react to that ….. Ah Haaaaa! …. as I was to learn during one of my lightbulb moments, you can choose how to respond and you can desensitise yourself to triggers and you can re-programme yourself and your hormones and it isn't that hard to do!

This incident taught me so much that I can only now be thankful for it in true Reiki Mantra fashion. My anger gave me the red light that my boundary had been breached and that I was continuously allowing this to happen throughout my life. Upon sitting quietly and contemplating it all, I learned from this altercation that it was time to change the way I reacted because someone would inevitably rile me again and I cannot do anything to change anyone else's behaviours – that's down to them (if they even want to). However, if I change my reaction into a considered "response", then I'm learning and I had to do so if I wanted my heart to heal and to remain healthy: I needed the angry, stress head Linda to grow to be a thing of the past or for special occasions only!

I don't know about you, but it seems to me that when I have a lesson to learn, it's pretty harsh. I've recently tried having a word with my Soul and told her that I'm listening and maybe the lessons could be more gentle from now on? More entertaining and fun, light-hearted and playful!!!

So, the key word here has to be "anger". One of the lessons I've learnt is that if you meet anger with anger then it self-perpetuates and just like the fire that is represents, it grows, spreads, destroys everything in its path. If we can recognise a negative emotion as it's directed at us, and diffuse it with a positive attitude, then we stand more chance of extinguishing the situation - for ourselves at least. We can stay in the eye of the storm and let others' carry on with their tantrum tornedo to their hearts' content. By taking ownership of our own behaviour, we stand more chance of having a positive influence on those around us. If, however, we blame others, then we haven't quite got it yet! We haven't realised that we have choice and freewill to respond however we want to. It's not an overnight process and I flounder sometimes, but I pick myself up and if at first I don't succeed, I try try and try again, just like Robert the Bruce's lesson from a spider.

*****

We are indeed programmed by our experiences and send out signals that attracts more of the same. For example, I was born looking different to others and had many operations on my eyelids as a child and so as a result I've always had to explain my appearances – and so I became programmed to "explain", and that resulted in my choosing a career in telecommunications sales where that natural ability that had been honed all of my life, then worked to my advantage.

I was happy to do so, I'd been trained and conditioned into explaining everything about myself so it was natural to me but I started to feel that every answer to any question, became an essay of a reply and I was tiring of it. In meeting so many new people here in ole ole land, there were naturally always a lot of questions from new friends and I felt like I was giving away a huge amount of information unnecessarily. For someone that chose to live in a remote olive grove, I was making everything about myself very public and I felt really exposed. As if to nudge me into rethinking my way of being, a friend had also said that she noticed that I explain myself and my decisions without being prompted and she didn't know why I did this and there was really no need to do that.

I thought that was really lovely of her and took it as a message from my soul that it was time to stop seeking agreement for everything.

The reason I was being prep'd by my soul became pretty clear during my recovery from my awakening. My friends and the medical profession wanted me to go down a particular treatment route which didn't sit well with me. I was constantly being quizzed, questioned and reasoned with, and each and every time, with different groups of friends, I had to explain myself, my thought processes, my research, my feelings, my intuitions, my plan and it got very tiresome. They disputed my reasoning and tried to convince me to do what the Doctors advised. I stuck to my guns and broke my life-long conditioning and stopped explaining myself. Instead I'd say something along the lines of "because that's the decision I've made".

One friend, for years had been constantly asking me "why?" or suggesting "couldn't you do x instead?" Having seen the light, I turned round one day and said "why are you questioning my judgement and my decisions about my life?" In just a week or two I had done it, I'd reprogrammed myself and my smoke signals - and magically, people stopped questioning me or asking for explanations.

I know that they all felt that they had my best interests at heart but it started to spoil nights out and conversations and what was supposed to be fun time but I had the lightbulb moment of "I don't have to explain myself" and it felt incredible and like a weight had been lifted off my shoulders.

As if to give me confirmation, when I posted on Facebook "my heart attack saved my life", someone posted simply "EXPLAIN!". I ignored her post and I didn't!

Within the week I got another fabulous confirmation at the local market when someone asked me question "Why are you going in that direction around the market?" and others seemed to ask me further strangely over-curious comments, all basically asking me to explain myself. For the first time in my life I didn't explain myself - I just said with a chuckle so as not to cause offense "don't be nosey"! Job Done! Lesson Learned A+

*****

Life after death

I've often pondered what happens after our body dies and I've had dreams, psychic insights, visions, taken workshops, taught workshops, taken part in dozens if not hundreds of Holistic and Psychic fayres and many of my friends are so inclined; I've done meditations, taken part in psychic circles, Ouija board sittings, philosophised with friends and colleagues and manifested the fantastic and the not so fantastic – from a simple parking space, to a lifestyle, to a break and as I'm the type of person who likes to join the dots so to speak, I've come to this conclusion:

We are energy occupying a physical body which we chose because we really wanted to taste food, feel the wind on our faces, paddle in the ocean, smell flowers and food cooking, enjoy physical pleasures, play music, listen to music, paint art, create things to please us and nurture our soul, feel the rush of excitement about being alive in a body; and embrace the challenges and the lessons that we are presented with in order to Rest In Peace RIP when our time on this beautiful planet is done and our body is spent. If we can find peace in this lifetime with ourselves as a single beautiful soul, then we're on the right track to truly RIP.

If we hold onto anger or rely on material possessions or others, or control or power for our joy then what happens when we have no body and it has turned to dust and everything that we are is purely energy – our personalities, our wisdom, our love – or lack of? I believe that the ailments we encounter on earth in this part of our long lifetime are clear direction of what we need to work on and just like a PlayStation® game, we're given clues along the way on what to work on and how. The internet is one of the most powerful tools at our disposal as are those around us who directly reflect to each of us individually what is alive inside of us.

Have you ever watched a film and the person you're watching it with perceives it differently? Or listened to music and got a different meaning to the lyrics than a friend? Because you have seen or heard what it means to YOU because that is what is alive in you. If it's positive that's fantastic. If it's negative then maybe it's something to work on so that you can rest in peace and take your beautiful positive energy with you.

In the meantime, whilst on this beautiful planet, our positivity is contagious and the more love and light we can shine around us, the more our World will become that because it is a direct reflection of you, me, of all of us. The only way to save our planet is to shine and empower other people to shine …. and the only way to shine, is to resolve our challenges to the best of our ability and to listen to our body as it tells us what we need to change through presenting us with diseases, ailments, accidents, and so forth.

And that is why I said no to Cardioversion and that is why I use herbs rather than pharmaceuticals as best I can and Hippocrates did say "let food be thy medicine"!

At this point I want to remind you that the whole point of this book is to inspire you but not to tell you what to do. I aim to inspire you to use your own intuition and get the support that you need to do what your intuition guides you to. I am not saying don't take diuretics. I'm saying I chose to drink lemon juice in litres of fresh spring water daily and massage my legs daily. The diuretics were an essential part of my treatment at the outset when the heart failure caused breathing difficulties due to the fluid in my lungs because my heart wasn't strong enough to pump it out.

I'm qualified in Manual Lymphatic Drainage Massage (MLD) and so set about helping my body to shift any excess fluid from my lower limbs. It's always advisable to check with your Medic before doing or having any kind of massage. With MLD you start at the top to clear the way for the fluid to move into so when starting to work on my legs, I started with my abdomen and swept my hands from the creases where my legs join my body, up towards my belly button. After this, I started above my knees and swept up to the top of my legs and then to my belly button. After a few minutes of this, around my knee caps and up to my belly button, after that, from my ankles all the way up. It improves skin tone, circulation and helps to shift fluid into the lymphatic system and then out of the body.

In trusting yourself it's important that you have opened a channel to yourself and are practiced at hearing what you have to say.

*****

Contact high

Chatting with a tee-total friend along the timeline of my recuperation, she asked me how this party animal was getting on without alcohol. I was a bit down and explained to her that I found it really difficult not getting silly and high from booze and it made me feel isolated from everyone around me at any given event, because they were literally on a different wave length but they were all having a great time. They had a different vibration and were bouncing off each other in the groove of the occasion whereas I – in the words of Paloma Faith – was stone cold sober. She told me that she could take herself into that zone at will as she'd been such a practiced drinker in the past. I decided that I could work with that and then I recalled an event a few years earlier when Igor and I had been a bit stoned and giggly at a pizza place on the Costa Del Sol, the waitress got really silly and giggly every time she came over to us but appeared fine when she was waiting on the other tables. She herself was perplexed by it. Igor informed me that this was known as a "contact high" and is a common phenomenon where those not under the influence of any given substance, pick up on the energy of those who are and experience the same high. What a bonus!

I decided to intentionally try this "contact high" and to tune into my squiffy friends and quite simply went out with the intent that I joined in. It came naturally which was fabulous but thinking about how I did it, I guess I focused for a nanosecond on my own energy within my body and then imagined it radiating outwards from my body to connect to theirs. I still smile when I do it and it's wonderful to connect with friends, share and exchange energies.

I believe that this is what happens when we're high or squiffy. Our guard comes down, our inhibitions drop and we easily and subconsciously connect with people as we're now on the same wavelength – we tune-in as if to a radio station and we become the same frequency (as an example, to 105.8FM) and we find the same things interesting or funny; but unfortunately, we also have to be aware that we can tune into people's insecurities, their aggression, their mood – whatever that is – because we become wide open. If we're the uninhibited one, we're the one that will exhibit this behaviour even if it is not our own. It's like we're possessed!

Anyway, it worked and I had a really good night. I felt part of the fun, uplifted and like I used to when out with everyone. You just have to decide to feel a part of it all. The mind is such a powerful thing.

Months later, this was life changing again. I no longer felt that I couldn't party or enjoy myself because I was sober. Far from it, I was really proud of myself that I could still party with the best, have as much fun but without the adverse effects and without waking in the morning with that awful amnesia and feeling of the dreaded "OMG what did I say to who? What did I do? Do I need to apologise to anyone?!"

I still found it challenging on how to reward myself at the end of a productive day. I loved the ritual of sitting with a sophisticated vodka and tonic or a glass of wine and watching the sun set behind the mountains. I found zero alcohol alternatives, some much better than others and I have to say that I get just as much joy from drinking a 0% Tanqueray Gin & Tonic with plenty of ice and a chunk of lime which has been run around the rim before adding it to the mix, as I used to from a 40%. I was in no way ready to turn to fruit juice and water entirely and fizzy drinks were never my bag – with the exception of tonic in a 'voddie sweedie darling' (that's vodka for non-Absolutely Fabulous TV show fans).

*****

<u>Energy exchange</u>

Going back to the energy exchange concept, James Redfield's novel - The Celestine Prophecy (1993) – explains that we exchange energies when we interact with other living things which is a fabulous experience. In social surroundings, we can have a wonderful time and feel thoroughly uplifted.

However, it's worth mentioning that sometimes this can be subconsciously abused by some people who want more energy that they give out. Ever feel drained when around certain people? It could be down to their control drama sucking the energy out of you. There are four control dramas as explained in The Celestine Prophecy (TCP) – Intimidator, Interrogator, Poor Me and Aloof. There is a TCP website where you can find further details which is very enlightening.

I've come to realise that people are here to give us the messages and information that we need for our life journey. By chatting with people, we naturally exchange energy and get the information and insights that will help us along our path and visa-versa.

I first read about this concept in The Celestine Prophecy about fifteen years ago but it had been archived by my mind. I started raving about this book to Beau and bought a copy for him but it would seem that he wasn't ready to receive its messages and insights as he left it behind when he moved on. However, in the true spirit of TCP it was then mine for the re-reading and I became consciously aware of it all once again.

Synchronicity then sent an online shamanism world summit into my awareness – the internet really is such a powerful tool - I LOVE IT. Once again this confirmed that people and our community bring us lessons and insights along our journey. This was a really important message for me to hear as my desire to steer clear of squiffy people, those under the influence or those who might press my buttons and trigger anger or anxiety, has me happy with my own company at home. However, I then realised that this would only hinder my journey and so my recovery. The only way forward is to manage myself and how I respond to situations, people and how I manage events, because becoming a happy hermit won't propel me to where I want to be and who I want to be.

I also completely related to the explanation that we can be halted on our journey by becoming addicted to someone who we feel completes us. However, when this happens we become only one half of the whole person that we should be- ie we are a C shape instead of an O shape. When we meet somebody who is the other half of the O, i.e the other C shape, then we interact with each other to such an extent exchanging our energies that we forget about both universal energy and our own mission here on Planet Earth.

When we take energy from each other rather than from The Universe, there isn't enough to go around and so we stop exchanging energy and try to keep it all for ourselves. Furthermore, we can take it a step further and steal energy from the other person by lapsing into our control dramas at which point it all goes Pete Tong because we are now in a co-dependent relationship and their and our own control dramas are competing in an energetic tug of war.

I am reminded of some lines from Eat Pray Love (Elizabeth Gilbert, 2006).
" Ruin is a gift. Ruin is the road to transformation." I particularly resonated with this as from a few weeks past my awakening, I started saying that the break was the best thing that had ever happened to me. It is directing me back on track for what I'm supposed to be doing here on Planet Earth and the journey is truly transformational for me and my world in the most amazingly positive ways.

That is the core of this book – how to use your own memoire justifying event to Wakey Wake-up Rise & Shine – in the deep meaning of each of those five words!

"We must always be prepared for endless waves of transformation." (Elizabeth Gilbert, 2006) I resonated with this because by my own experience, life isn't a ride that you can start and stop at will or press the pause button. We bought a ticket for this roller coaster and the trick is whilst screaming with excitement and fear, you got to enjoy the ride!

I believe that The Universe abhors a vacuum and so will continue to send transformational provoking events to you. Struggles in life happen when you don't see the signs and therefore don't make the changes for yourself. When this happens the Universe steps in and makes the change for you, often with all the style and panache of a sledgehammer! I've been on the receiving end of this many times! Thankfully sometimes I've seen the signs and made the changes in my own way, my own time and with consideration and spontaneity, but I'VE made them! If I didn't boy that sledgehammer packed a punch and sent me reeling into outer space! Once, you've spotted the pattern – make the change or it'll be made for you - act on it! I kept thinking in the months running up to my awakening "I've got to stop partying so much and use the gifts that I have, the healing, the qualifications including teaching, etc." I didn't act quickly enough and hey presto – point .... was a tsunami of transformation.

"You need learn to select your thoughts just the same way you select your clothes every day" (Elizabeth Gilbert, 2006). Thoughts are such a powerful energy. They can create and destroy. They can lift you up or drag you down. They can manifest the positive and the negative. They can affect other individuals, water and solid matter. Mindfulness is something that you absolutely must master in order to achieve well-being, peace of mind, happiness, fulfilment and more!

Inspired by Elizabeth Gilbert's wise words, the LOVE HATE IGNORE rice experiment that I'd heard of many years ago, popped into my mind, reinforcing the reason that I tell my heart how much I love her and congratulate her and my body when they have achieved something such as dancing, my heart going back into rhythm, perfect blood pressure – indeed, over-coming any hurdle - and I encourage you to do the same.

I've found that this has built a new found appreciation for my body and for respecting her and her feelings and what she is saying to me instead of stimulating my body with caffeine so that I can do more when she's actually telling me she needs rest, or having another drink when it's had enough (past tense), or doing just one more thing (and then another) before heading out of the door making myself late and so attempting to break the sound barrier in a 4x4 on mountain roads no doubt pushing up my blood pressure (even that sentence reads fast!)

I decided to actually do the LOVE HATE IGNORE rice experiment for myself and it features a little later in this book.

*****

Personal and spiritual evolution of mankind

In joining the dots once more, I decided to have a play with these ideas and I imagined my heart as atoms and I asked them all to beat in a regular rhythm.

There been a lot on the internet lately about experiments using photons and them doing what's expected of them "but only when they're being watched" (it's called the "double slit experiment" and well worth surfing the net about). In another experiment where DNA is extracted from a host, the host is then triggered emotionally and the scientists monitor the DNA within their body and compare it to the extracted DNA up to five miles away in a test tube. The results that both sets of DNA reacted identically and precisely the same time! I found that astonishing and so I figured I'd ask my DNA and atoms to beat my heart in perfect rhythm.

Over the past weeks, because I'd been using the pulse in my wrist to check on my heart's antics, I'd been focusing my intentions on having a strong, regular, stable rhythm pulse. It dawned on me that I needed to take my attention not to the symptom but to the origin of my pulse and health issues and so I switched my focus to my physical heart, I therefore visualised her as if looking directly into my chest when reciting the affirmations which I'd formulated in order to instruct my body back to good health.

I still find it so rewarding taking responsibility for my own wellbeing because I feel like I'm listening to my body and doing what she needs to be well.

I do get concerned when friends hide themselves away although I can totally understand it in all honesty as people can be challenging and when we're low it can feel too much to want to expose ourselves to.

However, I've found strength and wellbeing from being around others because it has brought to the surface the emotions that I need to deal with on order to get well which is a very important part of our life journey and why these challenges have been sent to us.

However, it's great to appreciate that we can get our energy from source at any and every moment by simply by taking in the beauty around us and also by feeling the love sent your way by friends and our animals of course.

Healing the emotions that caused this blip will ultimately enable us to heal without having to revisit it, because you'll have got it, learnt the life lesson, and people, as challenging as we can be, facilitate this by showing us what's alive inside of us, so we can deal with it and move forward enlightened, fitter and wiser for it. I have come to believe that we need to interact to get it.

I feel like a sponge, absorbing insights, facts, theories from every direction. One such fascinating insight was how we're transitioning from five sensory beings into multi-sensory beings because of the continuous process of enlightenment that we are going through. Wave upon wave as generations become more in tune with what's going on and different viewpoints are accepted. In the 1960's 'flower power', tree hugging hippies took mind expanding substances and saw the light and the error of humankind in their waging war on each other and molesting the planet without a second thought. They were dismissed and branded as being socially unacceptable and treated dreadfully by the authorities from what I understand.

But take a look today at the condition of Mother Earth and tell me that they weren't actually right all along. Gentle peace-loving people who wanted to respect nature, share the love and spread joy throughout the world were branded as anti-establishment lay-abouts.

Today, fifty years later and the planet is completely out of balance with animal and plant extinctions, wild fires raging out of control for week after week in the Amazon and Australia; sea creatures are dying on mass and being fished to crisis point, floods, earthquakes, crazy weather, storms and as I finish this, Coronavirus – Mother Nature is definitely kicking ass right now.   And then there is humankind where the vast majority have been conditioned not to listen to their intuition but to get in their car or on that train and get to work for 9am regardless of how their own individual body clock ticks. To take pharmaceuticals so that they can continue to go to work even when their body is saying "I'm run down, tired and unwell and I need to rest and heal". If we take x number of sick days in a month / year we have to explain ourselves to HR. The stresses of simply being alive in this modern age are staggering so it's no wonder that stress related illnesses are the number one cause of death on this beautiful planet we call home.

Compare this with caveman simply surviving with barely a spoken word, no technology and when flints as tools were pioneering, to the psychic enlightened beings we have the capability of being if we find the time to stop and smell the roses.

I have heard it said that the sensory input we receive from external sources such as computers, phones, TV, radio, social media, audio, advertising, newspapers, etc, that we receive in a single day, is more than a caveman/woman received in their entire lifetime.

Given our sensory evolution, the tools that we had back at the beginning of mankind are no longer sufficient to manage the power that we now have within us and our self-esteem is therefore taking a giant knock as we believe ourselves to be inadequate as we struggle to find balance that seems to be forever out of reach for many. We are more sensitive because of the enlightenment that humans are going through and so negativity, damage to the planet and the wrongdoing to every living thing that calls it home is painful. No wonder people turn to alcohol and substances to get comfortably numb. I guess that's called evolution!

But there is hope and that hope is within you as an individual. If your world has recently been turned upside down by an event and its life changing as mine has been, then I prefer to think it has been turned the right way up and now is that time for change. The smallest pebble in a pond makes a big ripple and the more of us who are the pebble of our own change, the greater the shift. Instead of pill popping and relying on pharmaceuticals or accepting our life as our lot and that's just the way it is, we each have the power to dig deep into our core and drag out the skeletons and release them with love and peace and understanding and find peace within ourselves and that will radiate outwards and enable the change to happen.

With this in mind, the more decisions we make for ourselves, rather than involve other people, the more we learn to trust our own intuition. It might go wrong sometimes but practice will make perfect as we'll become more tune with ourselves and our inner guidance. The more in-tune we become, the better decisions we will make and so we will trust ourselves more and more and then we will naturally grow into living our own fulfilling life full of love and joy and inner peace.

*****

Owning response-ability

Deciding upon a birthday treat I and Adrienne went to a health spa. I was only three months post-hospitalisation and when filling out the health questionnaire I was abruptly aware of the fact that I now have a heart condition, was on blood thinners and my blood pressure had been up and down causing severe dizziness and even a faint. Oh, Bloody Hell! I now had to think about these things that had previously only ever been a box on a form to ignore. In the true spirit of this book, I had to take responsibility for my own health and body here and so I even had to question what aromatherapy oils they were planning on using during my massage as these oils are so wonderfully potent that I needed to ensure that they were not going to have any adverse effects on my heart, circulation, blood pressure, bleeding, or absorption of the medication I was on. At this point I also realised that I hadn't yet laid on my stomach for forty minutes since hospitalisation and in all honesty I was a bit scared as to the effect this would have on my heart!

I could have pretended that all was OK but no one else lives in your body and no one else has to live with the repercussions of an action or inaction. It is up to us as individuals to ensure that things like this are considered. Whilst my friends were questioning me questioning the doctors in the hospital, I had to remind these same doctors twice that I cannot have an MRI scan because of metal wires in my face from operations as a child. They were not aware of the risk of rupture to breast implants with Cardioversion, so as respectful as I am of anyone's experience and qualifications, I advocate taking responsibility for ourselves because everyone has a head full of their own life. Apparently we each have between 60,000 and 120,000 thoughts per day whirring around in our minds and so it's not surprising that our needs are not necessarily latched onto by a third party as they're caught up in the gale force whirlwind in their own minds.

Three months post-hospitalisation I went to see the doctor in my local Spanish village to find out about my hospital follow up appointment and I told him that I thought that my heart is in normal rhythm to which he replied "Linda are you sure?" I said "yes, I think so." He got his machine out and it went beep beep beep "Linda it is in perfect rhythm 60 beats per minute it is like a clock ... how did you do it?" So, I told him some of the things that I have been doing ...which you already know being this far into the book ... and he said, "Linda you are a box of secrets, Congratulations".

As I reeled off all of my secrets, I began to wonder why I was doing so many different things to thrive rather than just survive? The answer popped into my head ... Because many different things caused the break it wasn't just a single cause. It was stress, alcohol, cigarettes, trauma, too much fun, heartbreak, anger, infection, giving out too much joy, trying so hard .... the list goes on and on. The upshot of it was that if the causes were multi-faceted, then the solutions must be multi-faceted too. One thing simply wouldn't cut the mustard.

At every opportunity I did (and still do) acupressure on myself, breathing exercises and visualised a normal heartbeat. I'd repeat affirmations, meditate and ask my heart what she needed. It could be food, rest, laughter, colour, herbs, etc.

When visualising, I created a picture in my mind of my actual heart beating in my chest. Not a cartoon or something to symbolise it, my actual heart as if I could see into my chest. At some point I'd made the transition from wanting a regular pulse, to wanting a regular heartbeat because I had the lightbulb moment that the heart creates the pulse and so that is what I had to focus my intent on. My actual heart was what needed my attention. So, my advice is to focus on the part of you that is creating the symptoms and that needs fixing; not the result. For example, if you have Crohn's or IBS, focus not on your poo being how you would wish it to be, focus on your bowels being healthy, with balanced gut flora and functioning perfectly to create optimum health for you as an individual. Then listen to your intuition as it tells you what you need to do to create that.

Some of my research is showing me things that tell me how much I've been exposing myself to risk factors for many years. Up until my recuperation and problems with erratic blood pressure, I had no idea that when we get physically cold, our blood pressure drops significantly. In addition low blood sugar causes anxiety and heart palpitations and rapid heartbeat. In a healthy body I guess our autonomic nervous system takes over and rectifies the situation and we're blissfully unaware of it all. However, in a vulnerable, fragile state, it can make a significant impact on us from moment to moment as everything is out of balance.

As I pondered on all of this, out of nowhere I got an insight which just popped into my head "don't celebrate too soon". How very rude of The Universe to inform me that despite my bravado and progress there is still much work to do. I was a bit miffed as I thought I was "there". Obviously not. Damn it! Not good to hear for an impatient redhead.

As if by magic the next day The Universe proved it's point and I fainted! I got up from the sofa and headed into the dining room and as I did so I felt a strange sensation. Strange because I didn't feel like I thought it would feel when one faints, but instinct made me grab a chair and to start to crouch down. The next thing I knew I was banging my head on the floor. I'd blacked out and the bruise on my deflated balloon of a derrière and the back of my head reminded me for days that I was obviously still quite high off the ground when my consciousness slipped away.

Within a day or so of that experience, I felt utterly sorry for myself because I could no longer party, drink, get silly, dance, pounce on unsuspecting men if the mood takes me. What am I now? Who am I? I felt unashamedly sorry for myself, took to my bed and I cried a lot. The next time this happened a few months later in the December, I'd got sufficient strength and resolve back to have a melt down in style. I had a bottle of 0% cava that had been chilling in the fridge, so I grabbed that and a box of handmade, dark chocolates from my lounge and I made myself a Linda McCartney sausage sandwich. I sat in my new four-poster bed making a real piggy of myself and sobbing to one chickflick after another. I didn't fight it or do the typically British stiff upper lip thing. I let it all out and it felt great as I embraced it as part of the process rather than an actual "it's not fair!!" episode

By mid-September when I went proudly to a Private hospital cardiology appointment with a friend as my interpreter and witness! The Consultant was wonderful and asked how I was. I told her I thought my arrhythmia had gone and I only felt my heart was out of rhythm when I got angry or upset or very tired or anxious. She said "oh no you've always got it, you just feel it more then". I was a bit disappointed thinking that maybe she was right but I got a hold on my head and thought NO I KNOW I'VE DONE IT, I KNOW I HAVE and so I held true to the beliefs in my head whilst secretly praying that I hadn't been deluding myself for the last month or two. A colleague did the ECG and she came through and took my pulse ..... and that's when a big grin spread across her face and she said, "Linda your arrhythmia has gone! congratulations how have you done it?" I told her about all the things that I've been doing, and she said "well keep doing them because that's very good. It's worked." Rock 'n' Roll! (well quite the opposite now actually!)

Go with the flow

As we walk our path of enlightenment, we'll naturally find that some people fall away from our lives or take less of a starring role. Some people may continue to treat us or behave towards us, the way that they always have because they haven't seen the changes that have taken place. Why should they, they have their own journey to be concentrating on. However, it's worth making a mental note at this stage, that we may need to tell them that we've changed and we don't think that way anymore, or that we don't want to part-take in this, that or the other activities – or indeed that we actually can't (or, we may not wish to say anything at all).

In finding ourselves less attracted to some people, it's worth seeking out those that we do resonate with; those that will encourage our growth and us theirs. Whatever your new interests and fascinations, the beauty of the internet is that we can find like-minded souls easily and build new relationships.

With my imposed lifestyle change and because my body and my mindset were going through such change, the bar didn't hold the same appeal as it once did. I seriously doubted at one point if I could carry on living here on the mountain as the social scene was a major part of the attraction and in my mind I couldn't be a part of that anymore. The Universe obviously heard my concerns (which I'd told absolutely no-one) and one of my friends whom I don't see that often happened to be in the bar one evening and made a beeline for me and completely out of the blue she said "you must stay here Linda. You have friends and we all love you very much and you are still needed here." I had never before appreciated how intuitive she was, and those words touched my heart like you cannot even believe to imagine and I welled up with relief and joy.

Uplifted, I still needed to find a social scene that would continue to lift my spirits rather than remind me of what I could no longer do; and that came through my friend Alex who was an absolute Godsend. He doesn't drink for health reasons and showed me that I could still have lovely times without alcohol and we went out for lovely lunches and dinners and relished delicious foods in poetic beach bars, lit with fairy lights and the waves and the moon lapped at the shore. It nurtured my soul and I did indeed feel so very happy. I was exploring new places and without any potential worry of drinking and driving – or, more to the point, worrying about not being able to drink because I was driving. I began to witness the limitations that people put upon themselves (as I had) because of the need for alcohol; in wanting to get back to local territory early in the evening or choosing a very local and predictable option so that they could drink.

In having significant differences of opinion with a few friends, I found that many like-minded people had experienced exactly the same thing at around about the same time. Rather than not being friends anymore, I'd like to think that we've completed that section of our Soul Contracts with each other (certainly for now) and we have nothing left to teach each other at this point in time. It's time to be around folk who can take us up to the next level and visa-versa.

I did indeed, seek out closer friendships with some that had previously been on the periphery of my life and I found that I was directed in new ways. New information came my way at a new level and I started to feel physically lighter, more mentally alert and motivated to share my insights – well, right up until I got Covid when the brain fog kicked in. Despite my heart history, I kept calm and starting taking my natural blood thinners for a few weeks. I'd got over the worst of it within a few days but slept like a dormouse for a few weeks and that was that.

As part of this process, I'd been invited to join a Distance Healing Circle and we all messaged and sent healing to someone in need, on a Thursday evening at 9pm. Even connecting with others remotely brings a sense of community and the intuits that we shared after the healing session were really quite profound.

I began to make a ritual of the evening, staring with a lovely warm shower with aromatherapy body wash I lit candles and incense, I got a glass of sin alcohol (as in without alcohol!) red wine and some spring water and I put on some lovely music courtesy of Enya. I adjusted the lighting, so it was calming and chilled for twenty minutes before the sitting.

The intention for the meeting was to release negative emotions and energy from our bodies and to tell every single cell in our body that we love it, entrust it to do its job perfectly to keep us in good health strong and energetic and enjoy life more each and every day. It was exactly what I needed on that day and I began to notice that we were becoming more in synch. If one of our number was feeling a particular way and asked for healing, chances were that several of us were also feeling the same way. We were reflecting each other without ever having met!

During this particular sitting I started to cry as I saw dozens of white doves and white butterflies fluttering about as I was performing the energetic and emotional release.

I felt weightless as I sat cross-legged in a yoga pose on my sofa and yet grounded. By the end of the twenty minutes I felt very strong.

Completely dynamically and without forethought, during these twenty minutes I forgave the cause of everything that had happened to me, I let go of the emotions and I knew as they were being released I never have to go through those things again - hence the tears I think. I thanked it all for being in my life and for bringing me to this point of awareness. I thanked the distresses that I had experienced throughout my life, that they have brought me to this point in time, where I feel peace and happiness, strengths and wisdom, optimistic and creative.

I have a driving desire to share my experiences so that others may choose a different path themselves rather than that which is offered by the mainstream. I know that it is entirely possible to cure yourself with the help of both traditional western medicine and alternative holistic practices and it's time to spread that word.

<u>Setbacks – or lessons?!</u>

After a roaring success at the Cardiologist I was riding high on life when there was a blip on the work front and I got really annoyed at the inconvenience caused to me. As I vented my annoyance I started to shake and my heart went out of synch, the arrhythmia was back and I was so disappointed in my heart. The crazy thing is, that looking back at this, two years down the line, I can't believe that I ever got so angry that I shook – ever. This journey is teaching me so much.

I really struggled with this fall from the pedestal where I'd proudly put my heart for all to see but I gritted my teeth and refused to admit defeat. I continued to tell my heart that I loved it and told her gently not to worry, you will be back in sync very soon. An element of doubt always crept in when this happened and I had to remind myself very strongly to keep the faith and remind myself that my mind is the power that brought it back into synch despite many others' scepticism. I told myself each time that I've done it once, twice, three or four times and I could do it again – and I did. Until one day, it didn't pop out of rhythm for over one year, over 18-months but when it did, it was only ever so slightly and she came back into her 60 beats per minute happily after a bit of TCL.

At the particular time mentioned above, I also realised that this could keep happening throughout my long life. If I was to come off the medication in favour of more natural ways of thinning my blood and controlling my heart rate and rhythm I'd have to do what I could to remain stress-free. I would therefore have to learn how to manage my reactions to emotional triggers, otherwise the worst-case scenario could happen because I risk provoking arrhythmia every time I stress and so forming a blood clot which could turn into a stroke or having another heart attack.

It's hugely important to look deep into what's going on around you. We are all being guided all of the time and the annoying work situation was there to show me what I needed to act on next! I feel that this incident beautifully demonstrates the importance of being around people so we learn and grow and become the enlightened species we are growing into.

I asked my guides in the universe for guidance on what to watch on Gaia channel and quite literally I opened the app and there right in front of me without any searching whatsoever, was The Science of Changing Your Mind by Dr Joe Dispenza, and he very eloquently brought back to the surface, my own beliefs. Here's what I took from what he had to say.

To facilitate the change that we as an individual want to achieve, we need to break the chemical programming of our body to emotional responses, to memories and situations.

Every day your routine means your body is used to producing and sending out certain chemicals at certain times and it is naturally trained to do that by you, your behaviour and your thinking patterns.

The chemical concoctions that the body makes up in response to upset, stress, anxiety, joy, etc. are remembered and automatically dispensed when that trigger is received by our mind or body before we even blink let alone think.

If we have a think about how we think, we then become conscious of that unconscious state and at this point we can reprogram ourselves and our chemical reactions.

He confirmed a long-held belief of mine which I've mentioned previously and so the message was re-presenting itself to me for my consideration:

Thoughts become actions
Repeating emotions become a mood
Repeating mood becomes a trait
Repeating trait becomes your personality

You therefore have to reprogram yourself not to behave in the same way to an emotional trigger because if you alter your actions, you'll alter your experience.

When you start to realise that you've consciously changed your reactions and so behaviours, you've made the shift from unconscious to conscious! At that point the chemical processes start to change and the circuits formed over your life start to quieten down.

When you start to rehearse and picture yourself in a new way of thinking and being, you naturally install the new hardware and software for handling this experience in the future in preparation for the trigger.

After that's happened a few times, it's then in your subconscious as are the revised chemical reactions of your body.

The quantum field then responds to your new state of being because you've changed your repeating trait and so your personality. Then, remember the smoke signals that you send out? You've now changed those and so you attract a different smoke signal answer and hey presto, life just got better.

Dr Joe put a long-held belief of mine into more physics-orientated words but I think it's interesting to note his words too:

Thoughts are the electrical charge in the quantum field.

The feelings are the magnetic charge in the quantum field and so how you think and feel broadcasts an electromagnetic signature that influences every atom in your life and draws the event to you. The Universe delivers but does it in an unusual way which makes it a surprise, so you then know that is The Universe that did it for you and inspires you to continue to do it.

So every morning think today 'I'll consciously create my day and thoughts .. choose your thoughts like you choose your clothes" and with this we change our electromagnetic signature and so what we attract. (Recognise this line from Eat Pray Love?)

Our body is designed for short term stress not repeated triggers or long-term, never-ending stresses.

We can turn on stress response by thought alone at which point our body believes it's happening and the fight or flight kicks and our body prepares for it chemically. These chemical reactions are addictive – think adrenaline junkie (guilty as charged on that one forever – well until my awakening!)

With the constant chemical / hormonal imbalance, we then get disease, anger, depression, aggression, hatred, prejudice, frustration, fear, anxiety, hopelessness insecurity and powerlessness.

(I had to keep stopping this video as it was so powerful I didn't want to miss and thing.)

Afterwards I had a good think because I do love joining the dots which is typical of being a Life Path number 7 (see The Balance Procedure in section 2). I deduced that because I'm such an emotionally led person, I am always going to encounter situations which potentially trigger me, resulting in my heart going into it's own crazy jazz rhythm i.e. it becomes really out of synch with the rest of my body, and believe me, when you go into atrial fibrillation / arrhythmia, each part of your body feels bizarrely mismatched. It feels like the cogs of a clock missing each other rather than working together "like clockwork".

(A couple of years later I was to get into astrology and realise why I'm so emotional. At that point I knew that I had to incorporate Astrology into my "Shine On" Masterclass Series (and Section 2 of this book) and so set about doing a course.

It turns out that I have six planets in water signs and water signs are notoriously emotional. The fact that my moon is in the sign of

Cancer is also a double whammy on that front so hey, I am being authentic (TBP) and being who I was born to be (astrology). However, because it happened so frequently, my own behaviour had become a mood and then ultimately a personality trait and I was known for being "over sensitive and emotional". Oh! Being a sunny Leo I hadn't spotted that one at all! My leonine ego had focused on being bold and energetic and life and soul of the party. My Sagittarius rising had focused on being crazy, wild and free. I hadn't even noticed the emotional side as I'd blow up like a volcano but revert back to my sunny Leo persona within minutes of venting my frustrations and so forget all about it. This is what we work through in my course.)

In looking for the answer on that day of realisation that I would constantly be triggered, the first thing that popped up when I turned on Gaia, was a speaker about changing your reaction to situations by retraining yourself how you react.

In time with practice of your new reactions, the chemicals that your body normally releases in those situations change and you no longer react that way. You become a new you and you've changed that aspect of your personality. And then the diseases that you've been suffering from fall away because they were attached to the old you, the old electromagnetic signature and they're not compatible with your new signal.

So, in realising that I've been a very emotionally reactive person, I acknowledged this as an aspect of myself to work on and it being a key part of my development and recovery. Learning not to respond so emotionally to things. That way my heart should stay in tiptop tik-tok time and voilà! I therefore set about changing my "reactions" into responses and the information poured my way over the coming years in oh so many different ways. Through movies, courses, intuits, the internet, friends, strangers, meditations – we just have to be present enough in each moment to notice it and make a note. That's one of the reasons that I have a journal app on my 'phone. I journal it immediately and reflect back through it every now and again. I wholehearted recommend doing the same.

Once again in The Balance Procedure revealing to me that I'm a Life Path 7, I was intrigued when I joined the dots between Joe Dispenza's electromagnetic theories and another golden nugget of information about our physical hearts.

It has been scientifically proven that the heart as a standard "pump" is nowhere near powerful enough to pump all of that blood through the 60,000 miles of blood vessels (100,000kms)! It is actually an electromagnetic pulse generator which spins the blood off into the arteries. This creates a vortex of self-perpetuating circulation through the human body, assisted by our own movements.

Our body works as a whole energetic being and so it stands to reason that our hearts and our thoughts and behaviours and so all of our electromagnetic signals are interlinked. Therefore, I have to wonder if only certain people only pick up on certain behaviours. Because it resonates with their own vibration, they "see" those behaviours which others just aren't aware of.

We are electric and so, if you want to go really deep, we can wonder at the effect of electromagnetic interference on our internal electromagnetic pulse generator I.e. our heart, from external sources such as Wi-Fi routers, Mobile 'phones, TVs, microwaves, even power sockets – and maybe take a break from all of that during our sleep time by turning it all off at source. I'll also discuss grounding techniques and crystals to counter these effects later on.

I always used to keep my 'phone on my bedside table overnight next to my glass of water, but since my awakening and having the time to recognise and process the awareness's that have come my way, I realised that this was a bad idea because of the EMFs generated by mobile 'phones. Indeed, when during my research I found a photograph that Emoto's team had taken of water exposed to mobile 'phone EMFs and it reinforced to me that it should be avoided.

On the other side of the coin, we can draw the comparison with making a crystal elixir as I have been experimenting with crystal energy in different forms. Often, I'll put my chosen crystals alongside and touching a bottle of drinking water and in doing so, create an elixir from the energy of the crystals. As I touch on in Section 2, Crystals chapter, they do not need to be in the water in order for their potent energy to infuse the water with their therapeutic properties. Indeed, some should not be put in water. The water tastes delightfully different after 24-hours of absorbing the crystal energy and more energised. By contrast, if I drink water that has been next to my 'phone, it tastes dead, strange and definitely unappealing. Going further down that rabbit hole, contemplate the fact that we ourselves are made up of 70% water and so keeping our mobiles attached to us 24/7 is going to have an adverse effect on our bodies for sure.

Incidentally, I have since bought different crystals to protect from EMF's - Shungite, pyrite, hematite and tourmaline, and wear these when sat at my computer or using my 'phone for long periods of time.

<u>'Don't take it to heart'</u>

Very quickly I was given the opportunity to try out my newfound information and to put into practice as I encountered a potential trigger the next morning. Because I'd decided to change my electromagnet signature, I realised that my "reaction" was coming directly from my heart as I could literally *feel* the pull in my chest. This was a new one for me and so I acted upon it.

(The difference between knowledge and wisdom is this: Knowledge is having the information. Wisdom is using that knowledge and actually acting upon that information).

I could feel the stress hormones beginning to course through my veins as since my hospitalisation I had become so body aware that my arms tingled whenever I got stressed or anxious. I therefore followed the advice on the video and I took charge of myself and I consciously decided not to put undue stress on my heart. Instead, I shifted that anxiety energy to my physical brain, but then wondered what my happen in my brain with all of that unwanted energy – could it bring on a stroke or a brain tumour? I realised that I needed to release this from my physical body completely – I didn't need it at all so why keep hold of it?! I therefore shifted that feeling to outside of myself, just to the right of my head, all by simply thinking about it happening. Our thoughts are indeed powerful. It worked and I didn't get emotional or upset about the situation as I had nipped the chemical reactions in the bud and stopped them from taking me over.

Then came my lightbulb moment about this trigger. Because I hadn't spun off into fight or flight mode, I recognised the deep-seated trigger was from my childhood and always being the last one to be picked for team sports and so rejection and so wanting to be loved.

Then I realised that I've been attracting rejection in different forms throughout significant and various different types of relationships. It was in my smoke signals, in my electromagnetic field and now I'd recognised it and could start the process of change. I used TBP card 4 for the heart chakra, with the affirmation "I am loved. I am welcome" throughout the coming days and weeks.

A couple of years down the line I had a further lightbulb moment. I was reflecting to those that were seemingly rejecting me. They, too were or had in the past, been rejected and so they too a similar hang-up. Between us we were self-perpetuating rejection. If only we'd all known all of this way back when these triggers were being created. This is the beauty of this moment in time in humankind's spiritual evolution. We're beginning to see why we're so messed up and we have the spiritual resources available to us to unravel them – in my humble opinion.

Sex

It's worth remembering that not all heart fluttering provocation has negative connotations! In exchanging messages with a rather dishy chap, my heart started to go into arrhythmia again …. "damn it!" I thought, "how is this making me stressed?!" I became frustrated with myself and disappointment washed through me as I focused and really tried not to let any stress hormones trigger and do the same. Then I realised - I'm obviously attracted to this guy and my heart is a flutter! . How very Edwardian I thought … My heart is literally flirting / fluttering. I relaxed and enjoyed the feeling instead of getting anxious! However, when we've been dealt a health wild card, it can stay with us for a long time and we can easily get paranoid about our what our body might do next. We have to learn to trust ourselves and in my view, the more responsibility we take for our own wellbeing, and the more active we are consciously about ourselves, the better chance we have of remaining fit, well, happy and healthy, strong and full of joie de vivre.

So there I was, several months down the line and I started to wonder about future romantic relationships. Then the stark reality hit me that I didn't drink any more which meant that any new encounter would have to be absolutely sober on my part without the benefit of a shot of Dutch courage on the rocks - Scooby Doo YIKES! Then, "Ew", just the thought of snogging someone stinking of booze and / or cigarettes made me wrinkle my nose and recoil, let alone the reality. Not just the smell but I really wasn't impressed by squiffy people's antics and certainly not for an intimate encounter.

No squiffy uninhibited shenanigans for me. I would have to face getting naked, sober! That meant that I would have to find a new level of body confidence. Not only the confidence that my heart would go the distance, but that I would be totally comfortable with my naked appearance. My body had been in pretty good shape with great skin and muscle tone, but with recent events I had become a skinny UK size 10. I'd lost three stone in two years and the final stone had just dropped off over two weeks leaving my fifty-two-year-old skin loose and crepe like. For the first time in my life I had bingo wings and my usually peach-like derrière was now a deflated balloon which looked very sorry for itself when I contorted myself to look at it in the mirror. My clothes were all too loose and although my cheekbones and jaw line were to die for (pun intended) and that I looked like a fashion model from the front, the rest of me needed some work before I was getting naked sober and in front of a potentially lover I can assure you – especially if they were sober too! I then pondered that maybe I should go for a fella who wears glasses and then I can seductively remove them in a pre-practiced sexy move. Hahaha. I literally laughed out loud at the thought of that one! "Yoo-hoo! ... Calling all those who haven't been to Specsavers yet!!!"

I tried to do weights but it still hurt my chest muscles which hadn't quite recovered. I wasn't strong enough to do any kind of fitness class yet, not even a full-on yoga class. It was very annoying!

I started to fret about how my will body react when I'm absolutely sober for the first time with a new man and post-heart attack and on meds? Oh dear God, overthinking alert! Then I started wondering about the fact that I have hung up my beer goggles for the last time and any potential romantic encounter would literally be the bare, naked truth.

Then there was the "do I tell them that I nearly died of a heart attack before we get jiggy with it?!" If I did it might put them off and I wouldn't get my oats, or they might get all "are you ok?" on me – Turn off alert! But then if I didn't and I started getting into trouble they wouldn't necessarily realise was happening and I could have actually died in the act! Take it from me, that the joke of 'hey, but what a way to go!' isn't actually funny when the joke becomes a distinct possibility it's not at all funny nor the way you want to go!

I resigned myself to sorting myself out for the time-being until I figured it out in my mind! I guess this is as good a time as any to tell you about the first time I did that!

One day, a month or few after the big heart event, I was feeling the tension in my body and I knew that the only way to release it was to go lone rangering and flick the bean! I've always had a high sex drive and found it to be therapeutic as well as highly enjoyable! This time, however, I had no idea if my heart could take the full body experience of an orgasm! I only mention this in these pages because after a major health issue, it's a real concern. The old adage of "what a way to go though eh ... wink wink nudge nudge?!", doesn't actually apply when you think you could well pop your clogs masturbating - especially when you realise that someone would then find your body in a compromising position .... on your own! But, in my view, it'd be therapeutic and flood my body with endorphins and I had to give it a go sometime, but this time I made a few preparations just in case I did die sorting myself out, I glammed myself up beforehand!

I put in my removable dental bridge (front few teeth courtesy of a horse-riding accident and then an Igor incident), I put on my make-up and brushed my hair and put on a satin negligee! I unlocked the door and took the key out so that someone could get in if it did indeed prove too much for my heart and I needed help or if I popped my clogs in the act! I hoped that if I was glamorous it might detract from the fact that I had been found with my legs akimbo, a stupid smile on my face and my hand undeniably located in my nether regions and so that wouldn't be the only legacy that I left! If I was going to go, I wanted to go down as a legend and not like Hollywood starlet Lupe Velez, who, in preparing to take her own life, apparently put on her glamorous make-up, did her hair, decorated her room and bed with rose petals, dressed in a negligee and lay on her satin bedsheets as she took an overdose. Unfortunately, as legend has it, her last supper disagreed with the tablets and as she rushed to the bathroom to vomit, she slipped and banged her head on the toilet, drowning in the toilet bowl. Nothing like the befitting Hollywood ending that she had meticulously planned, bless her. If I was to pop my clogs, I didn't want to be found as a toothless hag with ratty hair in a cat print T-shirt with my sheep pyjamas around my ankles! I just hoped that my cats wouldn't start eating me too soon and ruin the effect!

It was genuinely scary risking an orgasm. It was a real moment of truth I guess but something that has to be done at some point after any critical health event. If you or a loved one have ever gone through this, it's normal (well I hope it is, or I'm weirder than I thought!) It might not even have been death, it could have been a stroke or, well, let's not dwell on it any further – you get the point (pun intended), it is a naturally scary obstacle to overcome.

However, within the hour I had a big smile on my face and as the endorphins surfed through my arteries, these happy hormones made my senses become more acute and I could hear the birdies singing outside, I was aware that the sun was shining and there was so much good in the world and how wonderful life is – Everything was marvellous again!

I had a big satisfied smile on my face and my body was tingling with pleasure instead of tension, and so I did it again – I survived both of the whole body orgasms (obviously) and felt fabulous to boot! Whoohoo! Although an afterthought did creep into my awareness, that maybe I need to work on being greedy as I have a feeling it is a shadow part of my personality!

And, yes, every time I loved myself for some months afterwards, I'd do my make-up and hair to ensure that my departure would be glamorous rather than someone finding a hideous, scraggy haired, toothless crone in her house in the woods (well, olive grove but that's poetic license)! Putting it all on hold was not easy for the fiery, sassy redhead full of naughtiness and mischief that I was once was ... Boo hoo, I hadn't mourned that side of me at that point and I didn't intend to – just cryo-freeze her for the time being.

In pondering on all of that, I realised that I'd been too quick to give my heart away in the past and I began to realise just how precious my heart is. Without her I don't have life and so I'm looking after her. I'm making sure that I don't spend my heart's energy which creates those beats in my chest, on someone who isn't authentic. There is a balance between being open-hearted and loving and actually giving your heart to someone. I guess, instead we can practice "unconditional love" which is a very groovy but safe philosophy? I knew that at that moment in time, I needed to focus my heart's energy on simply beating and just staying alive and healing. Unfortunately, my dishy mate had unwittingly shown me that it wasn't actually that safe for me to go getting crushes and flirting too heavily with anyone as I needed to focus on rhythm and getting all unnecessary over a Mr D'Arcy type unfortunately wouldn't do me any favours if I was triggering arrhythmia!

So just like I had with the jealousy aspect of my recovery, I took myself out of the game and held in my mind that when the right person came along, my heart would be safe with them ... No stress, no anguish, no dramas which would literally damage my heart and I could actually die of a broken heart. How very Romeo and Juliet. 18-months down the line I was so much stronger that I started to have dalliances. I had to work through dramas and rejection – I guess I'd not focused on those as much as I'd thought as I hadn't been exposing myself to potential romances at all. However, this time, I did notice that I didn't dive in the deep end and when I recognised an old pattern beginning to unfold, I backed away. Boy did I have fun until those moments of realisation though. I was like a wild animal set free! In my mind and my journals, I simply set about reaffirming what was and was not acceptable (thank you Esther Hicks for that pearl of wisdom in a Hay House seminar) and created affirmations. I recognised the patterns and countered them. I realised that in order to attract "emotionally available" men, I had to allow myself to be "emotionally available" and that is a work in progress.

However, when I did venture back into the dating game and had the odd dalliance, I was really pleased to discover that my body was much more sensitive as I wasn't numbed with alcohol or nicotine and the whole experience was much more fun than a "drunken fumble". Because I'd done so much work on myself emotionally and spiritually, there wasn't any of the anxiety that I'd anticipated, nor any of the insecurities and because I'd grown into myself spiritually, I was quite happy at directing to the right spot and for that matter, in being authentic. It was fabulous!

Embracing the Change – you and others

For about six months I hardly went out socially at all. I had to put all of my efforts into regaining my strength and cultivating the will to go out as everything had changed and I started to worry as I wondered who the real Linda was when sober and straight? I'd joined my parents on their pub jaunts from the age of 11 years old and was very much a pub goer and party girl. I'd always been the last woman standing; the one dancing until dawn, laughing and drinking and having an absolute blast; making everyone else laugh, insisting they got up and danced and making sure that everyone had a great time. At one point in my past I found out that everyone at work in my London sales days thought I was "coked up" because I was so animated and crazy. When I'd told them "nope I'd never tried it", they didn't believe me for ages.

The Universe (my soul) heard my thoughts (of course) and when I popped out for the re-opening of a local bar I was deep in conversation when a friend bounced up behind me to say "hi". As I turned around to chat with him, dusk had crept up and the coloured fairy lights wrapped around the palm tree were all lit up behind him and I blurted out "Hi David, OOOO, look at the pretty lights!". He laughed out loud and said "yeah you're still the same Linda we know and love!" I wanted to cry with relief (in fact emotion has just swept through me as I write this) but instead I said to him "Thank you David, you have no idea how much that means to me. I really needed to hear that".

I guess this comes back to us chipping away at the marble to reveal the angel statue within as Michael Angelo described, and Anija Moorjani recalled: "We are essentially ourselves, but we have to let go of what isn't us" – and in my experience, it's alcohol that makes us a different person, not the sober self. The sober self is who we are, we just have to enjoy being that person and if we don't particularly like any aspect of who the real "us" is, then we can take steps to rectify that – that's personal growth. However, if we want to take substances (legal or illegal) to be the person that we actually wish we were then that's a falsehood (in my humble opinion). I was always the life and soul of a party but when I did experience cocaine, very quickly it turned me into a shadow of myself and I lost all of my confidence and felt that I couldn't go to a party without it. I felt like I'd sold my soul to the Devil. Thankfully, I got a grip and decided that I preferred being an adrenaline junkie au naturel. When I see people on it now, I see that they have no idea who they become under that influence and it isn't pretty. As far as alcohol is concerned, trust me when I say that we have more energy, make better judgement calls, are more motivated and trust ourselves so much more than without anything altering our mental state.

Several years down the line, I enjoy the odd glass of vino but I have to say that I'm too sensitive to it now to dare to drink much. I've realised that despite all my hard work, I can be easily triggered and it's not necessarily my own triggers that I display: I have found that, being a sensitive soul and an Empath, as my inhibitions / self-control falters under the guise of relaxing with a glass of wine, I am prone to displaying the emotions of other people - and as a bar is full of people, that could be anyone's shadow side as well as my own.

As we release the baggage that we've collected along the years, our vibration becomes higher and lighter as we're literally not holding onto heavy, negative emotions any more. My theory is that alcohol takes longer to wade through a denser, heavier vibration (and so person) and there is a higher tolerance. As our vibration becomes lighter, alcohol (etc) can pass though our bodies uninhibited much more quickly and so our tolerance for it becomes less and less. To use an analogy here: Picture an octopus' ink in the sea: In water, it travels and diffuses very quickly. However, if it were to be squirted into the sandy seabed, it would take much longer to travel between the grains of sand. It would have to find its way through the dense matter and weave this way and that. (I thought I'd get creative with the analogy there!)

However, as we're releasing that baggage and changing our behaviours, responses and essentially up-levelling ourselves, others might not see what's happening as they're understandably engrossed in their own life. Even if they see it, they might not understand what's going on, because as I've mentioned, until we've been through something ourselves, first hand, we can try to understand, but we can't actually understand it fully. As we start to grow we might not resonate with the same people as much, if at all anymore.

When going through a health scare, whilst our loved ones have a sense of fear for us, bewilderment, disbelief and shock, when it comes to it, no-one can fully appreciate what it's like to experience that lack of energy and the uncertainty that we have about our own future and not knowing if our body will ever be strong again, or if are we going to survive and if so, with what limitations?

If we have had to self-impose lifestyle changes to survive, the impact that makes on our very being, our personality, the side-effects of pharmaceuticals on our personality, the effect of the trauma on our personality, wondering who we are without alcohol, without our jobs and the people we once surrounded ourselves with and without our emotional crutches. We're not the only ones going through the changes so all I can say is make use of the drugs – pharmaceutical or natural– and be patient with them! We also need to understand that this is our life and not theirs and so it's up to us to make any changes necessary and hope that they too can adapt. This is our life of which they are a part but at this moment in time we have to look after number one and that's the whole O not the C mentioned in The Celestine Prophecy.

I know this from first-hand experience because my own brother had a heart attack two years before I did. Because he is still alive and there are a few thousand miles between us and I was busy with my own life, I never had an in-depth conversation with him about it all.

I didn't appreciate the trauma and lifestyle change that he was going through, nor his lack of energy. Indeed, I wasn't even aware of that until I had my own heart events and then we started to talk to about his experience. I was then devastated that I wasn't there for him more because I just didn't realise what he was going through because he always has been one to keep himself to himself and he didn't share.

Equally, people will only see what's alive in side of them and this was confirmed at a Cardiology review on Friday 13th December at the Comarcal Hospital here in Spain (NHS equivalent hospital).

I was absolutely delighted to show off my perfect rhythm heart on the ECG and to announce that I am no longer taking the betablockers. The Cardiologist was less than impressed with my decision to stop these pharmaceuticals and tutted disapprovingly. I reassured her that I am taking a herbal equivalent but that didn't impress her either. When she saw my ECG she said "the tablets are working". I said, well actually I've done a lot of work on myself" and listed my holistic practices (Reiki, acupuncture, acupressure, meditation, yoga, crystals, affirmations, working on emotional triggers and releasing the past during some serious emotional soul searching, mindfulness, etc.). She simply repeated "the tablets are working". In my lovely new calm state, I realised that she wasn't able to hear me right now, but maybe one day if other people tell her that they've done it too, she'd join the dots and cast her mind back to me and understand that diseases have emotional causes.

I've found that there is a strange struggle too. As our behaviours change, it may well be that others don't notice and continue to expect the same behaviours from us as they're used to. Even though we've changed, they don't necessarily see it and it can become quite disheartening that all of our hard work has gone unseen. Because the old behaviours are "expected of us", it might well be that we can't help but relapse during time spent with these folk and behave as they are energetically sending out those smoke signals and expecting to see the same back as they always did. I found it quite frustrating but again, we're all a work in progress. I guess that's why sometimes we have to make gentle shifts in our circle of friends to those that we resonate with once we've shed the old skin – otherwise we can get held in that old vibration. If we don't make the changes, we know that The Universe (our Soul) will take control and do it for us and my soul is pretty adamant when changes need to be made and takes no prisoners!

Post-health scare, everything needed "considering" and it got pretty tedious. I had to research anything that I wanted to use including herbal supplements, essential oils and even yoga postures and the position of my hands when I went to sleep! For the brain fog I had wanted to try Co-enzyme Q10, Ginkgo Biloba and indeed, everything else on the shelves for an alert mind, but given my heart history I had to research it all and make sure that it was safe to take.

Recently whilst sitting on the sofa I felt like my body was beginning to cave inwards. Bizarre I thought. I wonder what that's all about. Then I remembered Deirdre's words during one of her yoga classes earlier in the recovery process. She'd said that I should open my chest and focus on my posture as after a heart incident the tendency is to fold inwards. At the time I'd said to her that I'd always had a good posture so I didn't foresee a problem but I realised that this was what was happening. I guess my core had always been so very strong because of dancing, horse ownership and riding but since my awakening I had none of that to keep me strong. I just felt that it was now or never to get my strength back and I decided NOW.

I messaged my friend Tanya who inspired me to attend her yoga classes a couple of years ago but life had distracted me more recently I'd been hit and miss with her classes but always intended to go again. I felt it only fair to warn her that I wanted to go to her class and so I asked her if she'd be OK with me attending and she gave me some solid advice about consulting my Medics, not pushing myself and taking it really easy, to avoid anything that could make my heart race and to just relax and enjoy being there. I took her advice and throughout the class she made eye contact and checked in with me to make sure I was ok. It felt absolutely wonderful to be back in class.

I'd given it some thought and planned to go into Child, Mountain or Savasana poses as and when I needed to rest.

When we thanked ourselves for making the effort to practice yoga at the end of the class I got really emotional as I realised what a bloody fool I'd been pushing my body too far over the years, smoking, drinking and for not listening to her when she was tired. How I'd stressed and ignored the effects on my body thinking myself invincible. The years had crept up on me like a panther stalking it's prey and suddenly I was that 52-year old business executive having a heart attack that was so far off when I was in my 20's and 30's flying high.

The following week throughout the yoga class I discreetly checked my pulse and i was delighted that my heart stayed steady. My Intercostal muscles ached and really made me realise how quickly strength and muscles weaken. Once again, at the end of class when we silently thanked ourselves for making the effort to practice yoga, I felt myself about to cry.

In the interests of continuing to embrace the changes and to now listen to my body I went home to sleep and bask in the sun!

Princess Jade – Reflections

Reflections of what is going on within us emotionally, are much more obvious with our animals as they are emotionally honest – remember the saying that "pets are like their owners". As an Equine Massage Therapist and Bach Flower Remedy Therapist I'd see this all of the time when I was called into to treat a horse that was behaving badly for example; maybe it was nervous, anxious or angry. As I tuned into the beautiful big beasties and listened to their owner describing what was going on, I'd start to create the bespoke Bach Flower remedy, blending a unique potion of up to six of these fabulous remedies. Each blend was specifically for that individual horse in order to address its varying emotional states that were showing to be out of balance. Almost every time, as I listened to the owner, I was mentally compiling exactly the same list of remedies for them as they'd be equally anxious, nervous, angry, skitty, etc! Horses have been used in treating humans via Equine Psychotherapy for many years because they are so acutely in tune, that they will demonstrate a person's behaviours, even if the person is in denial that this is going on inside of themselves. Because horses are so vocal and big and physical, we can't help but take notice. We know it when they're angry or afraid, it's all in their body language. I'd "happened" across a book during my fifteen years with Penny-Horse, called Riding Between The Worlds, by Linda Kohanov. It was about her insights and experiences which led her to create EponaQuest where horses work to heal us humans in this way.

I would sometimes go to see my Penny-Horse when I was at the end of my tether in the bar for one reason or another. I'd go with the intent of having some quiet down time out in nature, but she would very clearly demonstrate that despite my calm facade, inside I was an emotional wreck. I'd inevitably breakdown as she misbehaved or bit me (which was out of character for her) and a flood of emotions would release. She became my rock and I adored her for her overt emotions – something which I had disabled in myself for fear of what I would do, say or even cry in my very public house.

I would watch the very same happen to my stable-mates and to my clients. Dog owners would ask me for a remedy for their dog and I would see that they needed one too. I now offer a discount for

Pet/Owner remedies as the two are so intertwined, I see that I need to treat both, not just one.

In the November after my heart had told me that she'd just about had enough, my beautiful cat, best friend and constant companion of eleven years had reached the final stages of her life. I was fretting ... was she comfortable? Did she know she was dying? Was she scared? Was she ready? Was she in pain?

Then I recalled that night in A&E when I didn't know that I was close to dying. I was in and out of sleep – or was it consciousness? I don't know, but I saw Princess Jade going through the same process. She would appear to be asleep in the middle of the floor in a crouched position with her face against the floor and just as I had been she was only vaguely aware of what was going on around her; she too was tired and peaceful, just as I had been.

She was going with the flow of what was being done with her and when I carried her to bed, or the sofa; and when I stroked her she purred so very softly so I could hardly feel or hear her any more. I could barely feel her usually strong life-force energy and knew that her time was near. I realised that she was probably no more aware of her situation than I had been of mine and I managed to find comfort in knowing that she therefore wasn't distressed

After a couple of weeks of trying various treatments (holistic and from the vet) she wasn't improving and in seeing her in the state that I've described above for several days, I woke one morning and just knew that today was the day to take her to be put to sleep.

Apart from anything else, there had been a few dogs around over the last month or so, that were up to no good and a few neighbours' cats had fallen to them. I couldn't bear the thought of that happening to her in this fragile state. The heavens were calling her on that day and so I asked that her guardian angels were there waiting to welcome her and care for her during this time of transformation. I later realised that it was a new moon on that day and so it was a beautiful day to be released from her mortal coil back into spirit.

As I've mentioned, life and our animals around us, are mirrors and when we change our own vibration, then things around us change to reflect our new ways, or things/they disappear. Since my hospitalisation, I'd done so much work on changing my vibe, releasing the anger that I didn't know that I had, changing the way I reacted to things, and even consciously changing the chemicals my body pumped out in response to emotional triggers. My anger was a different beastie now.

I wholeheartedly believe that my little princess just couldn't follow suit as she still had so much stress in her tiny little heart. She constantly growled at the other cats, ran away from human visitors or hissed like a wildcat if they went to stroke her. I was told by the vet in the week prior to her passing, and also by a cattery owner a few years previous, "she really doesn't like me. She really hates it here" In other words, 'Don't bring her back!' I believe that because she didn't shift along with me, she disappeared from my world.

All of her anger and fear manifested into the gut problem that killed her because when the vet called me with the result of the post-mortem there was nothing to show why she had stopped eating. There was no blockage, no foreign body, no inflammation, no disease, nothing; and despite the fact that she had not eaten or drunk anything for six days by the time she was put to sleep, they found poo in her bowel.

In my world of mirrors and looking for the signs, this showed me that she literally could not digest this new way of being and as she was too entrenched in her reactions, she was unable or unwilling to make the changes. This was demonstrated by her digestive system stalling and not restarting.

I lit a candle for her every night for several weeks and none of the other cats went near her chair for two weeks after her passing back into spirit.

Love Hate Ignore Rice Experiment

(colour photos can be found on my website, WWRS page
www.LindaJaneW.me)

Some years ago, I'd heard about a experiment using rice, the aim of which is to tangibly demonstrate the power of words, thoughts and so energy, on physical matter – why is that important? – all will be revealed ...

I was curious whether the outcome was true or exaggerated and so I decided that rather than rely on hearsay, especially when quoting it within these pages, I should give it a go; and so I did indeed conduct the "Love, Hate, Ignore rice experiment".

I cooked some white rice and divided it into three jars. For two weeks, twice-a-day, I spoke loving words to the "Love" rice, hateful words to the "Hate" rice and I completely ignored the "Ignore" rice.

Bizarrely, though not surprisingly, I started to feel really guilty about sending hateful vibes to the "Hate" rice, just summoning up those feelings made me feel dis-ease within my very being and really uncomfortable vocalising them; so much so that I feared it would affect the experiment. I thought about it and the solution was that I started to blame the rice for making me feel that way and told the "Hate" jar that it was it's fault and how could it do that to me?! (I wonder how many times someone has done that to you or indeed, you to them? In doing so, it absolved me of guilt and enabled me to carry on being hateful in my words to the rice – makes you think.

Something else strange happened when I was struggling to find hateful things to say. The archives of my mind spontaneously cracked open and I started reciting some of the things Igor had said to me during his depressive episodes: "I don't like you, I don't love you, I don't want you here in my space, my daughter doesn't like you, my friends don't like you, I fell out of love with you and I've been using your body for sex for over six months, you're an inconvenience, you cramp my style". Whilst no words from Brad came forth, his negativity was always more in the form of actions and gas-lighting, but negative energy fired at anyone within range nonetheless. I only mention Brad because you may have experienced the force of negative energy rather than words – so this is for you too, as words and thoughts are energy and if someone is aiming them at you, the outcome will be the same.

(I actually feel rather nauseous as I'm reading this several years down the line during the rewrite process, as I experienced years of this and I really can't for the life of me understand why I stuck around to be subjected to such abuse. It does, however, clearly show me how much I've grown from the process, and I hope that this in itself will inspire anyone reading this .... read on, it gets better.)

I sent positive words to the "Love" rice: That I'm really pleased that it's in my life and thank you for taking part in this experiment; that I cherish it and appreciate it; I'm so grateful for the nutrition I would get from eating it, I think it's amazing, I think it looks lovely, I think it's really fabulous, I love it, I'm so happy that it is in my life, etc.

(This is a good moment to consider that when witches cast a spell on someone, it is using the power of words and thoughts, hence they are called "spells". This demonstrates clearly that these words don't necessarily need to be our own as when you think about it, obviously the rice isn't saying these words to itself, we are directing our thoughts and so energy them at it. If we take this knowledge and apply it to having negative expectations of someone, they can't help but live up to that expectation if we're sending them those vibes!)

The Result:

Thirteen days later the results and the proof of the rice pudding really is in the eating but when you take a look at the photos below you probably won't feel like taking a spoon to it!

(colour photos can be found on my website, WWRS page
www.LindaJaneW.me)

Yes, the "Love" rice was still pretty much the same as the day I put it into the jar, white and fluffy – so being loved it stayed in great shape.

The "Hate" rice was indeed black and green mould which really shows the power of words and thoughts when compared to the "Love" rice.

Seeing tangible evidence of the effect of words and energy between these two jars was amazing enough but then I was really surprised by the state of the "Ignore" rice. I expected that to be pretty indifferent but if the colour is anything to go by, it would seem that even receiving negative hateful energy is better than being completely ignored! It was yellow and was in really sorry looking state, barely holding it together. One of my friends is a qualified Nanny and says that children will misbehave to get attention because any attention is better than none at all. This too is worth having a good think about, when considering those around us eh?

Conclusions:
So this begs the question what happens when you ignore your body's cry for change? Well here's the answer ... The IGNORE rice is what happens.

When you take a pill to suppress the symptoms of an ailment, unless you also take action and listen to what your body is telling you, you are ignoring your body instead of hearing it and paying attention to it.

It's important to include stress, depression and anxiety under "ailments" because of you're on the right track then life is a joy and none of these are prevalent in your mindset for long.

So what needs to change? Changing your lifestyle, your behaviour, what you're putting into your body in terms of food, chemicals and liquids; what you're exposing yourself to energetically. What you do for a living, what you do with your time, changing your thoughts, changing the people you are surrounded by or your living circumstances. Which one(s) apply? The answer is within you yourself.

These results have also made me take time to realise that if we ignore or neglect someone, the devastating effect that can have on them. When I started to realise what was happening with the rice, ten days or so into the experiment, I made a conscious effort to smile at elderly people as our paths crossed because one often hears of how invisible they feel as the hand of Father Time sweeps the years into an ever growing pile.

As for the "Hate" rice, now compare this to your own body. If you are constantly telling yourself that your body is too fat, too thin, too short, too tall, not good enough, hair not right, etc, we are turning the actual cells of your body into the mouldy rice – i.e. disease!

Turn this around for a second and think what the effect is on someone else if we constantly disapprove of them, hit them with machine gun fire of anger or resentment and tell them they're not trying hard enough.

The "Love" rice speaks for itself doesn't it! How absolutely wonderful that as The Beatles sang all those years ago "All you need is love".

This experiment absolutely enforces the belief system that all diseases have emotional roots. If you are happy and at peace with yourself. If you appreciate who you are, what you've been through to bring you to this point in your life, and love yourself and others for this experience, then your body should surely be akin to the "Love" rice.

The thing is that you can just as easily do this to someone else's body by telling them that they are not good enough, you don't like them, they are inconvenient, etc, etc. Words and thoughts are energy and energy is POWERFUL.

So if we compare the rice to the physical cells in our bodies which includes the tissues, muscles, bones and organs, then what about water aspect of our body? Water makes up approximately 65% of our body and is diffused throughout our cells and organs, and in the form of various body fluids including blood, lymph, tears, sweat, etc.

A Japanese gentleman named Masaru Emoto conducted experiments by freezing water which had been exposed to different words, emotions, music and environments. His company's website and the internet in general, contains many photographs of the results which show that when water is exposed to hateful words the water crystals are unsightly, irregular and dark. However, when water is exposed to words such as peace and love; or prayer and positive affirmations, freezing it produces the most beautiful and unique water crystals that you can imagine. Check it out online.

In addition, the crystals also go into different and intriguing forms when exposed to different genres of music and so I personally feel that it is really important to expose ourselves to music that is literally on the same wave length as us individually in order to bring about harmony in our body and to promote healing from within.

I also read into it that this is what we are doing to our own body with self-deprecation and also when we accept a relationship which is toxic. Whatever that relationship is, we would be constantly telling ourselves that we are not worthy of happiness and we do not deserve to be treated respectfully.

If we bombard ourselves with such negativity or we allow ourselves to be on the receiving end if it, then this is the effect that this energy will have on our body. Our body is our anchor to this beautiful world where we can taste, smell, feel the wind in your hair and the sun on your skin, make love, dance to music and so it's worth looking after.

Throughout the entire recuperation process, even during not so good times when things were extremely challenging physically and emotionally, I always thanked my heart and told her she was doing a great job and that I was very grateful to her for continuing to beat and give me life. I continuously thanked her for hanging on in there and when my heart did indeed respond to all of the holistic practices that we were working with and popped back into rhythm, I congratulated her and shared my delight with her as I beamed and smiled inside and out! Even now, if I tell my heart how beautiful she is and how well she is doing, I can literally feel the energy swell in my chest – seriously – try it!

With that in mind, I wonder what the outcome would have been had I told myself that I was doomed? What if I'd told my heart how useless it was or referred to her as an inconvenience or a nuisance? Basically, I'd have been throwing "hate" rice energy in her direction and look what happened to that rice.

However, what if I'd ignored my body's cry for a change to the way I was living and I'd continued smoking and drinking and stimulating my body with energy boosters such as caffeine and energy drinks to push it when it was tired? The "Ignore" rice demonstrated that clearly too.

in the words of The Beatles "all we need is love" so to be ignored is pretty awful - especially for a Leo such as myself. I therefore recently decided to have a play with Reiki energies and whilst I was conducting a healing session on myself, I focused my thoughts on each of the physical systems and body parts associated with that chakra. I told each cell and each drop of water within each and every part of my body in turn, that I loved it, valued it and appreciated the role that it played in creating heath and wellbeing for my entire body. Afterwards I not only felt amazing, but I started to connect with my pets more. My heart took a little leap every time I stroked one of my cats; similarly when I was playing with Vagabond my dog. I literally started to feel the love – something that had been emotionally unavailable for quite a few years it would seem – until now! As I tried this in working with a friend and client during a Reiki session, I didn't tell her what I was doing. However, after the session she told me that she had thought during the treatment "allow yourself to feel the love". She had and she did indeed feel it. Incredible isn't it. Don't take my word for it – try it for yourself. You'll find this meditation in my Zen Den Facebook group.

Forgiveness

During the earliest days of my recovery and before I starting writing, I happened across a documentary about "Forgiveness". Practicing forgiveness is something that I've always done naturally but I had never actually put a label on it as a one of my characteristics. I guess I never stopped long enough to analyse myself - I was too busy healing others or out having fun. In the writing of this book I had this self-realisation and I'm so happy to label myself as a forgiving person. Even in forgiving someone, we don't have to accept their presence in our lives. We can forgive from a distance. If someone triggers me and despite my best efforts, that continues to happen, then it's best that they're not in my life as I don't want to be that person – because remember, a behaviour, when repeated regularly enough, becomes a personality trait. We have decide who we do and don't want to be and if we can't overcome the trigger, remove ourselves – in my humble opinion.

I've researched and discovered that forgiveness reduces our heart rate, improves sleep, lowers blood pressure, reduces our stress levels, lowers fatigue levels, transforms anger and hurt into healing peace, reduces anxiety and empowers positivity.

I love the analogy that if we hold a glass of water in the air, it becomes heavier and heavier - and it's the same with a grudge. If we hold onto things for the duration, then the only person who suffers is us. We can so easily torment ourselves by re-living something over and over again and winding ourselves up into a frenzy like the Looney Tunes cartoon Tasmanian Devil who gets into a rage and trashes everything in his path during his vocal hissy-fits. The hurt, betrayal or anger that we feel really does feel heavy inside our chest and how can we blossom and dance in the sunshine with a heavy heart. If we don't work the emotions out of our vibration then there they will stay and attract more of the same and we will become a prisoner for the rest of our lives with the dis-ease manifesting into disease. We can't 'just let it go' in my opinion. We have to rationalise it in our minds before accepting it.

The Balance Procedure puts us in touch with our intuition so we know exactly how to do that. At the end of February I had to do exactly this once again and it took me about ten minutes to resolve it in my head after balancing on card 4 for "I am Love, I am Inspiring" and with the intention of my heart returning to a strong healthy rhythm. Incident after incident had taken my stress levels way high and my heart was going crazy. I used card 6 for seeing things from the helicopter view and the thoughts streamed into my mind put together a mental jigsaw for the reason for it all. I felt the weight lift from my heart as I achieved an understanding that enabled me to accept it and put it behind me.

My mum has always said to me "you're so forgiving, no matter what anybody does to you, you always bounce right back up" and that says it all really so in the words of Forrest Gump complete with southern drawl "that's all I got to say about that".

So how do we forgive? Well, for a start, if we reassess the situation and look at what we've learned from it, then we can give thanks for the lesson. If we realise that someone is only being themselves, how can we hold a grudge about that? If we don't like the way we behave, we don't have to stick around, but essentially they're showing us what's alive in side of us. If they're questioning us, is it because we're secretly doubting ourselves and they're just showing us that. It can get very deep, but for now, this is a great way of looking at things.

For example, taking it back to yet another time when I was so angry with Beau when I felt that he let me down; this had stayed with me for a several weeks until I saw the light. When he had cockily said to me at the time, "I haven't made you angry, you're choosing to be angry", that incensed me all the more but with the progress that I made in the writing of this guidebook, I realised that this was indeed a lesson being delivered from Beau. I did indeed have a choice but my chemical reflexes had reacted with anger hormones (without any conscious effort as I'd yet to hear about the ability to reprogramme our own chemical responses to situations).

Beau and I had often pondered on the reason for our meeting and connecting so intensely. With the wisdom of hindsight and time and piecing together the jigsaw of my heart's dis-ease, I strongly feel that he was pretty much the only person cheeky and direct enough (with the added benefit of being tall, dark and handsome) to be able to hold my attention long enough to get through to me – albeit with a metaphorical sledgehammer at times!

As for my purpose with him, well you'll have to ask him about that but I do know from mutual friends that I did a lot for him as a person. I have nothing but forgiveness, gratitude and love in my heart for him and isn't that so much better than any kind of blame game. I've taken responsibility for myself, my actions and my tolerances and I have indeed had to block him from my life rather than become triggered so frequently that my behaviours relapsed into a personality trait. I chose me and my own personal progression and I'd outgrown the circles that he was going around in repeatedly and I refused to be sucked into that whirlpool any more.

With this also came the realisation that although his behaviour was unacceptable to me, it is quite possible that his behaviour wouldn't matter at all to anyone else, because we all have different triggers. All I needed was clarification on what I was and wasn't prepared to accept from my perspective and that's what these lessons are all about – nudging us towards our peace of mind.

In addition, by now I had my suspicions that Beau was a narcissist as no matter what I gave him, he always wanted more and blatantly so, even getting irritated when something wasn't good enough (considering that he literally had nothing at all, I thought he'd have been appreciative for a home-cooked meal and creature comforts but he'd often criticise quite significantly).

Being kind-hearted healers, we are apparently a shining light to narcissists as we want to help people which they recognise. Narcissists apparently want their way on everything as the World really does revolve around them and them only and they are ruthless in getting it. Social media is full of the fact that they can totally mess up people's heads and I've even seen advice on how to get revenge by messing with their minds. Alarmingly in the same article advising how to mess up a Narcissist's head, it also gave an insight into the fact that a Narcissist wasn't born that way but rather was formed by abuse, neglect or some awful incident in their life. I was appalled as with this knowledge, the author of that article was then giving out advice on how to mess with them even more!?! You've got to be kidding me! Compassion, forgiveness, understanding – even if it takes a few hours or days to get the negative waves of emotion out of your system before you can achieve a more positive frame of mind, I truly believe that we have to do that in order to free ourselves and move forward with a lighter step.

In my opinion, if you don't like the way that a Narcissist plays their games, just don't hang out with them! If you enter into their mind games they will win because it's their game and they make up the rules. You can't blame a Narcissist for being who they are just like you can't blame a zebra for having stripes or a koala bear for being a tree hugger. I think I've encountered a few in my time and it was my peril for sticking around. No one forced me to, but in hindsight, I also had a lot of laughs with them bringing their tendencies to their attention and making light of it with them, before deciding that our friendship didn't fit and I did indeed move on.

However, I can now gratefully accept where any one person or situation has brought me in my life (geographically, emotionally and/or spiritually) and accepting that throughout the course of my life, people will only have roles to play in certain scenes in the movie of my life, because life itself is dynamic. If we relax and go with the flow of our soul's will (The Universe) rather than hold onto situations that no longer fit, that may well mean that we'll no longer connect with the same people as our reflections change. If they don't make the same shifts, it's a mismatch. I feel that this isn't something to feel rueful about as it's proof that we're evolving. Those around us have the same option but maybe they're not ready, or life is taking them in another direction. From my perspective, I'd rather grow towards the light like a plant rather than put myself into the shade to stunt my growth.

Forgiveness isn't necessarily easy to achieve and one particular time I recall, when words and actions were so hurtful to me that I tried so very hard for days to find it within myself to forgive - but I just couldn't find it in myself to actually do it. My heart had gone out of rhythm as a result and I was weak and tearful but I went to Tanya's yoga class knowing that it was the right thing to do. At the end of the class as we finished our meditation practice, as if reading my mind, she said "forgive anyone with the understanding that they are on their own journey". Coupled with the asanas and the meditation I actually "felt" forgiveness in my very being and I kid you not, my heart returned to a beautiful regular rhythm within the day. I realise that all of this sounds really Disney at times but I promise it's all the absolute truth throughout the book. I'd also like to add here that yoga isn't just about holding poses. As mentioned in the Yoga Chapter in Section 2 of this book, the movement itself enables the energy of emotions to release from our bodies and frees us.

In forgiving, my body literally showed me that my emotions were at ease again. Had I continued to hold the unpleasantness in my vibration, then my heart's irregular beat could have caused a stroke, a heart attack; it was affecting my energy levels and would have continued to do so. Our heart is literally a generator sending our blood spiralling through our arteries and veins. When it's not working effectively, that is literally going to adversely affect every single cell in our body as would the discombobulated energy.

It's also crossed my mind that when our thoughts circle around and around it may be because we need more information as we simply don't have enough to form an opinion or come to a conclusion and understand what's going. If our heightened confusion is about somebody's behaviour then we need to remember that human beings can be as dynamic as a leaf on the wind, forever changing in mood, direction, higher and lower, around and around sometimes coming to rest, sometimes in full flight. We don't necessarily know what has gone on in their world, nor what's going on currently in their World as we only see a snapshot. Therefore, we can't always think our way to a comfortable conclusion and if they are causing us that much dis-ease in our own mind, then maybe it's best just to realise that, stop trying to make sense of it and simply accept that's just who they are. We can then decide if we want to share that person's energy and space, if they complement our own life or if they're best kept at a distance or even ousted altogether.

Just like everybody else they're being themselves in fact that admirable for being true themselves instead of conforming to social etiquette. Aquarians are particularly good at that. Brad used to walk away from someone at a party who was boring him. No explanation or excuse, he'd just turn on his heels and off he'd go; leaving me nodding politely and trying to look interested in what was being said.

I guess it's important to realise that some people are there for a specific time and purpose and as life is dynamic and we are all learning and growing as an individual, what was a good fit doesn't necessarily stay a good fit and when it's time for a change, we shouldn't be afraid of that. Everything around us is a reflection of what is alive within us and so when we spot something that we don't appreciate in someone else we are being shown what we need to work on. Once we've begun to make those changes for ourselves with affirmations, TBP, and all of the other tools mentioned within these pages, we don't see those reflections. In shifting to a different vibration ourselves, we don't pick up those smoke signals anymore (sorry to mix metaphors!), that aspect becomes invisible to us.

It's possible that that person changes with us or we could naturally relegate them (or be relegated) to the role of being an Extra rather than a Co-Star in our own life movie. That's the beauty of this dynamic universe. If change doesn't happen, they could continue with that behaviour and mirror others until that person learns the lesson (or not) – remember how earlier I describe how a spiritual baton is passed from one person to the next to continue to present us with the same situation if we dismiss people from our lives before we've learned that lesson?

Fitness

I've always wholeheartedly agreed with the moto of the zodiac sign Leo, which is "never run when you can walk, never walk when you can stand, never stand when you can sit, never sit when you can lie down" and in any task at hand I found myself automatically calculating the quickest most effective way of doing things to save energy and time around the house, picking up an armful of stuff so I only had to make the trip once, dropping things off on my path. However, began to realise that I had to start improving my cardiovascular strength and fitness and so I actually derived joy from going backwards and forwards, backwards and forwards around my house and garden during my chores, by way of exercise. I used a Smartwatch which my friend Alex gifted to me. This gave me vibrations of approval when I achieved certain goals, but I have to say that I became obsessive looking at my paces stats and using the ECG features on it. That, combined with taking my pulse and using the sphygmomanometer to take my blood pressure throughout the day was consuming my mind.

When I realised I was getting obsessive, I knew that I had to seriously get a grip on myself as I felt myself spiralling downwards and subconsciously fear was overtaking me and the machines were there technically to reassure me. With a friend's gentle nudge, I resolved to rely on what my body was telling me rather than a machine and in snapping myself out of that fear headspace, I also got back on track using The Balance Procedure and affirmations to manifest "I am strong, fit and healthy" and more. Having said that, I think it's really worthwhile having these instruments to fall back on and give ourselves peace of mind or to tell us that it's time to take action - including getting help.

Fast-forward to a couple of years after this experience when I felt as if I maybe had low blood pressure as I was a bit lightheaded. I was about to take measures to rectify this when my intuition spoke to me and suggested that I should check with the sphygmomanometer – it was actually a little high which was completely unusual, so it was just as well that I listened to myself. I took action to bring it down using acupressure and breathing techniques and taking a Rescue Remedy pastel.

Vagabond

Despite feeling well and happy and whilst I'd achieved so much in terms of wellbeing over the last 18-months (my heart function had risen from 17% to over 65% which is normal), I began to realise that my physical heart didn't seem to quite get what it had to do. It still felt like it needed reminding and retraining and that instead of being a strong purposeful muscle, it was a bit of a wobbly jelly. I moved a loudly ticking clock into my bedroom so as to act as a metronome during my sleeping hours and give my heart something to keep time with. Over the coming weeks "get a dog" kept popping into my awareness. Being a confirmed and life-long Mad Cat Woman, I pushed that thought away several times and then one day I stopped in my tracks and the lightbulb went on above my head as I realised that it was my intuition speaking to me.

Almost the same day, I saw a puppy at a market where I was doing card readings. It was up for adoption and adorable. "Is she naughty?" I asked the fosterer "very" was the answer. "Ah not for me then. That's nervous breakdown territory as far as I'm concerned!" and I beat a hasty retreat.

On my way home I found myself speaking out loud to myself "Well Linda, if you're going to get a dog you need to decide what you need and want. Well Linda, you've always loved Alsatians but your house isn't very big so it can't be a big one – you need a smaller one; and you don't do naughty puppies so it needs to be past that stage but not too old. Oh and good with cats and hens. Basically, you need the perfect dog for you". Twenty-minutes later I was home and sat having a cuppa with my friend Harley who had been doing some work at my place. I told her about the puppy and she said "oo, are you after a dog then? I know one that needs a new home. He's an Alsatian but he isn't very big and he's two-years old". My mouth fell open and my jaw hit the floor! I relayed the conversation I'd had with myself on the way home. Two days later I went to meet Vagabond. As we pulled up the mountain track towards the friend's house, Vagabond popped up on the garden wall and then came bounding down, straight past Harley and to me. He jumped up and put his paws on my shoulders and looked straight into my eyes. It was love at first sight and he came home with me. That was 18-months ago and I never knew that I would adore a dog so much!

He has indeed strengthened my heart emotionally as well as physically as he has brought the most amazing companionship, love and entertainment into my world and an unexpected bonus is that I feel protected (and I didn't actually realise that this was lacking in my life).

My heart isn't just strong, it's actually stronger than it's been for many years. Because I can't resist those big brown eyes which are so persuasive, and because I see the joy that he experiences during our walkies, he motivates me into nature when I would really rather crash on the sofa. Most days I walk 3km with him and I'm exploring the area where I've lived for several years but been completely unaware of my surroundings! Being out with nature lifts my spirits. I see bats and hear the frogs, walk past beehives; smell the orange blossom and scrump the old orange or avocado!

An unexpected bonus is that when I went back to yoga classes after a few months off because walkies had taken priority (and I initally didn't have the energy to do both in one day), I wholly expected to be back to square-one as I'd let my practices fall.

I set my intention at the beginning of the class to just enjoy whatever my body was able to do, not get impatient with myself or push myself beyond my limits which I'd tended to do in the past. Historically I'd found myself breathless, a bit awkward at times and trembling in poses and wishing the class wasn't so long.

My mind was blown as I moved easily and freely from pose to pose, breathing smoothly and evenly and holding each pose for as long as I wanted to. My legs and arms were physically strong !!! THAT WAS UNEXPECTED! Wow Wow WOW! My wonderful yoga teacher, Tanya, noticed and commented after the class too, confirming that I was back and then some!

I still thought that this was just as far as the yoga class went as I was still very much in the mindset that I was weak (post-hospitalisation). A few weeks later, I set about doing something physical in the garden and shocked myself as I realised that my strength was indeed significantly beyond what it had been even for a couple of years prior to heart hissy-fit. When out walkies with Vagabond I'd always found flat areas to walk such as the empty riverbed but I started to try out my new legs and found that they were strong and carried me easily up the mountain. My heart and lungs were equally strong and were embraced the challenge.

It's really shocking how quickly we can fall into a weakened mindset and can stay there indefinitely if we don't take action. Vagabond was the perfect little angel to snap me out of that way of being, physically and mentally.

Not so long ago, I woke up to the fact that the "I'm tired" mentality was still present from my Covid experience a month earlier. We had returned from walkies and I went to plonk myself down on the sofa with the thought in my head "I'm back from walkies so I'll be tired and will need to just sit down instead of doing the chores around the place"; then I realised that I wasn't tired, I was holding myself upright and I still felt strong and energetic.

This is the self-talk that The Balance Procedure empowers us to keep at bay and/or shift from our reality and instead, create the days that we would rather have for ourselves. I had worked with the affirmation, reciting it daily throughout the virus days, that "I am strong, fit and healthy". I was only unwell for 2 ½ days. After that it was the brain fog and sudden onset fatigue. I worked with acupressure to stimulate my brain synapses, just as I had post-hospital discharge; and took a tincture of Periwinkle Lesser.

Foods

In being drawn to write about foods, because this book is pretty generic rather than aimed at a particular ailment, as much as I would like to write about how I changed my diet dramatically, I didn't. I've eaten a healthy vegetarian and sometimes vegan diet for years and years and so the best advice that I can give to you is eat the foods that you are drawn to. Hippocrates did indeed say "Let food be thy medicine" and interesting garlic, ginger and turmeric are all-natural antibiotics and they all also thin the blood. It turns out that infections can thicken the blood so isn't that amazing that Mother Nature gives us a natural remedy to address the infection and thin our blood – she really does ROCK! These days, whenever I have a health hiccup, I research online for which foods will help and which will exacerbate the problem. Caffeine as we know, will stimulate our body, and as much as we might feel like we need a boost, if we're already edgy, coffee could metaphorically fuse our circuits and make us scattered as opposed to a calming chamomile tea which will allow us to function more effectively purely because of its soothing effect.

I'd found eating what my body wanted quite challenging when I first moved to Spain, I had been a Vegetarian for over a decade and Vegan for several years. Turning my back on dairy was very difficult as I loved cream cakes and cheeses but the animal husbandry involved in its production broke my heart (pun intended) and the more I learned about the dairy industry, the less I could eat milk based products and the very thought of it repulsed me.

In the UK it is easy to buy vegan alternatives but Spain had a lot of catching up to do back then and certainly eating out vegan was virtually impossible so I was forced to resort to chips and bread just to fill my stomach and then eat properly when I got home if I had the energy after a night out on the razzle. My hair had started to break and my energy levels dropped and so I had made the decision to become a flexitarian and eat what my body told me to.

Straight away, I reintroduced fish and eggs into my diet and I couldn't get enough of what once turned my stomach at the very thought of eating. That was in the summer about the time of the rash appearing on the back of my legs and so I wondered if it was a food intolerance but as you've already read, it wasn't; nor was it down to the vitamin B12 deficiency.

Several months before my hospitalisation, I had a craving for steak. No other meat, just steak. It was in my head almost constantly and I had to seriously fight the urge to order it when I was dining out with the girls. After a month or so of denying myself, I caved in and ordered it when I was at one of the local bars. I wasn't sure how my digestive system would cope or if I'd even be able to actually eat it but I can assure you that I was more like a ravenous lion when it appeared on the plate in front of me, to the point that I found myself eating it with my fingers, much to the amusement of my friends! One of them took a photograph to mark the occasion and I even look like a ravenous lion with my red mane and the look in my eyes was that of a carnivore.

I ate steak many more times and it tasted divine. I tried chicken and my digestive system did protest. It was purely steak that my body wanted. I was really interested to learn that a friend had had a serious foot injury many years previous and at the time she too was vegetarian. She developed gangrene and was told by the Medics that it would have to be amputated to save her life. She point blank refused and instead listened to her body and guess what it told her to eat – Yep, Steak! No other meat, just steak - and yes, she cured her gangrene and kept her foot.

During the summer months of my early recovery I was craving salt and so I was never without a bag of salted peanuts and plain salted tortilla chips and I salted my food significantly. My blood pressure has always been on the low side and at this stage I was on several different medications for my heart, all of which had the "advantage" of lowering blood pressure. I was getting a bit dizzy throughout every day and when I took my blood pressure it was invariably low – sometimes worryingly so and on one occasion I remember it being 64/46. Although the credibility of the machine is now suspect, the dizziness did confirm that and so yes, listen to our body is good advice. I drank litres of water to keep myself and my blood hydrated and I was also drawn to drink loads of coconut water which contains natural electrolytes to maintain an equilibrium of body salts and minerals.

Then in January and I noticed that I'm no longer craving salted peanuts and after a blood pressure spike I bought plain, unsalted monkey nuts and I was hardly snacking on tortilla chips. I use very little salt in my cooking and I haven't bought coconut water in weeks but I'm aware that this may all change as the weather hots up to 35°+ during the summer months.

It's a good idea to find out if any foods are contraindicated with medication. I was told that there was no need to worry but I've heard that with some blood thinners grapefruit, cranberries and vitamin K rich, green leafy vegetables are out.

In the early days of my recovery I was very drawn to making green smoothies from celery, apple, kiwi fruit, spinach, fresh ginger, moringa, fresh lemon juice, flaxseeds and a dollop of probiotic soya yogurt. Along the way of my research I had found that we are naturally drawn to foods of the same colour as the chakra which is deficient in energy. Interesting then that the above are all green which is the heart chakra, and yellow which is the solar plexus.

Many of the celebrity chefs advocate eating seasonal produce and I do believe that the reason for that is because these contain the therapeutic properties needed for optimal health at that time of year. For example, oranges are high in vitamin C and they are a winter crop which is a time when flu and colds are rife and strawberries help prevent sunburn and are prevalent in the UK summer season.

Hand in hand with foods, go vitamin and mineral supplements. Magnesium for example is very good for arrhythmia but should be taken a few hours before or after pharmaceuticals as it is known to affect the absorption of tablets. Magnesium also has a laxative effect and so if you're a bit bunged up so to speak, then taking this will help to loosen everything up. Iron supplements on the other hand, and eggs, will bind the contents of your bowels.

Now here's an innovative way of looking at food preparation which I'm sure will spice up your view on convenience foods, take-aways and even your own cooking. When I was learning Reiki many moons ago, I was taught how to use this life-force energy to cleanse food. At the time I thought that it was a bit over the top but I stored it in the old grey matter of my brain until such time as it was needed. The teacher had told me that she used it when on holiday to prevent an upset stomach and I could resonate with that as a practical application. Some ten years later I saw an eastern European movie called Black Cat White Cat, which is absolutely brilliant. During this, a heartbroken woman has to make the wedding feast for a couple and she is sobbing whilst preparing the food, particularly as she's in love with the groom, and he with her (but it's an arranged wedding). Later, as the wedding guests feast, everyone starts crying uncontrollably as her heartbroken energy went into the food whilst she was cooking it! Suddenly, the grey matter fired up and popped out that Reiki tuition memory and I got it!

We have no idea what energy has gone into the making of convenience foods, raw ingredients or take-aways and so being able to use Reiki on our food not only cleanses the energies, it also empowers the nutritional value too.

Again, years later a friend and I were ordered about by the Manager of a Chinese take-away when we walked in to place our order. We were exchanging shocked glances with each other as she told us where to stand and as she shouted at the Cooks, the Waitresses and us! When we started to giggle she got even more angry and then when I went to take the carrier bag of food, she tugged it back – twice. Trust me when I say that we both cleansed that food with Reiki before eating it! Imagine the energy that had got wrapped up with the making of it and neither of us wanted to consume it!

To go with my medicine cabinet of aromatherapy oils, I have a shelf full of supplements including magnesium, echinacea to boost the immune system, probiotics for a healthy gut, turmeric, multi-vitamins and minerals, vitamin B12, calcium, herbal tinctures, CBD oil as well as the herbal alternatives for pharmaceuticals. With the exception of the herbal Betablocker and Magnesium, I don't take any of them daily. I listen to my body and I body dowse too, and if my body sways forward as I hold the bottle to my heart then I take it and if it sways backwards I don't. It's a simple way of hearing what your intuition wants to say to you.

Regardless of what time of year it is, it is absolutely essential to keep our fluid intake up and our body hydrated. Our systems just can't function without sufficient water and we are about 65% water after all and if we're recuperating from a serious health issue, it's even more important. Our heart is 73% water, similarly with the brain; lungs 83%, skin 64%, muscles and kidneys are 79%. As we lose water throughout the day, it's really important to keep ourselves topped up as sufficient water is needed for digestion, hydration, heartbeat, blood pressure, blood sugar, blood fluidity, muscles and tissues of the body and to prevent fainting. I always drink a glass of water before I even get out of bed now, as I've been dormant for maybe eight hours and so I reckon my body needs it straight away.

When the cortisone cream prescribed by the Medics had zero effect, I went for food intolerance testing and found that I'm sensitive to the nightshade family which includes tomatoes, aubergines and potatoes. Being a northern lass at heart I love potatoes but now limit them in my diet in favour of rice, grains and pasta. I feel that if I am going through a blip in my health then this is a good time to avoid these foods and not give my system the extra work of digesting and managing something which is going to stress my body.

I love using olive oil where possible and use or a 100% vegetable spread instead of butter and my diet is rich in vegetables, chickpeas, beans, lentils, tofu, fruits and I tend to buy the decent gluten-free products such as pasta and crackers to rest my system so that I can happily eat normal bread.

I guess I believe in moderation and balance as too much of anything – even the good stuff – is bad for us. We can always ask our body and body dowse. Just hold the foodstuff with one hand against your heart in the centre of your chest and ask if this food is beneficial to you right now. I also do this with supplements and it changes on a daily basis. If you sway forward, that's a yes; backwards is a no. Our body knows and this is a really simple way of asking it.

During my hours of research and looking for new ways of doing things, I happened across a series on Gaia and four of the episodes were interviewing Dr Brownstein, an Endocrinologist from USA, who now practices integrative medicine (a combination of holistic and traditional western medicine). I was really interested to learn that the majority of people a) need to take 1tsp of good quality sea salt every day in addition to whatever they add to their food; and b) that high dose iodine supplements can significantly reduce signs and symptoms of ADHD and autism. Not only that, but the thyroid when deficient, significantly adversely affects every cell in the body and it cannot function properly.

I'd noticed over the months that my voice had changed and rather than sing like a bird, I now squawked like a parrot when I belted it out to Blondie in my car. I couldn't understand it until Jeremiah mentioned to me one day that my thyroid seemed a bit enlarged. I immediately made the connection and he set about working on the relevant acupuncture points; and I took some iodine supplements. When testing for thyroid function, apparently, according to Dr Brownstein, most tests only cover some of what is actually needed unless you specifically request the full spectrum of thyroid tests. For this reason, many underactive thyroids are missed and so ADHD medication is given.

Dr Brownstein stated a case study where a youngster's mother was told by his school that he was so disruptive that he must go on ADHD medication in order to be allowed to stay in school. Reluctant to do so, she went to Dr Brownstein instead who found that his thyroid function was extremely low. After just ten days on high dose iodine supplementation the youngster's behaviour, concentration levels and academic skills were vastly improved to the point that his teachers thought he was being medicated.

For my own part, I found that after taking iodine for several weeks, my handwriting improved and after several months my hair, nails and skin strengthened significantly and I got my voice back (although some may dispute that!).

Although my weight had never really concerned me, I'd be so health conscious regarding foodstuffs that I'd denied myself many guilty pleasures for years. Now, as I was unable to drink, smoke or enjoy the occasional puff on the peace pipe, I had to have a vice and be naughty, or I really wasn't being me at all(!) - and so I turned to sweet stuff. I started with 70% dark chocolate and maintained my healthy diet as best I could, with handmade dark chocolates from the local market (the fella who makes and sells them is so lovely that the energy of his wares is uplifting too), and once my energy levels returned, I made vegan desserts such as banoffee pie – made with dates, bananas, walnuts, ginger and coconut milk and that's all; and avocado chocolate mousse made with banana, avocado, coconut milk and raw cocoa. Of course, I couldn't resist the odd chocolate mousse at a bar but I also had to be true to my authentic holistic-self too and so found a healthier way of being. Stewing apples with sultanas and spooning it over crumbled walnuts and pecans with a dollop of refrigerated (tinned) coconut milk – oo la la! I also made my own fruit and nut chocolate bars by melting the 90% cocoa chocolate from the health food shop and stirring in my own mix of chopped cranberries and raisins, smashed nuts and seeds, along with a dash of orange juice.

A friend of mine, Juliette Bryant, also gives some amazing vegan recipes in her e-book "Divine Desserts".

PTSD (Post Traumatic Stress Disorder)
The trauma that we experience is something I think that many will push into the archives of their minds – just as I had. It had started to peek out whilst messaging friends in my Healing circle one day, I mentioned that whilst writing the original version of this book which contained many of the gory details, I sometimes got very gloomy. One of the others told me that she too had started to write a book about her own event but she couldn't continue past chapter four as it brought it all back into her present-day reality and it was just too much for her and she'd had to stop writing it.

In writing the original edition of WWRS, when I realised how sad some of my past had been, as much it was cathartic, I'd find myself sobbing. However, such was the sense of relief and release as the tears flowed that I was inspired to mention that crying is a very important thing to do as it sets the tension free from our body. I ended up laughing and crying at the same time as I thanked my body for liberating the past from my vibration and I also started to see that these were all lessons to be learned. In acknowledging that everything was a lesson, I was able to start moving away from the blame game and also to accept my part in events from others' perspectives.

I also started to energetically protect myself when working to release events of the past and I noticed that when talking with people about it all, it brought it all back into my present which disturbed my body, my heart would sometimes pop out of rhythm for a day or more and I'd feel my solar plexus tighten uncomfortably.

Just after I was discharged from hospital in May, home alone, when I went to bed I would sometimes find the darkness of my bedroom horribly uneasy and my body just wouldn't rest let alone sleep. My friend Pauline had asked me if I'd experienced this and I was so relieved to hear that it is a common complaint after going through a traumatic event. As I became stronger, I was happy to turn off the bedside light but every now and again I'd go through phases of preferring the light on.

For several months, my body was still struggling to find its equilibrium and for no reason I'd get weird symptoms such as a blood pressure spike, or dizziness, or low blood pressure, my heart could pop out of rhythm for no reason, my solar plexus tighten up, sometimes I'd feel weak sometimes I'd be breathless, sometimes I'd be strong, robust, bouncy, healthy and happy, sometimes, everything seemed to affect me dramatically. In addition, for at least a couple of years, I'd sometimes wake up with an erratic pulse, hot and bothered, breathing maybe a bit off and I'd wonder if I was having another episode. I'd inevitably need a pee now that I was awake and stressed, and I'd wonder if I was going to drop dead on the way to the bathroom, or have a stroke. I'd take action and work on my acupressure points, take some Rescue Remedy and pop a few drops of lavender essential oil on my pillow and whilst I was "managing it", it didn't actually dawn on me to question why these thoughts were occurring in the first place.

As the months passed, whilst my body was slowly getting stronger, my mind was regressing as the severity and reality of events started to unfold as new information came forward. I'd connected the dots and realised that actually I'd probably had several small heart attacks before the big one. That somehow, I'd missed the fact that I'd actually gone into heart failure. The list went on. My mind regularly went into Amber Alert as I was aware of every twinge or ache in my heart, chest, my body. The side-effects of some of the medications mimicked a heart attack i.e anxiety, chest pain, weakness and breathlessness, tingling in the hands and feet, etc. I was aware that some were fine, others were a sign of a possible impending stroke. I'd wake in the night and in the morning and check if I could still move my fingers and toes or if I'd had a stroke in the night. If I had a bad dream, I'd wake with my heart racing and all over the place and I'd struggle to relax.

For many months, every night I got into my bed, I had a flashback to that night when I had an eight-hour heart attack, home alone; and I wondered if it was going to happen again. For months I took my phone everywhere with me – even to the bathroom "just in case". Every time I got out of bed, I wondered if I'd collapse and every morning and every evening that I got into the shower I wondered what would happen if I dropped dead in the shower – how long before I was found and what state my lifeless body would be in by then. I originally thought that the shower concern was purely because that happened on a TV show that I'd seen and so I assumed that my brain took it on board. However, only a few days ago (three years post-hospitalisation) in chatting with my friend Avra, she told me that on that day, as I was going into heart failure and before I made those SOS calls to my friends, I'd told her that I'd showered and had not been able to raise my hands above my head as my heart was too weak to give me the power to do that. My brain had obviously connected the dots once I'd seen that TV drama and also realised how close to death I actually was.

I often didn't feel like going out and made excuses to myself, even on really important occasions such as funerals, birthdays, weddings. The underlying thoughts were that I had a perfect excuse not to go as I'd had a heart episode so no-one could expect me to go and I genuinely felt that it'd be too much for me. I really just didn't want to go out and be around drinkers as I'd developed a deep distrust of them, as indeed, I had of myself and my body's abilities! Whoah! There's that mirror again, showing me what I was feeling inside through those around me!

Sometimes, I'd catch sight of myself in a mirror and I'd be astonished that I looked nice and happy – because that mirror did not reflect how I was feeling inside – insecure and fragile. It was very bizarre. However, most of the time, my head didn't feel a dark place to be and I was pretty upbeat. I did notice that I wasn't being a social butterfly very much and if I did go out, I'd sit in the one chair all evening. Then, one day, someone mentioned that I might be suffering from PTSD (Post-traumatic Stress Disorder). I researched and oh! Yep, actually I think i am!

There was more, but you get the drift. One day a friend mentioned that maybe I was suffering from PTSD and I knew that she was right. I set up an appointment with a Counsellor but somehow I actually forgot to go, which astonished me. She hadn't called to confirm, nor did she message to ask where I was, nor did she respond to my apologetic message; so I concluded that my soul said no! Instead, I tuned into myself and recruited the help of a friend of mine who had recently qualified in Transformational Hypnotherapy. We did the hypnotherapy discovery session via Zoom and she recorded a hypnosis for me to listen to every day for 21-days to empower my mind to reprogram itself. It was incredible and definitely the right pathway for me. Within the week my perceptions had shifted and within three weeks the PTSD had gone. I felt strong, happy and confident in my body's ability to support my life and with no doubts whatsoever. It was phenomenal.

A short while later a spiritual friend and Mentor of mine, told me that by having this hypnotherapy, I had probably saved my own life as unresolved trauma is strongly linked with a diseased pancreas. As mentioned throughout, different emotions directly affect their corresponding organs throughout the body (more on this in the Acupressure chapter in Section 2).

When I was at the height of the PTSD experience, in order to bring peace and calm to myself, I did continue to use my crystals daily either by choosing which necklaces, bracelets and rings to wear or sometimes I'd take myself back to bed and do a complete chakra cleanse and balance on myself. It's an incredibly peaceful therapy and I drift off into a meditative state with the crystals placed on my chakra points. As mentioned in the Crystal Healing Chapter in Section 2, the crystals with the right vibration for you as an individual will find you. To this day, or should I say night, I sometimes hold a piece of amethyst in my hand as I drop off to sleep, and/or put a piece of rose quartz under my pillow.

In summary, I guess the point of writing this chapter is to draw your attention to the fact that PTSD can happen to anyone who has experienced trauma and that includes the medical trauma of a health scare. As a species, we humans are surviving a lot more than we used to, say thirty years ago, and so because we are still here in our body, we remember what happened rather than dying. We are also becoming so much more sensitive as we evolve spiritually.

Drama, stories and staying in the Eye of the Storm

As a Leo, drama comes naturally to me (too much so at times, but this is why I was born a Leo and given that to work on during this lifetime), but all of us can embrace dramas all too readily – it's entertainment of sorts at the end of the day, hence the popularity of soap operas. We all have Leo in our birth charts somewhere along the line, and as the heavens constantly shift, Leo energies will affect us all at times (see Astrology Chapter in Section 2).

Real life drama does, however, use up our energy, our time, our thoughts and distract us from a more creative and blissful way of being. Because we give dramas all of this energy, our soul (The Universe) believes that we like it and welcome it and so sends us more – because it's seen the smoke signals.

It's not an overnight process when we decide to make this change to our being, and not to embrace drama quite so much. We can stay in the eye of the storm or indeed watch from afar and not allow ourselves be sucked into it. Over the last few years and in recognising that I needed to look after my fragile heart all the way back at the outset of this episode of my Dark Night of The Soul, I felt that it was time to balance this aspect of my personality and to steer clear of dramas. By "balance", I mean accepting that drama will pop up, but not to get carried away by it, and to work on resolution rather than fuelling it – or indeed, leaving others to own and resolve their own drama and for me not take part.

At times other people's tornadoes land close by and try to suck me in but I use The Balance Procedure to gain clarity, I take some deep breaths to keep my heart steady and to give myself the time and space to hear what my intuition says, I turn off the radio or the TV. As you've read in these pages, I have been sucked into others' chaos for decades, but in stopping and smelling the roses with my

"Awakening", I was finally able to learn some of the lessons and back away as gracefully as I could muster.

Therefore, sometimes, when the constant dramas or confusion becomes too much, it's possibly a time to change the players in my world and those manifesting the dramas continuously have to exit stage left. To send out a clear message to my soul, I also implement the Esther Hicks "this is not satisfactory" chant so that The Universe was in no doubt that these dramas are unacceptable to my world.

Even getting engrossed in "the story" is giving vast amounts of energy to a situation and so it'll surely self-perpetuate as we've become a drama dynamo and unwittingly we're giving it the power to keep going. If it's a fab and groovy story then wonderful! If not, cut it off from its energy source, be mindful and think of something positive instead. Give that the power of your mind and your being and let that come into reality instead; in doing so, we free ourselves out of that spiralling tornedo and start to see the light again. The Bach Flower remedies, mindfulness, TBP, crystals, acupressure, all these and more give us the tools to do that.

I've always loved using a multi-pronged approach and so in working on calm, and whilst sat contemplating any situation, I also work with acupressure on my hands. I work intuitively as a few years ago, on one such occasion, my fingers seemed to take on a life of their own and simply stroked my hands ever so gently all across the palms, the length of my fingers and thumbs and the backs of my hands. I was overwhelmed by a feeling of peace and calm which I wasn't expecting as I continued this practice and I felt what can only be described as "bliss".

"Of course!" I thought, holding hands with a loved one is a really nice feeling, but being a Life Path 7, my curiosity was sparked and so I researched hand holding – and hey presto. Hand holding is known to relieve stress by decreasing stress hormones and produces oxytocin which makes us feel loved and happier. It reduces blood pressure and can also relieve pain as the effect of the above makes us relax our muscles. Holding hands provides us with a sense of security and helps our nervous system to relax.

Although the article was aimed at holding hands with another person, it confirmed what I had achieved for myself as I'd found a beautiful level of inner peace. That lead me to wonder if that's how a "stress ball" de-stresses. I'd always assumed that it we vented our angers, stresses and frustrations on said ball by squeezing it, that was the stress buster. It's working on our acupressure points and activating the hand-holding comforts.

Epilogue

As I constantly re-read this book to try and make sure that I've covered everything that I wanted to and explained things accurately, I'm amazed at my own journey. I can see for myself how I've evolved over the years which is reflected in my writing style, the messages that I've shared and how the original dramas have morphed from blame games into lessons for me to learn and for which I'm grateful.

I have to say, that not once have I regretted my decisions and have looked for the lesson in every "negative" event and there was always one there! It tends to present itself with repeated occurrences so just look for the patterns and get your cartoon lightbulb moment and then balance on it, work with it, do what your intuition tells you to do with love and positivity. When we accept that there is a lesson to learn and we embrace our part in whatever has happened, we can forgive – in fact we should be thanking anyone involved for showing us the light at the end of the tunnel.

The benefit of hindsight is indeed something else. I remembered that up until my awakening, I always had a feeling that my time was running out. During my relationship with Brad I was almost in a panic to do things whilst I still could even though I was only in my thirties and early forties. I also recalled that during my 20's, I'd jokingly say to anyone that talked about pensions that I doubt I'd make it to 50-years old and so why worry about it?

I've now embraced my intuitive, psychic side all the more because I have slowed down sufficiently to actually recognised it and to hear it and just as I knew that my brother, Alan, wouldn't reach 30-years old, I wonder if I knew that my time was indeed limited. However, as I was having an absolute ball in my life, I didn't notice that my time had ticked away and when the clock struck midnight on that fateful night (and it was midnight when I went to bed and had the major heart episode), my stagecoach turned back into a pumpkin.

If I had undergone the cardioversion, I might well have missed this entire journey and been forced by my soul (The Universe) to revisit it or I may well have floated up through the pearly gates the next time because I didn't have the tools to manage my heart myself - Who knows? I am pretty convinced that the emotional events since my awakening would without a shadow of a doubt, have relapsed my heart back into a state of arrhythmia until another electrifying appointment possibly set it straight again for a time. Without the tools and awareness that I've discovered along this quest, I feel that I would have had to have continued medical intervention indefinitely and that is why I strongly advocate taking responsibility for our own well-being whilst integrating everything available to us.

As it is, I feel that "Holistic" means addressing the whole and there is indeed a balance between traditional and alternative therapies in order to preserve life and that balance is constantly shifting as our minds, our bodies and the environments in which we spend our time change. I believe that it is up to us as individuals to become self-aware enough and owning the accountability for our own health and to find and release the emotions that caused our body to play-up in the first place. If we need to integrate pharmaceuticals whilst we're on this learning curve, then so be it.

Once we've identified the triggers, we can work through them and / or avoid them in the first place but taking the approach of an ostrich sticking its head in the sand and popping the pills, pretending that we're cured isn't actually fixing what's going on inside of us.

If we have a relapse in our symptoms, then I think that it's because we've been exposed to a trigger and we need to make a change in our life or our thought processes as I've described throughout **Wakey Wake-Up Rise & Shine!** I was reminded of a major epiphany when these words dropped into my mind, a lightbulb when on overhead and I felt my body relax "don't take it to heart". I realised at that moment, that for many years, I had taken *everything* to heart – and look what happened!

It's important that we have the courage to be honest with ourselves and accept that even though we were born perfect, we have to chip away at the debris that has attached itself to us along the way making us imperfect and get back into a state of bliss. If there was no debris, then we would have no growing to do and the journey of our life would be surely be a bit dull!

Our bodies are amazing. They are our link to this beautiful planet and our life, and they show us what we need to work on emotionally via events, disease, illness and accidents. In digging deep into myself to find the root causes I've been able to see the lessons so far, learn from them and release them like doves from a coop and regardless of your decisions about medical intervention, you owe it to yourself to preserve your body so that it lasts for years and enables you to do joyful things and make the most of every day that you open your eyes, because when we stop running around on that hamster's wheel and smell the roses, that scent tells us that we are already living in Paradise!

Today, I am strong, happy, in control, I am motivated, I am confident in my decisions, I am optimistic for each and every day and into the future. I appreciate the body that is Linda and I know when to rest and do so without guilt-trippng myself. I can hear what Linda and my heart is saying to me more than ever before and I dare not ignore her – well Linda is a formidable force after all and how very stupid of me to even think that I could ever get away with not paying her the attention that she deserves! Be your own formidable force with love so that you can say:

I am Powerful, I am successful

I am a Free Spirit, I am Imaginative

I am authentic, I am Spiritual

I am Love, I am Inspiring

I am Creative, I am a Pioneer

I am Visionary, I am Flexible and Passionate

I am Intuitive & Psychic, I am Inquisitive

I am Wealthy and generous

... I am an Avatar baby! (to be said in Austin Powers voice)

And if I have a wobble - I have the tools to get myself back on track and so too can you.

I intend to continue spreading the word through social media (LindaJaneW13), courses, Inspirational Speaking engagements and Masterclasses - all the while taking this book to events because this book is the very reason that I survived and that's what my intuition tells me to do!

Keep Smiling Inside Shiny Happy People and I hope you enjoy the Wakey Wake-Up Rise & Shine page on my website which has a gallery of colour pictures to accompany this book! www.LindaJaneW.me

Namaste

Pauline's Tale

While writing this guidebook, I became aware of the fact that it wasn't just me going through this event and that those closest to me also had their own experience going on in tandem. My life was changing forever and so was theirs. They were experiencing terror, upset, trauma and if I had died, loss - and they were pretty much powerless as to the eventual outcome.

I wondered whether to retain this chapter in this second edition, as it is dramatic, it is a story and I'm rapidly growing away from these aspects of my being. However, I felt that there are some really valid points in here which could well help others with their own journey, directly or indirectly; and so I kept it, albeit in an edited format:

At this point in time, my friend Pauline and her husband Dougie had been in Spain for almost six years and lived on the other side of the mountain ridge from me. They are very active in our fabulous social scene here and Dougie hosts the Open Mic nights at the local Spanish bar where our tribe all congregate by the dozen to sing, dance, laugh and chat non-stop.

I asked Pauline if she could share events from her perspective to enable readers to understand what your nearest and dearest were possibly going through during your event. I suspect that just as I was blissfully unaware of the impact that I'd made, others may be too.

Throughout the interview Pauline cried, Dougie cried, and I cried – thankfully we all managed to laugh at the same time too.

One thing that stood out to all of us, was that there are significant gaps in my memory of events that afternoon and throughout my hospital stay. Even though I was there, I have no recollection whatsoever of certain things. Even digging deep into the grey matter of my brain to see if I could pull a memory out of the hat, I drew a blank.

I can't remember calling around my friends on that day and until this interview I had no idea that Holly had called Pauline to raise the alarm after I'd called her to say I was in trouble. I have no recollection of friends visiting me in hospital even though I was chatting with them and although my friend Avra was apparently with me for quite a while, the only thing that I can remember is seeing a worried look on her face and wondering "why?" During her visit I apparently made an appointment with a private Cardiologist but when they called to confirm this two weeks later, I had zero recollection of having made it.

I guess the significance of this is if you or someone close to you has had a similar event, you need to be aware that there might be significant gaps to be filled.

Pauline's involvement in my story started on the Monday morning after what we now know to have been a heart attack, when she and Dougie picked me up from home and took me to the local Spanish GP, as they too had an appointment. Pauline's Spanish is slightly better than mine and so for that reason, coupled with her concern and by way of moral support, she came into the consulting room with me.

Pauline's opening words "it was horrible. I was absolutely terrified for you".

On the day that it all went horribly wrong and my short term memory went AWOL during messages and conversations with Pauline, she too thought that I was having a stroke and was terrified for me, not just in the moment but for the repercussions of such an event. Thankfully kept her wits about her when I suggested that I use the inhaler that I'd found in my handbag, she told me "NO!" in no uncertain terms. If you knew Pauline, you'd know that although she's a pussycat at heart, you don't mess with her – thank goodness!

I certainly have to thank my lucky stars that Pedro was working on the olive trees nearby and when he got Pauline's call, he dropped everything and came to my aid. Apparently, I was a bit strange when he arrived at my house and during our very slow decent in his truck down the mountain to the local A&E, my whole demeanour was weird, and I was bright and bubbly and kept giggling in a child-like manner which continued for hours. However, my spark had apparently gone, and I was in a different dimension to everyone else, but I can remember looking at them all and thinking how worried they appeared to be.

As I gave my family history to the Medics with Pedro translating, they were astonished at the degree of my family's heart history and Pauline says that she sat there aghast thinking "For fuck's sake, why didn't she tell me that her grandfather died pouring a cup of tea at her age?" Why didn't I? Well he was always an old man to me and so I was as shocked as anyone that I was now his age!

Pauline was by my side as the Medics gave me two injections to get my heart to relax and normalise my heart rate but when these didn't have the desired effect everyone went into a completely different mode and rushed me off to the main hospital twenty minutes away, blue lights flashing with Pauline in hot pursuit until it was no longer safe to do so. She even followed the ambulance through a restaurant carpark to avoid a traffic jam which did make us giggle. I have zero recollection of the ambulance – being put into it, the journey or anything upon arrival at the other end – *nada*!

Pauline has a medical background and told me that I was behaving in a completely different state to what she was observing on machines that I was wired up to. However, I was completely "out of it" by the time I got to the main hospital and the general consensus of opinion is that I got there in the nick of time!

When she arrived I was in a wheelchair and on a drip - I don't remember being triaged, seeing a Doctor or having a drip inserted and apparently, even at the time I didn't take in what was happening and I wasn't retaining any information. This was all very frightening for Pauline as she realised that she had the responsibility of taking everything in on my behalf. I was so disconnected from reality that when the needle dug deeper into the crook of my elbow as I flexed it, I didn't know what was causing the pain, but still I remained flippant about the whole thing to the point that Pauline remembers thinking "I know I'd be completely different to this – I'd be totally scared and probably in tears!"

For the next hour or so whilst the hospital staff did their thing, I weakened and Pauline tells me that she kept stroking my arm to keep me engaged and says that it was like watching the life fade out of me and she thought that I was about to pass out and off into the next realm. At this point in the interview we all started sobbing at once as the reality of how very close it all was hit us, but even then laughed at our ourselves!

Eventually she watched with absolute relief as I was admitted to the observation ward and she tells me that my whole body just melted into the reclined treatment chair. Both of us were utterly exhausted from the adrenaline fuelled drama but when they told her that she would have to leave for a few hours, she refused to leave until they told her what was going on but at this point there was no definitive diagnosis as we were told that I hadn't had a heart attack and I didn't have an enlarged heart.

The hospital wouldn't let me hold onto my phone or my handbag much to my irritation and they told Pauline to take these with her and return at 8pm. She says "Leaving was just horrible as I had no idea what would happen to you. I was an absolute wreck! The role as your significant other had landed in my lap that day and I was responsible for you and so I knew that I had to hold it together and I was listening to everything that they were saying and trying to take it in and then make judgement calls on your behalf. When you think about it, we hadn't even known each other very long or very well at this stage."

As she sat in a café having a coffee and a sandwich, she realised that she didn't have any money with her and had to rummage about in my handbag "which was a weird experience" in itself. I had some money tucked into my mobile phone case and so she noticed that I had lots of missed calls from our friend Tina B. As she called to relay events, she completely broke down and sobbed down the 'phone as it was all so traumatic

Tina B had said "I'm coming down, I'm coming now!" but at this stage there was no point, no-one was allowed in to see me for several hours and so the responsibility of my very existence remained firmly with Pauline who was sat clutching my handbag to her so tight and didn't let it out of her sight as she felt that my whole life in that bag. Pauline tells me "I felt so incredibly sad and couldn't get my head around the fact that I had all of your stuff in my arms. From your house to the local hospital and then on to the main hospital had been quite a significant amount of time and I couldn't help but wonder what the long-term effect of your heart pounding at such a high rate for so many hours would be because of the lack of oxygen to your brain, your heart, your vital organs – and so how would it affect your life - and this scared me as much as anything."

Pauline told me that when she returned to the hospital at 8pm I was apparently on a nasal oxygen tube; I was exhausted, and my peculiar laughing had stopped. It was then that the Doctors confirmed that I did indeed have an enlarged heart and that I had had a heart attack sometime over the last week. I still didn't take in the severity of my situation - I didn't even want to stay in hospital overnight and when I asked the staff if I could go home they apparently looked at me as if I was nuts and Pauline looked back at them with "please God don't let her out" written all over her face!

Dougie can't remember what happened when he got home as he was too stressed, but he did say that the pair of them had three or four days of absolute fear whilst I was in hospital as they have lost a few friends over the years. Dougie tells me that when Pauline arrived home that evening, she completely broke down and sobbed her heart out. They were both terrified that they were going to lose me in the days to come and having seen me at the hospital they seriously wondered whether I was going to make it.

Dougie tells me with a bit of a smile that with the emotion of it all, "Pauline was more than just a little bit cross" with me for not mentioning my family history as if she'd known, she would have bundled me into the car on that Thursday night regardless of my protests! One of the things that has hit her the hardest is, "what if you hadn't woken up the next morning?! As I drove away from the hospital it absolutely tore me apart".

Although I myself am really clued up medically, I was so unaware of my internal landscape back then and there seemed to be a rational explanation for everything that was going on with my body but the years had crept up on me like a game of What Time is it Mr Wolf?

And suddenly I was the same age as my Grandfather was when his life was snapped out of him as he poured a cup of tea.

Dougie told me that it was a terrible time for everyone in our community because we are all so close and people were distraught. The news provoked the same reaction from all who heard "What? Linda?! How can Linda have had a heart attack?!!" I can honestly say that until this interview, I personally didn't realise how terrible it was for everyone else! As he pointed out, we've all stayed here in Spain at the top of the mountain because we are all so close – we are a family, a tribe – and when one of us is unwell or going through a difficult time, we all rally round. Such is the bond between us all, that I can honestly say there was something to live for and so I fought to make sure that I did just that and enjoy every single day here in paradise with my amazing friends.

So, the advice from Pauline and myself to everyone, is even if you think that it's a waste of your and A&E's time, it's still worth getting checked out because we have a responsibility to those around us to actually listen and not ignore their contribution. When something is happening, they can see what's going on and we can't because I certainly couldn't see myself and I was so adamant that I was ok.

Joining the dots, when my dear Dad had a heavy clock drop on him from above a doorway, I was persistently explaining to Mum that he'd had a significant bang on the head and perhaps we should make the serious judgement calls rather than him because he wasn't able to see what we could see and hear. Similarly, in hindsight, I was unwell and my judgement impaired, but I carried it off so well that no-one knew – not even me!

Pedro and Pauline apparently came to see me on the Sunday and stayed for an hour and I'm told that we both cried! I have no recollection of this at all. Even now, when I'm told of events that happened and I try to recollect them, I don't know if it's a memory I'm retrieving or if I'm imagining what it would have looked like when people came to see me. I've always had such a good memory and can remember lines from movies verbatim, so this is extremely weird for me personally.

With this in mind, I may well have been told things throughout my hospital stay and simply not taken them on board so in reading this, I'd say do bear this in mind and if you find yourself in the significant other position, listen to what's going on.

Even though it would appear that I was unaware of the severity of my condition, one thing that I knew without a shadow of a doubt is no more smoking and drinking. That lodged firmly in my mind and I took it very seriously even though it still took several hospital reviews for it all to sink in. To Pauline and Dougie, this is the only evidence that I actually took in anything as I've remained positive and buoyant for the vast majority of the time. Maybe it was that I was heavily medicated and there was so much going on with decisions to make, people around me constantly, being in the alien environment of a hospital coupled with the language barrier. It could be that I didn't have time to process what was actually happening.

We got quite philosophical during the interview for this chapter and came out with some interesting points which I thought I'd share.

When body is in survival mode, every bit of energy is being utilised to stay alive and heal the heart which is in jeopardy.

The brain has an amazing function constantly checking that everything is working properly and so when my brain went into survival mode to keep me alive, it was using the minimum of energy to keep itself going and diverting my body's energy to the important functions such as life support and so maybe this is why some memories are irretrievable because from the brain's point of view memories aren't important it just wants you to survive.

During my research I discovered that delirium can be caused by medication, a stroke, heart attack, lung or liver disease, a fall, low sodium or calcium, fever, urinary tract infections, pneumonia, flu, toxins, dehydration, pain, and more.

Symptoms of delirium include confusion, reduced awareness of your environment, lack of focus, easily distracted, withdrawn, poor memory of recent events, difficulty speaking or recalling words, rambling speech, difficulty reading and writing, calling out, hallucinations, restlessness, agitation, anxiety, fear, paranoia, euphoria, personality changes and more.

If someone close to you goes through something similar and seems in high spirits as I apparently was throughout, you must get medical attention immediately to prevent permanent damage to the central nervous system.

To end of a light note, I promised Dougie that I'd relay this tale that he told me during our interview. Apparently one of his mates had had a heart attack when in his forties and when Dougie had gone to see him and found him connected to machines in hospital and looking grey and unwell, he cheekily hid a porn mag under his coat. To cheer his friend up, he said "hey, take a look at this mate, this'll make you smile" and held open the mag for him to see. Apparently, the heart monitor went bonkers and the ward Sister came marching in, confiscated it and gave him a big telling off! Hahaha!

It just shows you though, if only a visual image can have that effect on a heart, imagine what a completely interactive, energetic, in person interaction has on our heart – positive, negative or mischievous!

My heartfelt thanks go to Pauline, Dougie (RIP my lovely friend), Pedro and the hospitals' staff as without their actions I wouldn't be here today. Namaste Shiny Happy People.

SECTION 2

I am a firm believer that achieving well-being involves a multifaceted approach as the chances are that there was not a single cause for our ailment or mindset, but rather it has been an accumulation of things over the years; and so it is important to use different methods to untangle ourselves into wellness. Each has it's own place and it's own unique set of therapeutic attributes, and of course there is some overlap between aspects of each, such as working with crystals and Reiki simultaneously.

In these pages, I aim to bring to you my own experiences and insights into just some of the methods that I have practiced and frequently in conjunction with each other.

Sometimes I am drawn to use Reiki, sometimes I know that I need to combine some of the Bach flower remedies into a single treatment bottle and take this for a few weeks and all the time I'm doing The Balance Procedure daily and going to yoga classes weekly and popping one crystal or another under my pillow or in my bra!

Healing Crisis

In using complementary medicine such as crystals, Reiki, aromatherapy, massage, etc., it's good to be aware of something called a "healing crisis" which can continue for a day or two after a session. Because such therapies involve releasing and balancing our emotions so that we can return to a state of relaxation and peace of mind, they can bring events that have been stored in cells and water within our body and so our vibration, to the surface to be sent away. With that can come symptoms akin to the flu with aches and pains as well as tears and even outbursts and sometimes a memory can be brought to the surface to evaporate away from you so that it will no longer cause you dis-ease. It's a really cleansing process and doesn't last long.

As I've mentioned, I've burst into tears a few times along this journey and have always felt much better for it. Last night I resorted to a Disney movie to keep them flowing and yep, it worked a treat and my lounge floor is littered with soggy tissues and my face is puffy. As a result of all of this book writing, I've recalled the practice that was considered a normal part of being a woman a couple of decades ago, and I put on a movie that I know will have me sobbing throughout! Having a good cry and laugh at the same time brings an invaluable release. I have a rueful expression on my face as I wonder if Brad's caustic comment if I cried in front of him "oh that's it, turn on the waterworks", resulted in me pushing my emotions deeper and so I lost the ability to cry freely? As we both found out, that was really unhealthy as when the wine took a hold, a Batman style "POW" of emotion erupted out of my body in his direction. That's gives a whole new meaning to "healing crisis" doesn't it.

The fresh air and spending time with Penny-Horse charging about the countryside were my therapy then. Here are some other wonderful ways of working with yourself to bring down stress levels and have a positive effect on our body's dis-ease and so disease.

Our bodies are not designed for long-term stress; just short-term fight or flight to get us out of trouble (or into it!) and we literally damage ourselves if we allow stress to continue. If we're at the top of our stress threshold daily, then that's when the slightest thing tips us over the edge into stress-head behaviours such as anger, crying, having a meltdown and so on. As mentioned previously, the more often we behave in a certain way, the more that becomes "our personality" rather than just the occasional outburst. We might not see it, but those around us do. It might just be one or one set of people (such as work colleagues) who see this aspect of our personalities, because we're always stressed at work. They think that's who we are full-time.

I teach Masterclasses in many of these therapies as well as other wisdoms as they come to me. Take a look at my website for further information: www.LindaJaneW.me

Acupressure

The forerunner to acupuncture is acupressure which is reported to have been a traditional Chinese medicine practice 2500 years before acupuncture and as it does not involve the use of needles anyone can safely practice it – with the usual precautions in pregnancy. There are over 300 energy points along the 14 meridians which can be stimulated to clear energy blockages and promote well-being for every organ and system in the body and boy do they work!

Meridians carry energy around our body. Just as blood vessels, i.e. veins and arteries, carry blood around our body, Meridians are energy vessels and carry energy to every organ and part of us in order to bring us to life. When an energy vessel gets blocked, it results in a physical problem such as a disease or an ailment. Acupressure clears these blockages so that life force energy can flow freely through us to each of our organs and all living tissues, and balances it out to bring a state of wellbeing.

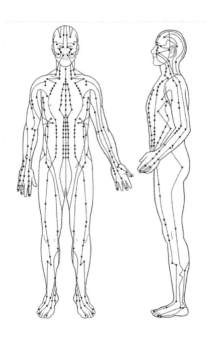

(A full colour diagram of the meridians can be found on my website: www.LindaJaneW.me on the Wakey Wake-Up Rise & Shine page.)

Acupressure is phenomenal for pain relief, diseases, nerve issues and even brain function.

For example, when I returned home from hospital I was struggling to find my words, my memory was pretty bad and brain fog had closed in on my usually sharp mind. It made me realise how precious our minds are and I was quite scared about the possibility that it was a permanent fixture, possibly as a result of a lack of oxygen to my brain at the time of it all with my rapid heart and short-term memory loss. However, I did consider that it might just be post-traumatic, a lack of caffeine or a side-effect of the medications. Whatever it was, I wasn't about to accept it and so in true Universal fashion, once I'd acknowledged it, I was sent the information by the Cosmos and I "just so happened" across some information about rehabilitating stroke victims with fingertip stimulation.

By tapping each fingertip with the tip of the thumb on the same hand, backwards and forwards repeatedly stimulates the synapses in our brain, makes repairs and encourages our brains to work properly again. It's recommended for those who have had a stroke and so in order to lift the brain fog I decided to give it a go. Much to my surprise, to begin with it was a real struggle to even unite my fingertips to my thumb-tips – I just couldn't coordinate them at all. Given that I'd been a very fast typist for 30 years and a Massage Therapist, I had always been particularly dextrous. To me that said it all and I felt that this exercise was essential for my rehab.

Fast-forward a couple of months and brain fog and the difficulty with synchronizing my fingertip tapping had become a thing of the distant past! I truly had got my mind back. So when post-Covid, the brain fog closed in again, I set about fingertip stimulation and by this time my heart was so happy and strong, that Jeremiah was happy to suggest Periwinkle Lesser tincture which is tremendous for brain fog and memory as well as regulating blood pressure which the dreaded lurgy had adversely affected somehow. I worked on the thumb web space to regulate blood pressure too.

Acupressure being the forerunner to acupuncture is healing art of using the thumb and fingers to press on specific locations in the body. It is one of the most effective self-help healing modalities, not least because you can do it pretty much anywhere, any time, without the need for any equipment. In other words, you can use acupressure on yourself as a preventative measure, to maintain wellbeing and/or heal yourself. I personally eventually realised that it was far better to practice acupressure on myself daily whilst sitting watching the TV for example, than to wait for my heart to pop out of rhythm and then work to get it back into rhythm. By working on myself every day, even for a few minutes, my health started to strengthen and episodes of atrial fibrillation or anxiety decreased significantly.

Acupressure itself can release muscular tension, promote circulation of both the blood and the body's vital energy (Qi, Chi, Ki & Prana) and enable the body to relax deeply. Indeed, whilst working on your own acupressure points, you'll often find a sigh or a wonderful deep breath spontaneously happens; your breathing slows and deepens and your shoulders drop. But remember, that practice makes perfect and it might take a few goes before you really find your body responding. By relieving stress, acupressure strengthens the body's resistance to disease and promotes wellbeing. As I've mentioned throughout Wakey Wake-Up Rise & Shine, our body is a barometer of our own, very individual feelings. It doesn't matter what others think of your feelings – if you are feeling something, it is for a reason. If we ignore our feelings and continually allowing ourselves to be angered, upset, worried, bored, pessimistic, etc. Then this dis-eases of our emotions manifest in illness. It is by no means an overnight process and by the time our body has accrued sufficient dis-eased energy to be presenting us with symptoms, we have made it harder on ourselves to reverse the process – but taking responsibility for our own wellbeing becomes so rewarding that it becomes addictive and easier by the day.

By working on the points that are specific to our own ailments, we can really accelerate along our road to recovery rather than dawdle like a Sunday driver.

In practicing acupressure, we are balancing the energy that our organs absolutely must maintain in order to achieve good health. If you're taking tablets, then be aware, that these may not be not curing you, but rather they maybe masking the imbalance and your body is likely to protest in another way – in my mind, these are the side-effects of medication; when we suddenly find another ailment pops up. It is often essential to take medication for a while because by the time our body has manifested an illness, it has been out of balance for a long time emotionally and it will take a while to get ourselves back into balance. This can involve lifestyle changes including our living circumstances, work life, social life, diet, not to mention re-educating ourselves how to "respond" to triggers rather than "react". In other words, we may have to change which people we have around us, and consciously decide how to change the way we feel when those that remain, behave or speak in a certain way. This all takes time. If only we'd all listened when our emotions said "not happy, I do not like the way this person speaks, behaves, my job, how bad I feel the morning after the night before", etc. Etc.

But, we're human, we didn't, but this is where we can rebalance ourselves with acupressure every single day and start to listen to our body, our intuition and be oh so grateful to the body that gives us life on this beautiful planet.

By way of further explanation, an imbalance in the bladder meridian results in feelings of habitual fear, indecision, jealousy, suspicion, holding onto grudges – and hence the expression "I'm pissed off" – and this often manifests in cystitis – an infection / irritation of the bladder. During my days as a Medical Secretary for a Urologist, I found that his patients with kidney stones were rather hostile, angry and rude – one actually made me cry due to his outpouring of anger at me over the telephone. In Louise Hay's "You Can Heal Your Life", she explains that the emotional cause of kidney stones is large chunks of unresolved anger. If we look at the resultant imbalance of emotions associated with the liver, we see rage, resentment, anger, irritability, jealousy, frustration and depression – something which is sadly evident in many problem drinkers. What defines a "problem drinker"? ... My ex-husband who is an alcoholic put it succinctly: "A problem drinker is when your drinking causes you or others, problems".

When we look at these imbalances, we can start to see which organ and so meridian is out of balance, with blocked energy or insufficient energy or stagnant energy maybe. And this is where acupressure can start to gently yet effectively, bring us back to ourselves, the person that we were born to be in good health, with joy in our heart and peace in our minds.

Acupressure is one of the practices covered by the term "Traditional Chinese Medicine" (TCM) and as part of this way of thinking, I was fascinated to learn that organs supply each other with energy and therefore if one is deficient, the next organ in the wheel doesn't receive sufficient energy to be able to function effectively, and so a domino effect of energy deficiency occurs and eventually the whole body becomes dysfunctional, as shown in the diagram below:

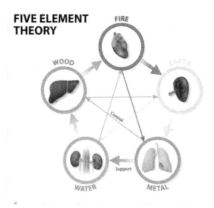

Full Colour picture can be found on www.LindaJaneW.me on the Wakey Wake-Up Rise & Shine page.

Whilst we can have blood tests to assess organ functions, tests only analyse what the machines are capable of measuring. Therefore, unless a machine has been created to measure TCM energy, it won't tell us this vital information. By practicing acupressure on ourselves we can make positive inroads in energy distribution throughout our organs.

An example of dysfunction may begin with partying too much and so challenging our liver. This would need to draw more energy from the organ upstream from it (the kidneys) who won't then be in optimal condition to do their job effectively on a physical level, filtering toxins out of the body and purifying the water retained for the body to use. In addition, in TCM terms, the kidneys also "control" the heart and make sure that it doesn't get too overenthusiastic and use up all of its energy. Er, well suddenly I understand why my bouncing around Tiggeresque style all my adult life, has taken it's toll and my heart couldn't take it any more.

➢ Liver partying.
➢ Kidneys, didn't have the energy to control my overenthusiastic heart (when I love, I'm all in, with both feet, totally and see the whole thing as a great fun adventure and I'll do ALL that I can to magic projects into reality with all the gusto, energy and enthusiasm of a Spaniel puppy – even when I got metaphorically smacked on the nose by a rolled up newspaper for being too boisterous, I'd bounce back up and off I'd go again) – oops! (Kidneys I owe you an apology for not learning sooner, to ground myself, and pace myself and observe, watch and wait (This wisdom has indeed finally reached me after my "wake-up call" and I'm more of a Cheshire Cat than a Spaniel puppy these days).
➢ Heart ran out of joy, enthusiasm, energy,

When we want to assess how our organs are from a TCM perspective, we can ask ourselves:

- Which organ(s) do we have issues with?
- Which of these emotions do we feel are out of balance (either too much of it going on, or suppressed): Fear, Anger, Joy, Overthinking, Grief.
- What symptoms do we have (if any) or take medications for?
- Which tastes do you crave: sweet, sour, bitter, salt, spicy.
- Do you find yourself easily: crying, laughing, singing, deep sighing, calling sounds

The answers to these questions gives us clues as to our TCM state of health.

Negative emotions held in the organs:

- Lungs: Disappointment, sadness, grief, despair, anxiety, shame & sorrow.
- Large intestine: Negative: Sadness, grief, worry, physical weakness, introverted, depression, irritability, discouraged, distressed, apathy.
- Stomach: Mania, hypomania, confusion, severe anxiety and hyperactivity.
- Spleen & pancreas: Worry, over-thinking, pensiveness, obsessive, remorse, regret, obsessions and self-doubt.
- Heart: Hate, guilt, shock, nervousness, excitement, longing and craving, lack of joy.
- Small intestine: Brain fog, lack of judgment.
- Bladder: Jealousy, suspicion, holding long-standing grudges.

- Kidney: Fear, loneliness, insecurity, shock (when it overflows from the heart).
- Liver: Anger, irritability, frustration, resentment, jealousy, rage and depression.
- Gallbladder: Timid, indecisive, easily discouraged.

The Qi (Chi, Ki and Prana) of the body can be drawn into the body by breathwork including yoga practice, by practicing or receiving Reiki and other TCM practices. The concept of acupressure is that the body produces it's own qi and so is self-sufficient in its ability to heal. It is just a matter of stimulating acupressure points on the body which instruct the body to send qi to rebalance and heal. It is also produced in the internal organs and circulated through the body via meridians. Just as veins and arteries carry blood throughout the body, meridians carry this life force energy throughout the body, thus giving each cell in the body, the energy the do its job, whether that is a liver cell, a blood cell, a cell that makes up part of the intestines or other organ, or a muscle cell, etc. The meridians are each named after one of the ten internal organs as it passes through that organ and their function is interconnected with the emotions associated with that organ and there are specific acupressure points along the line of the meridians.

It has been scientifically proven that the electrical impulses at that these acupressure points is significantly higher than the current running along the meridians – the energy here is highly charged and so applying pressure here provokes a significant response from the body to heal itself. Unlike Reiki when the Reiki Practitioner channels Ki, Chi, Prana, to the client, acupressure triggers the body to send its own energy to heal – depending upon which acupressure point(s) has been stimulated. E.g. heart points will heal the heart, lung points - the lungs, kidney points – the kidneys, etc.

Acupressure is also highly effective for pain as, when stimulated, they release endorphins which dampen the pain signals in the nerves.

Acupressure points can be located at landmarks on the body such as an indent close to a bony prominence, in an elbow crease, between muscles, etc. Where points are "close" to such landmarks, the distance from that mark is measured by x number of thumb's widths from there. This is unit of measurement is "cun".

After locating the point, we can stimulates it by pressing directly on the muscular knot of tension or directly into the hollow or indentation near the bone with the thumb or the fingers.

Points that are painful when pressed are considered areas where excessive energy has accumulated and so a soothing technique is called for. Points that welcome touch are considered areas of energy deficiency. Points are typically addressed on both the left and right sides of the body. Interestingly, when first working on myself I didn't know which method to use but when I tried each in turn, I naturally felt which method felt right and in which direction, ie clockwise or anti-clockwise. If I went anti-clockwise it would sometimes feel irritating but in changing direction and going clockwise, immediately my body relaxed, I would sigh and drop my shoulders and feel my face smile. Being aware of your own body's responses is a fabulous way to assess your true feelings on anything in life.

Ordinary pressure is considered tonifying to the point and can be used for both excess and deficient energy conditions. Locate the point and with moderate pressure, gradually press directly into the point with a thumb, fingertip, knuckle or even a blunt instrument (such as a pencil with a rubber on the end) at a 90-degree angle from the surface of the skin, hold for a few seconds and then release gradually. Repeat this for several minutes.

To address points that feel particularly painful or excessive, perform a stronger more dispersing technique using the tip of the thumb and applying a deeper, stronger pressure to break up the excessive and stagnant energy in the point. Hold the point until the excess energy is released. You may well find that you become tearful or shudder as the acupressure struts its stuff. As you may recall from earlier in WWRS, the first time that I applied pressure to a particular heart point I yelped as the pain was excruciating and it was a real shock. It was even more of a surprise when seconds later I burst into tears and sobbed my heart out – see what I mean about using particular expressions that relate to your own individual condition?!

To address energy deficient points, and to encourage more Qi and blood to the area, use the flat part of the thumb, relax the hands, and use moderate pressure on the point to draw energy into the area. I have found that as the energy is drawn into the acupressure point, the indent seems to plump out and a gentle sense of wellbeing starts to accumulate in my body and my being, giving me the feeling that everything is going to be OK.

Acupressure itself is a vast subject and so the way I suggest going forward, is to research online, in books, YouTube to find which points are relevant for you and your health condition. I also recruited the help of Jeremiah – my Acupuncturist – to show me which points I could trigger as my homework between sessions. We can also do an acupressure massage on ourselves over a number of days, working on the acupressure points for along the meridians. This is one of the modules in my Shine On Course, which you can find details of on my website: www.LindaJaneW.me .

In the area of TCM that I've studied, each organ provides energy to the next organ in a specific order in an eternal circle of wellbeing. The liver provides energy to the heart and therefore if our liver is struggling because of excessive alcohol intake, prescription drugs, toxins, recreational drugs, etc., then it will use all of its energy to repair itself and so it will not have enough going spare to pass onto our heart, and our hearts will then become deficient and heart disease set in in whatever form. I found my heart health and general wellbeing improved massively when I started taking the herb Milk Thistle which is well known for it's ability to support the liver.

Flower Power - Aromatherapy

I've found some amazing aromatherapy oils during my quest which have really helped to bring about relaxation and lift my spirits, cure viruses and colds and draw infections out of my body.

The oils are created by distilling the flowers, roots or bark from plants which creates an extremely concentrated oil with a powerful scent. Some of the most popular ones include Lavender, Eucalyptus, Citronella and Rosemary but my own sizeable collection also includes Ylang ylang, Fennel, Lemongrass, Teatree, Frankincense, Geranium, Black pepper, Cedarwood and many more. I also enjoy buying pre-blended aromatherapy concoctions for "respiratory", "calming", "refreshing", digestive, etc.

Even during the most anxious times of my recuperation, sometimes the smell of lavender flipped my stomach despite it being well known as a relaxant, analgesic, anti-inflammatory, great for insomnia, depression and restlessness. Instead, I'd see how my nose responded to chamomile and / or rose as these have soothing therapeutic properties too. We have to listen to what our body is telling us constantly, and most importantly act on that rather than go ahead and do it / don't do it anyway. The more we listen, the more we learn to trust ourselves and the healthier and happier we can be.

When choosing which essential oil to use, wave the open bottle under your nose. If it smells lovely to you then your body is telling you that's a good choice in this moment and its therapeutic properties will benefit you. If on the other hand it smells foul to you, then your body most definitely doesn't need it right now and it could even be harmful to you so don't use it. I joined the dots after I thought that some of my oils must have perished over time because they smelled really awful to me on a given day; but when I did an equine aromatherapy course it was explained that horses will shy away from those which they don't want and try and grab the bottle if it's the right aroma. When I returned to the "stinky" oils at a later date, they smelled divine again.

I love joining the dots as I'm a life path 7 and in The Balance Procedure, one of our traits is: "Finding the underlying answers in everything relating to nature and the meaning of The Universe is typical of a 7, who will link the practical to the theoretical and the conventional to the unconventional".

With this in mind, I did a bit of research about expensive perfumes as of course their ingredients include essential oils and I guess this is why one person can smell amazing and another, wearing the same scent, not so great – or indeed, if we think it's perished it could be because we don't need those ingredients at this moment in time.

My favourite is J'Adore by Christian Dior and about nine months after my wake-up call, I treated myself to a bottle as I suddenly felt like wearing perfume again. In writing this chapter, out of curiosity, I was drawn to research the ingredients to see if there was any link between the ingredients and why I was drawn to wearing it again; and here goes:

Lemon – energising, calming, detoxifying (liver), antiseptic, anti-fungal.

Lime – antiviral, antibacterial, reduce fever, astringent, antiseptic, disinfectant.

Mandarin orange – antispasmodic, circulatory, hepatic (liver), nervous relaxant, sedative, tonic.

Neroli – cardiac problems, digestive issues, anti-stress, antibacterial, antiviral, sedative.

Jasmine – improving mood, overcoming stress, balancing hormones, anxiety, depression, insomnia.

African orange flower – I actually couldn't find anything about this one.

Ylang-ylang – pain relief, anti-inflammatory, improve mood, libido, promote wound healing, reduce scarring.

Tuberose – antidepressant, calming relief in stressful situations, sedative, relieve restlessness, nervousness and physical tension.

Rose – hydrates skin, minimise scarring, anxiety, depression, headaches, menopause, migraines, menstrual cramps, reduces stress, stimulates circulation, sharpens the memory and boosts the mood.

Woodsy – nurturing, calming, recharging, strengthening, balancing, elevating.

Vanilla – Fights infections, antidepressant, reduces inflammation, lowers blood pressure, improves libido, PMS symptoms, prevents cancer cells' growth, antioxidant.

Well, what can I say, except that I think my Soul is guiding me once again. How wonderful to have all of these therapeutic properties in one divine scent and bottle and so I'm off to mist myself in it right now!

Whilst qualified Aromatherapists and Perfumers have the expertise, I unfortunately don't at this time and as aromatherapy oils are so wonderfully potent, I don't feel able to recommend any particular oil or blend. Nature is as powerful as pharmaceuticals in my world and so we need to use our own nose and maybe do some research to choose wisely for our own wellbeing and health and they too have contraindications.

Rosemary and Clary Sage for example can bring on a miscarriage in pregnancy and whilst many oils are fabulous for relaxation and the heart, over-exposure can have the opposite effect. Indeed, a friend of mine used to drench herself in a particularly powerful designer fragrance and on one occasion when she grabbed me into a hug, the scent remained on my clothes and I had a migraine within the hour. I always kept her at arm's length after that but I did explain why!

Because essential oils are so potent, we need to manage the dosage as we do pharmaceuticals in order to achieve our desired state so research online and in books to find which oils are appropriate for you and how and when to use them. I suggest searching "aromatherapy for ……. " and see what pops up.

When working with neat essential oils, we need to dilute them in a carrier oil so that they don't burn our skin. Anything from a teaspoon of olive oil, coconut oil, aloe vera gel, even a moisturiser will do the trick although professionals tend to use sweet almond oil or jojoba oil.

One last word is that they are so potent it is never advised to take them internally and severe overdosing can be fatal. Also be aware that they are highly flammable and so should be stored and used carefully and away from a heat source. Otherwise, enjoy nature's bounty.

Astrology – The Value of Your Natal Chart

Why are you the way you are? How do you know what you need to work on in this lifetime? As you read through this chapter, you'll realise that looking at your whole natal chart (which zodiac sign each of the planets in our solar system was in at the time of our birth) gives you a more more complete picture of who you were born to be. This shows us that there is so much more to you and your personality traits than just your star / sun / zodiac sign. That is simply one aspect of over twenty aspects of your being. It's incredible and will empower you to learn so much more quickly why you are the way you are. It explains your positive personality traits as well as your shadow side – or should I say, what others perceive to be your negative personality traits.

For example, as mentioned in this book, I was considered "over-sensitive" but since investigating my astrology chart, I can put a different viewpoint across as I now understand that I'm *very* sensitive because my moon is in cancer and I have six-out-of-eleven planets in the water signs (water signs are all about emotions), so I can't help but be very sensitive to mine and other people's energies. It is who I am.

Equally, historically, I have given people that I care about, too many chances because of Chiron's position in my chart. I have had a problem with creating and upholding boundaries, I literally feel their pain amplified – and I can get stuck in a suffering rut as I attract one lost soul after another. It's not their fault, it's more about me being held back because I either get horribly upset and behaved out of character for so long that it became my personality; and of course I felt obliged to rescue and/or fix them. This has involved me putting my own life on hold and pouring my own energies into picking them up and putting them back on their feet. When this happens constantly, it's a massive drain with not that much in return as it's not long before they're onto their next drama!

Once I became aware of Chiron's influence, I was able to extract myself from this repetitive cycle and happily create boundaries and recognise that by rescuing, I was enabling people to repeat their mistakes again and again and in doing so, I was stopping them from learning their lesson – and in doing that, I finally learnt my lesson. In doing that, I stopped attracting the same old situation and was able to take a giant step forward in my own personal growth! Whoohoo! At Last!

This is the power of astrology awareness and that is why I have included this chapter in both my book and my Shine On course when we discuss who you were born to be by looking at your chart.

How does astrology work? Imagine sitting back and staring up at the sky at the moment that you were born, and viewing the heavens as a complete circle of 360-degrees. Divide that circle into 12 equal slices of 30-degrees each. Each slice represents one of the constellations of stars that is a zodiac sign.

The slices always follow the same order in an anti-clockwise direction – Aries, Taurus, Gemini, Cancer, Leo, Virgo, Libra, Scorpio, Sagittarius, Capricorn, Aquarius, Pisces.

Each of the planets that we work with in astrology (The Sun, the moon, Venus, Pluto, Jupiter, Mars, Uranus, Mercury, Saturn, Neptune, Chiron, Black Moon Lilith) is somewhere in the heavens – in one of those slices. It might be daytime and we cannot see them, but they are there 24/7 and they are each constantly moving around this 360-degree circle, moving from one zodiac slice / constellation to the next. Each moves at a different speed around the circle and some planets take decades to complete a full 360, whilst the moon does so in 28-days.

At the time that you were born, if you'd looked up, you'd have seen that the sun was passing across whichever "star, sun or zodiac" constellation / sign you are. The sun was in the Leo slice at the time that I was born, hence I'm a Leo.

Each of these zodiac signs have different personality traits associated with them – both positive and "challenging" (negative). However, in embracing the shadow aspects rather than hiding them and pretending that they don't exist, we can truly grow and upgrade ourselves as we do so.

***

Each sign of the zodiac is also associated with one of the four elements: Water, Fire, Earth or Air - each of which has its own attributes:

Fire: Warm, hot , passionate, dramatic.

Water: Gentle, emotional, feelings, sensitive to others.

Earth: Sturdy, reliable, practical, sensual, don't mind doing the dirty work.

Air: Spend much time in their heads; talkers, thinkers, intellectual.

***

Even deeper meanings come with the three categories described as the "Qualities" of: Cardinal, Fixed and Mutable. If for example, you're great at starting things it could well be that your sign is one in the "Cardinal" group (Aries, Cancer, Libra, Capricorn). If you have great staying power then your sign is likely to be in the "Fixed sign" group (Taurus, Leo, Scorpio. Aquarius); but if you tend to go with the flow and you're a bit rubbish at completing projects, chances are that your sun sign is "Mutable" (Gemini, Virgo, Sagittarius, Pisces).

***

These Zodiac signs are as follows:

Aries (Fire. Cardinal): Spontaneous, enthusiastic, outgoing, open, frank, loves starting new things.

Taurus: (Earth. Fixed): Sees the beauty in everything, steady, stubborn, sensual, don't like being rushed.

Gemini (Air. Mutable): Chatty, witty, humerous, fabulous communicators, flirty, gossipy, playful, imaginative.

Cancer (Water. Cardinal): Loving, caring, nurturing, self-starting, sensitive, little insecure, driven by the moon phases.

Leo (Fire. Fixed): Confident, stable, show-off, dramatic, generous, grabs life by the horns, powerful, creative, extravagant, assertive.

Virgo (Earth. Mutable): Adaptable, organises and brings order, serve others, perfectionists and loves to master all that they do. Practical and dependable. Alternative health is likely to intrigue them.

Libra (Air. Cardinal): Relaxing to be around, indecisive, fair and just. Ruled by head rather than heart. Seeks harmony, diplomatic, tactful. Artistic, social.

Scorpio (Water. Fixed): Mysterious, secretive, jealous, passionate, hurts with words. Intense and determined.

Sagittarius (Fire. Mutable): Generous, lucky, show-offs, optimistic, freedom-loving, philosophical, loves travelling, brutally honest!

Capricorn (Earth. Fixed): Hard workers, focused, face life head on, ambitious and understand how to achieve it. Committed, wise, loyal.

Aquarius (Air. Fixed): Crazy, forward thinkers, non-conformist, inventive, values scientific and universal truths.

Pisces (Water. Mutable): Imaginative, receptive, intuitive, takes down boundaries, psychic, dreamers, mysterious, easy going, changeable.

***

Each of the planets is responsible for a different aspect of our personality:

Sun: Who we really are for this lifetime and what our focus is. Positives: Self, self-image, willpower, vitality, power, authenticity, authority.

Negatives: Ego, vanity, selfishness.

Moon: What I need, how I feel, emotions, sensitive.

Positives: Compassion, feeling, nurturing, instincts, intuition, warm.

Negatives: Neediness, moodiness, timid, emotionally repressed.

Mercury: How we communicate, express ourselves, negotiate.

Positives: Natural communicator, intelligent, quick witted, information exchange.

Negatives: Gossipy, superficial, inconsistent, unfocused, over-think, indecisive.

Mars: How we chase down and get what we want. Desire, action and how we argue.

Positives: Determination, courage, action, initiative, spontaneity.

Negatives: Rage, brash, aggressive, argumentative, destructive and brutal.

Venus: How do I fall in love? Romance and riches. Music. Key to your heart. Sensuality, luxury, beauty, health. What do you need from a lover?

Positives: Loving, gentle, caring, cooperation and peace.

Lazy, manipulative, weak-willed, jealous, vain.

Jupiter: Luck. Good luck charm. Believe in yourself, Opportunities.

Positives: Faith, excitement, adventure, joy, exploring, likeable.

Negatives: Overindulgence, pompous,, risks, foolish, over-confident, overbearing or complacent.

Saturn: This lifetime's lessons. What scares you. What saddens, depresses or limits you. How responsible you are. Patience levels. Self-discipline. Karma.

Positives: Commitment, discipline, integrity, longevity. Hard working.

Negatives: Fear, barriers, depression, hard-heartedness.

Uranus: Where I can't be controlled! Innovative, free spirit, independent, doesn't like authority,

Positives: Progressive, unexpected surprises, breakthroughs, non-conformity, dares to be different.

Negatives: Chaotic, unreliable, rushes in, loose cannon, wreaks havoc.

Neptune: Where we romanticise life and what inspires me. The planet of extremes. Alcohol and drugs – including drug-induced / natural divine states of being. Deception vs fantasy. Poetic, artistic vs Martyr. Trance, spiritual, paranormal. Meditative states

Positive: Enlightenment, inspiration, dreams, connection to the divine, mysticism, seeing things through rose-tinted glasses.

Negative: No boundaries, substance abuse, deluded, disappointment, worry needlessly.

Pluto: Where we control through power and manipulation! Breakdowns / reborn. Magic. Shift deadwood from your life. We erupt and lose it. Healing crisis. Healers.

Positive: Don't mess with the Lord of The Underworld! Magician. Transformation, birth, death, resurrection. Detoxification.

Negative: Destruction, power struggles, violence.

Chiron: The Wounded Healer.

Positives: Shows our vulnerabilities. Where we are extra sensitive. Gives us clear direction on what to work on to heal ourselves.

Negatives: Makes us have to change or go under. Karmic debt.

When we combine the information from the planets and the zodiac signs, we begin to realise who we were born to be and so the full picture and the insights begin! For example, in my chart, the moon is in the sign of Cancer. Moon governs how we express and manage our emotions, our innermost needs in our home and private life. Hence, as I have 4 planets in Cancer (Moon, Venus, Mars & Jupiter) and so I'm an emotional and very nurturing person when it comes to dealing with the aspects associated with the above plants - which is a lot of water and a lot of emotions and some might find that particularly overwhelming.

We can then add in our ascending or rising sign, which is taking a look at which sign / constellation was on the eastern horizon at the moment that we were born. Our ascending / rising sign, is our social image that we display in public and so how we come across.

In my case that's Sagittarius - and given that being a show-off is an attribute of both that and Leo, I'm a bit full-on at times! But, at least I understand that now and can be aware that I can easily overwhelm at times if I'm not careful!

From our natal chart we can then look at where the planets were in relation to each other in the heavens and begin to understand which aspects of our personalities / life are going to flow; and which are the challenges for us in this lifetime. These are called the "Aspects" and include: Conjunctions, sextiles, opposition, Square and Trine.

We can then look at the twelve "houses". Each of these looks after a different facet of our lives such as career, romance, home, communication, family, etc.

As we begin to explore what was written in the stars at the time of our birth, we can begin to appreciate why we are who we are and accept ourselves, forgive ourselves, appreciate ourselves, work on ourselves, recognise our shadow side and decide what we're going to do about it without guilt or blame. It's a beautiful process and that's why I decided to include it in my Shine On course as a module in its own right; and to include a very brief insight herein.

Flower Power - Bach Flower Remedies

I first discovered the Bach Flower Remedies when I was working with horses as a newly qualified Equine Massage Therapist.

The more I worked with animals the greater my connection became and I started to tune into their mental and emotional issues and so the massage for which I was called to them was only a part of the treatment that they needed in order to achieve peace in their minds, which then had a domino effect on their body and their behaviours.

Whilst the massage released tight muscles and brought a happy demeanour for a while, their more deep-seated pains would take more than a massage. I realised that these incredibly sensitive creatures, more often than not, were completely misunderstood and their feelings ignored – ah, here comes that mirror again. Almost every horse at one time or another has been separated from their herd, their mother, their family, being sold, being mistreated or bullied into a horsebox or shouted at or worse, when they were simply telling people that they were grieving, in pain or frightened.

I had to do something about their emotional dis-ease and these powerful flower remedies found me, along with a Diploma course in how to offer treatments to animals as well as people.

Interestingly, I noticed there was almost always a direct reflection of the horse's behaviour and emotions, with that of the owner and so I aimed to treat both and I believe that confirms the saying that 'pets are like their owners'. They are emotionally honest and open and show us unashamedly what we are pretending not to feel.

If I were to go to see my beautiful Penny-Horse in an upset state, she would mirror exactly that to me, even if I was showing the outside world that I was fine. For this reason, horses are often used in psychotherapy practices.

The Bach flower remedies naturally and gently release emotions which are causing us dis-ease – and to be honest these emotions are probably causing those around us upset too. If we become jealous, angry, resentful, over-protective, overzealous in our opinions and actions it can be distressing to the recipient or onlooker too.

Dr Bach worked for years with trial and error, preparing and testing thousands of plants until he had his eureka moments and found the remedies that he wanted, to address different emotional states. In doing so, he found that when he treated the personalities and feelings of his patients, their unhappiness and physical distress would be alleviated naturally as it released the dis-ease and so inspired the body's own healing ability into action and released the disease too. If we stifle our emotions this is when dis-ease is given so much power and unhappy energy that it cannot help but manifest into reality and the easiest way it can do that is with disease in our own body.

The remedies are made by using one of two methods using natural heat either from the sun or by boiling in spring water. In both cases the heat transfers the energy from the flowers and plants into the water. This is then filtered and an equal quantity of brandy is added to the energised water as a preservative. This creates the mother tincture.

There are thirty-eight Bach Flower Remedies to address thirty-eight different emotional states and Rescue Remedy is a combination of five of these. We all have these emotions but if they get out of balance and become too strong they cause us and those around us, distress. As a Bach Flower Remedy Therapist I combine several of the remedies below with spring water into a treatment bottle to make a bespoke remedy and bring about peace of mind.

Clients simply take four drops, four times a day directly onto the tongue, into a drink or even over food – which is an easy way to administer to animals. The time it takes to make a difference depends on the individual – it can be hours or a couple of weeks. There is a minuscule amount of alcohol in the treatment bottle but otherwise the remedies do not interact with medication, you cannot overdose on them and they have no side-effects.

Bach Remedy Quick Guide to Ailments and Emotions

Agrimony – Smiles and hides inner worry or grief and pretends everything is fine

Aspen - Apprehension, unknown fears

Beech - Over critical, intolerant, fussy

Centaury - Weak willed, subservient, too eager to please others

Cerato - Lack of faith in our own judgement

Cherry Plum* - Fear of losing control, suicidal, fear of doing dreaded things

Chestnut Bud - Inability to learn from our life lessons / repeating the same mistakes over again

Chicory - Possessive, controlling, hurt and tearful – what about me?!

Clematis* - Dreamy, absent minded, unable to focus or concentrate

Crab Apple - Cleansing - physically & mentally, poor self-esteem. A belief that we're not worthy

Elm - Overwhelmed by responsibility – it's just too much, I can't cope!

Gentian - Despondency, disappointment, lack of faith

Gorse - Hopelessness, despair

Heather – Over-talkative to keep someone there. Lonely

Holly - Anger, Jealousy, Suspicion

Honeysuckle - Living in the past, homesickness, always refers back to the good old days

Hornbeam - Mental tiredness, procrastination

Impatiens* - Impatience, irritability

Larch - Lack of confidence in our own abilities "I can't do that!"

Mimulus - Known fears, nervousness, phobias

Mustard - Gloom, depression for no apparent reason

Oak – When we persevere despite being exhausted

Olive - Physical & metal tiredness, exhaustion

Pine - Feelings of guilt, unworthiness

Red Chestnut - Fear for others, irrational worry, projecting worry onto others "you can't do that, what if … ?"

Rock Rose* - Extreme fear, nightmares

Rock Water – Punishing ourselves, rigidity

Scleranthus - Indecision, inability to choose, it brings balance

Star of Bethlehem* - Shock, trauma, accidents – even from the past

Sweet Chestnut - Extreme anguish, despair

Vervain - Over enthusiasm, perfectionism

Vine - Dominating, need for control over others

Walnut – To ease through changes, protection from outside influences

Water Violet - Proud, upright people, superiority

White Chestnut - Thoughts buzzing around in our head, over-talkative mind that won't stop

Wild Oat - Inability to see our direction

Wild Rose - Apathy, lack of enthusiasm

Willow - Resentment, bitterness

* These five are the ingredients in Rescue Remedy

I have found Rescue Remedy invaluable throughout my life to help me and my friends to deal with anxiety, stress or worry and trauma. If I was in an unhappy relationship, the slightest shift out of my comfort zone would have me in a dreadful state and desperate to get home to safety but when I discovered this little potion I was delighted.

After my awakening whilst I was working on my new lifestyle and the challenges that came with it, Rescue Remedy was a quick fix because it works in minutes and within half-an-hour I'd forgotten what the problem was and was able to focus and move forward. It was a tremendous benefit whilst I was working out what I needed to change within myself or my environment, to reduce stress levels, etc.

I also sometimes have the Rescue Remedy pastels which do not contain alcohol and so are suitable if contraindicated with medication or for someone with an alcohol issue.

Mindfulness

Mindfulness is being aware of what we are thinking, and consciously changing our thoughts.

For example, if a negative thought or worry is circling around in our mind and sending us down that helter-skelter into torment, we need to recognise what is happening and think of something positive in order to bring ourselves back up.

A really simple tactic is to make a mental note of what makes you happy whether that be a sunflowers, animals, forest, beach, sea, etc and when you catch yourself about to spiral downwards with a negative thought, bring that visual image into your mind and give it the power of your thoughts to break the spell.

Maybe introduce that into your daily life via a screensaver on your 'phone or a picture on the fridge or dressing table, to lift your spirits and remind yourself.

Remember:
- Your day hasn't been created yet so you can make it happen
- Don't worry about something that hasn't happened yet – it doesn't exist so it can't harm you
- Life flows for a happy person
- It's much harder to be angry or negative than it is to simply allow yourself to be happy

The power of thought delights me – most of the time! Have you ever pulled a sickie then been sick? There have been sufficient occasions in my working life to have spotted the pattern that if I felt like a duvet day and put on a croaky, poor me voice and called in sick (desperately hoping to get an answerphone or voicemail rather than a real person) I'd inevitably get the migraine or bad stomach that I'd acted out during the call!

Such was the power of my intention to convince my boss that I was actually sick, I was unwittingly sending out that signal to The Universe and it said "OK Linda. Here you go ... one migraine coming your way". Eventually, when I wised up to this, as soon as I'd hung up the 'phone, I'd look up to the heavens and say "I was acting! I don't want one thank you very much!"

Foods affect our mind:

Happy foods: Bananas, kiwi fruit, mushrooms, pineapple, dark chocolate

Hyper foods: Orange food colouring, sugar, fizzy drinks, sweets, caffeine – tea, coffee, cola

Calming foods: Chamomile tea, vanilla, celery, peaches, blueberries, dark chocolate!

Downer foods: Gluten, caffeine – can frazzle your mind and make you shut down

One of my long-term clients in the UK was suffering with dreadful anxiety and when she first came to see me for a Reiki session, she lay curled up on the couch shaking from head to foot. Her husband had to wait outside of the room as she wouldn't have been able to cope with him leaving the building without going into a full blown panic attack.

Over the weeks she improved tremendously with her Reiki, back massages and sometimes a bespoke Bach Flower remedy which I prepared for her. When I happened across the information that depression and anxiety is scientifically proven to be linked to an imbalance in our gut flora, I shared these findings with her and her husband and advised them to change their brand of yoghurt to one that is bioactive.

Her anxiety almost vanished and she became so much more confident and able to go out on her own or with a friend.

The Balance Procedure

As I've mentioned in Section 1 of **Wakey Wake-Up Rise & Shine**, my great friend and mentor Adrienne Green found me at a Holistic Fayre. Such was the impact of The Balance Procedure on my day that I cancelled my arrangements to make sure that I could attend the level 1 workshop that she was running a few weeks later. I later took part in her level 2 Practitioner level workshop and subsequently became a Trainer in The Balance Procedure as I absolutely loved its simplicity and effectiveness.

I have never looked back and The Balance Procedure (TBP) has become a major part of my life and empowered me to create my reality and to fix myself, my heart and my world. I used TBP whilst I was in hospital to manifest what I wanted to achieve and as soon as I was discharged and I realised that "this was far from over", I made TBP a fundamental part of my own daily treatment plan.

Not least I used card 4 of TBP – Heart – to instruct my body to heal itself with the affirmation "my heart is the perfect size and shape for my optimum health" and "my heart beats in a strong, regular rhythm at around 60 beats per minute". I practiced this several times a day with absolute determination as this was my time to strut my stuff and make it happen.

The tools used with The Balance Procedure are a handbook and nine Universal Symbol cards. You don't have to believe in anything but yourself and if you haven't yet achieved that, this will empower you to do so readily. I absolutely love teaching The Balance

Procedure via Zoom and in-person as my passion is empowering others to do and be all that they would wish for themselves.

The nine cards focus our attention on what we desire, whether it is relaxation, to create something using The Law of Attraction or to gain clarity on a situation and so make a decision. TBP takes us out of a stressed "fight or flight" state into a relaxed and calm state. Instead of running around in panic mode, when we are relaxed, we can see things clearly and listen to our intuition and we just know what to do.

We can use TBP for a particular situation, event or life in general. For our life path, our birthday year, to be who we were born to be - and the more we use it, the more creative we get with using it.

As I've mentioned throughout Section 1, your intuition is your best friend and has your best interests at heart. It wants you to survive and to be happy and to achieve whatever purpose you were put on this planet for.

Sometimes when I'm in a stressed state I'm not necessarily aware of it and so I find the emotional guidance scale below invaluable to identify when I need to use The Balance Procedure to bring my energies back into balance and so into a relaxed state. Jenny Cox who created The Balance Procedure has adapted the emotional guidance scale from Jerry and Esther Hicks book 'Ask and it is Given' (2004, Hay House).

I would like to thank Jenny and her husband Alan, along with Jerry and Esther Hicks' team for consenting to me publishing it herein as follows:

1.   Joy, knowledge, freedom, love, appreciation
2.   Passion
3.   Enthusiasm, eagerness, happiness
4.   Positive expectation / belief
5.   Optimism
6.   Hopefulness
7.   Contentment
8.   Boredom
9.   Pessimism
10. Frustration, irritation, impatience
11. feeling overwhelmed
12. Disappointment
13. Doubt
14. Worry
15. Blame
16. Discouragement
17. Anger
18. Revenge
19. Hatred
20. Jealousy
21. Insecurity, guilt, unworthy
22. Fear, grief, depression, powerlessness, despair

If we feel anything from 8 – 22, this demonstrates that we are out of balance

Intuitions come through thoughts but we have to actually action them in order to make the difference to our world. The more we work with TBP, the more we trust our intuition and so the more we take the action as it gives us a hotline to our intuition whenever we need to hear from it. Our intuition loves this and so will talk to us more and then it really does become our best friend with a mutual and equal trust.

Because our intuition wants the best for us, it directs us to shed the behaviours that are holding us back, let go of any skeletons in our past and ways of thinking that no longer work for us. This includes fears phobias, addictions, repeating mistakes, etc. When we start to believe in ourselves and that we have control of our life, it gives us the confidence to be who we want to be.

During a Balance Procedure coaching session or workshop, using the numerology aspect of TBP, we calculate our Life Path number which is the sum of each individual number of our date of birth. Throughout the book you've heard me mention that I'm a Life Path 7 which is the sum total of 1+3+0+8+1+9+6+6=34, 3+4=7. When we're out of balance with who we were born to be, we simply balance on the corresponding card, in my case card 7 and this brings us back into balance for our life purpose.

Once we've learned how to use TBP in a workshop, coaching session or by your own methods, using the symbol cards gives us the ability to rebalance our energies and bring balance and harmony to our world in any given moment. I've always been a free spirit – much to the annoyance of some! - but at times my wings were clipped and I was far from the person I was born to be and I was lost. With TBP I have found a continuous process to access and balance my energies and draw in the energy that I need to maintain myself and give myself software upgrades. Life is a continuous journey after all.

TBP gives us access to the universal energies of maths (numerology), zodiac, planetary influences, crystals, colour, the elements, the chakras, Reiki and sacred geometry, with the positivity of affirmations. We don't need to research these (although naturally, if any spark your curiosity, you may well find yourself wanting to learn more). However, all the information is in the TBP handbook with bullet points on the back of the symbol cards and we learn how to use these during the workshop or coaching session.

Using The Balance Procedure, we can quickly and easily ascertain which of our chakras are out of balance (and so is likely to be causing the physical or emotional symptoms associated with that chakra) , and bring it into balance in moments using the cards and as I teach during the workshops.

The difference between knowledge and wisdom is that with wisdom you actually put into practice what you know.

You can find out more on my website: www.LindaJaneW.me specifically about this workshop or as part of the Shine-On modular course.

The Chakra System

1. The Crown Chakra

2. The Third Eye Chakra

3. The Throat Chakra

4. The Heart Chakra

5. The Solar Plexus Chakra

6. The Sacral Chakra

7. The Base/Root Chakra

The word "Chakra" is a Sanskrit word which translated means "wheel", it is believed that Chakras are non-physical energy centres which are situated slightly away from the physical body and allow the flow of energy through the body. It is understood that the Chakras are akin to spinning wheels which move in a clockwise direction, and each wheel has to spin correctly to ensure that the next wheel to it also spins correctly, like cogs in an old watch, thus aligning and balancing the body's energies. If the wheels do not align correctly then it is believed that the body is not balanced correctly.

The Chakras' energy frequencies are lowest at the base and highest at the crown. Indeed, during a recent Gaia program, I learned that the faster a wheel goes, the higher the vibration is emanating from it - and in turn, this vibration / frequency changes colour - and it starts at red, ending up at the highest visible frequency of violet, in direct correlation with the chakras.

During a chakra balance session, we aim to realign the Chakras, which may have become out of sync due to stress, tension or illness, to restore harmony and balance to ourselves.

When we practice Reiki we generally work on the seven main chakras and similarly so with crystal healing, The Balance Procedure and many energy based healing systems because they are the gateway to the systems and emotions of the body and our mind.

There are seven major Chakras:

First - Base Chakra (also known as Root Chakra)

It is associated with the adrenals, and is connected to health and survival, and may relate to fear, obsessive/compulsive disorders and possessiveness.

This Chakra has a physical association with the skeleton, hair, teeth and nails; excretion and when imbalanced can be linked to digestive disorders, obesity, constipation and frequent illness.

A person with an imbalance in this Chakra can feel as if they are ungrounded and unfocused. They may feel weak, lack confidence and be unable to achieve their goals.

When balanced the Chakra is associated with stability, security, good health, optimism for life.

Crystals that relate to this Chakra include Red Jasper, Garnet and ruby.

Second - Sacral Chakra. It is associated with the reproductive organs, the kidneys and the bladder; the ovaries and is connected to relationships. This Chakra has a physical link to sexual reproduction, body fluids and male/female hormones,

When imbalanced can be linked to impotence, frigidity, uterine and bladder problems. A person with an imbalance in this Chakra may bury their emotions and be overly sensitive, can also lead to sexual difficulties and energy blocks which affect creativity.

When balanced the Chakra is associated with a zest for life, pleasure and desire.

Crystals that relate to this Chakra include Carnelian, Orange Calcite, Blood stone

Third - Solar Plexus Chakra It is associated with personality, emotion and strength. This Chakra has a physical link with the stomach, digestion and metabolism, skin, the pancreas, muscles, tendons and ligaments.

When imbalanced can be linked to lack of confidence, bad temper, stubbornness, ulcers, diabetes and poor skin. A person with an imbalance in this Chakra may feel depressed, insecure, lacking in confidence and may worry what others think. People who are under stress will show imbalance in this chakra, shock and stress have a greater impact on this Chakra as it is the solar plexus that negative energies relating to thoughts and feelings are processed.

When balanced the Chakra is associated with confidence, peace and inner harmony.

Crystals that relate to this Chakra are Yellow : Citrine, Topaz, Amber and Yellow Calcite, Brown Tiger's Eye

Fourth - Heart Chakra   It is associated with the thymus gland and is concerned with empathy and sympathy.

This Chakra has a physical link with the lungs, heart, arms, hands and immune system, and when imbalanced can be linked to heart, respiratory and circulatory problems, ulcers, fear, and resentment.

A person with an imbalance in this Chakra may feel sorry for themselves. Be afraid of letting go, feel unworthy of love or feel terrified of rejection. If the energy does not flow freely between the solar plexus and the heart, or between the heart and the throat, it can lead to energy withdrawal into the body.

When balanced the Chakra is associated with sincerity, caring and loving.

Crystals that relate to this Chakra are green and include Emerald, Jade and Green Aventurine – but also rose quartz for love of self and others.

Fifth - Throat Chakra   It is associated with the thyroid gland and is concerned with communication. This Chakra has a physical link with the throat, ears, mouth and nervous system,

When imbalanced can be linked to allergies, throat, neck and shoulder problems, shyness and tension. A person with an imbalance in this Chakra may feel unable to relax. If this Chakra is out of balance it may affect our ability to express our emotions, frustration and tension may result.

When balanced the Chakra is associated with creativity, open and honest feelings and sincerity.

Crystals that relate to this Chakra are blue Turquoise, blue lace agate, Sapphire, Aquamarine and Sodalite.

Sixth - Brow Chakra (also known as Third Eye   It is associated with the pituitary gland and is concerned with inner vision.

This Chakra has a physical link with the brain, nose, eyes, face and ears and when imbalanced can be linked to headaches, migraine, sinus issues, eye disorders, pituitary problems and insomnia.

A person with an imbalance in this Chakra may be oversensitive, be afraid of success, and be non-assertive and undisciplined. If this Chakra is not functioning correctly it can lead to headaches and nightmares.

When balanced the Chakra is associated with intuition, memory and perception.

Crystals that relate to this Chakra include Lapis Lazuli, Clear Quartz, Opal, Apophyllite and Amethyst

Seventh - Crown   It is associated with the pineal gland and is concerned with thinking and decision making.

This Chakra has a physical link with the nervous system and cerebral cortex, and when imbalanced can be linked to apathy, depression, confusion, epilepsy, inability to make decisions. A person with an imbalance in this Chakra may be unwilling to open up to their spiritual potential and show an inability to make decisions..

When balanced, the Chakra is associated with spirituality, understanding, wisdom and open mindedness.

Crystals that relate to this Chakra are: Clear Quartz, Opal, Sugalite, Amentrine and Amethyst and any crystals or gemstones that are white or clear.

Crystal Healing

I've had a passion for using crystals for many many years and teach informal workshops online and in person as well as accredited Practitioner courses for those wanting to carry out crystal healing professionally for clients. Crystals have amazing therapeutic properties and I intuitively choose my jewelry on any given day to provide me with the energetic backup that I need. I've also been known to put stones in my bra as well as my pockets and yes, it's raised a few eyebrows when wearing a summer dress and a crystal suddenly drops from about my person and rolls across the floor! It happens so often that I just laugh now and explain "it's from my bra!"

Crystal Therapy is an ancient way of healing by putting the stones onto chakra points on and around, the body and as explained in the previous chapter, each chakra (energy centre) resonates with a particular crystal of the same colour.

You can use by them by putting them on or around yourself and/or a fully clothed person to induce deep relaxation, healing, release stress and alleviate pain. Crystals also balance the body's energies which will help to maintain a healthy mind, body and spirit.

History of crystals

Crystals have been used by ancient civilizations including the Egyptians and there is evidence as far back as 2000 BC of medical cures using crystals including ground Lapis Lazuli which was made into a poultice and rubbed into the crown of the head to draw out spiritual impurities. Today we use Lapis Lazuli for protection from psychic attack, headaches, sinus issues and to assist with meditation. You'll notice that it is the colour of the 3rd eye chakra which is your psychic ability.

Native Americans are famed for their use of Turquoise and would consult their crystals several times daily to guide them and Obsidian was used as arrowheads - you may have seen this used to kill the White Walkers in Game of Thrones!

Mexicans used polished Pyrite as mirrors and the Mayans used quartz crystals for diagnosis and treatment of disease. In China quartz crystal balls were considered to represent the heart of dragons which are powerful, wise and enlightened. Jade is the stone mostly associated with China and is used for harmony, attracts good luck, friendship and it's cleansing abilities release negativity.

The very way in which crystals are formed, creates a unique energy vibration. If you recall, the Periodic Table from Chemistry classes at school, include every single chemical element known including hydrogen, carbon, nitrogen, oxygen, iron, calcium, etc,

Each crystal has its own unique recipe from the Periodic Table, cooked for a given time at a certain pressure, temperature, and affected by the electromagnetic field in the area they were formed. This all goes into creating a unique energy which is harnessed in the most beautiful crystal form.

Because we, and everything else in the universe, are all made up of the elements found in The Universe, the energy in crystals matches that of our own and so their energy can empower us to heal ourselves on a physical, emotional or spiritual level.

Examples of some crystal recipes are as follows:

Amethyst SiO_2 +(Al, Fe, Ca, Mg, Li,Na)

Diamond $Cn+$ (Al, Ca, Cr, Fe, Mg, Mn, Si, Sr, Ti)

Pyrite FeS_2+ Co, Ni, Sb + (Cu, AU, Ag, Zn)

Tiger's Eye $SiO_2+FeOOH$

Turquoise $CuAl_6[(OH)_2/PO_4l_4 . 4 H_2) + Fe$

Some people who want to use crystals have a particular purpose in mind and so when selecting a crystal, you want one which matches your vibration although as anyone who knows crystals will tell you, they pick you. For example, right before a "cat incident" in Morocco with Igor and his friend when I had a double serving of men behaving badly, I'd been mooching around the shops which were all like Aladdin's caves to me and being a magpie I was in heaven. However, a Carnelian necklace called to me and I just had to have it and wore it for the next few days during which time the mud hit the fan and I found myself alone in Marrakech. Some weeks after the event I discovered that the therapeutic properties of Carnelian include: grounding, overcoming abuse of any kind, trusting yourself and your perceptions, positive life choices and courage. Once again, thank you Universe!

When we ask crystals to heal us, it works by raising our vibrational frequency and we often crave certain crystals because we have a great "vibrational match" with them. For me it's Labradorite. I have two rings and several pendants and I have to stop myself from buying chunks of it when I go into a crystal shop.

This vibrational match means that proximity to this crystal raises our vibrational frequency, thus making us feel "good." Selecting a crystal for a particular purpose is a great way to help yourself without having to devote much energy to it.

The proximity of the crystal is constantly affecting your own frequency, guiding you upward toward your goal. Similarly, a crystal that does not have a good match may drain you by lowering your vibrational frequency and we also need to cleanse them after use to recharge their energies.

When purchasing stones be sure to feel the energy of the stone. Some people walk around a shop or store with stone in their hands to feel for any energy that it brings into their body. Some of the most beautiful stones get put back in the case, or on the shelf, while others that might not be the most aesthetically pleasing end up being the one that 'works best' for you.

Don't be afraid to hold the crystal in your hand or thinking about holding it if you're buying online for example and state your purpose: "I want to heighten my meditation practices" or "I need a crystal to help my stomach pains". Always state the purpose in a positive way i.e. don't say: "I want to stop feeling angry", try "I wish to feel inner calm and at peace when my boundaries are breached" as positive affirmations set the intent and allow the flow of energy, whereas negative sayings will trigger resistances.

Interestingly, when I first met Igor I decided to take him a present of a crystal when I was working at a Mind Body Spirit fayre one Saturday. As I didn't know him very well I asked for the right crystal to present itself. My hand went straight to a pretty ordinary looking white stone with grey veins called Howlite which I discovered teaches patience, helps to eliminate rage, pain and stress. It is a calming stone which reduces anxiety, tensions and stress and encourages emotional expression and when I presented it to him, he told me that it was perfect.

Close your eyes while you state your purpose so you can focus inward and your emotions will tell you whether it's right or wrong. If you get a good feeling, that's the one! You can also body dowse with a crystal and if we sway forward that's a yay, backwards a nay.

We have to cleanse and re-energise our crystals regularly as they can attract and absorb all kinds of vibrations, both positive and negative, it is crucial that we cleanse them to remove any negative energy – this includes any stones in your jewellery.

Remember that energies and vibrations as well as diseases, could have been accumulated by the crystal from the point that it was mined, shipped, handled, sold, shipped again, potential buyers who have handled them etc. Opal for example is considered unlucky as it is an absorbent stone and if the owner died of a disease, the sweat from the fever was said to go into the stone and then pass onto the next owner who would come down with the disease too.

In cleansing crystals, we can use Reiki, spring water, salt water, other stones which have cleansing abilities such as Amethyst and Lepidolite and then placing them in the light of the full moon is a beautiful and poetic way of recharging their energies.

When we use a crystal, it is a practice to be savoured and made into something of a ritual by holding it close to us and asking it to direct its energies for whatever our intent. This is often called "Programming".

I treated myself to a Chakra crystal set complete with Chakra symbols engraved in gold on each palmstone and as you'll see on my Facebook page Smileinside13, I sometimes take myself back to bed on a rainy day, setup a yoga nidra meditation on my 'phone and place crystals on my chakra points. I pull over the duvet and off I go into a most beautiful zone as this is an incredibly dynamic combination.

Workshops and courses on my website www.LindaJaneW.me

Reiki

Reiki is a generally considered as a hands-on healing technique which we use to heal ourselves and others. If we are working with clients, they are fully clothed, lying on a treatment couch and I like to cover them in a warm blanket so they can be truly relaxed and peaceful. I often do a Reiki treatment on myself when I'm in bed as I'm lovely and warm, in calm surroundings and if I fall asleep then the Reiki will continue working overnight. It's a wonderful practice if you're prone to waking up in the middle of the night and then can't get back to sleep.

As I've mentioned during **Wakey Wake-Up Rise & Shine**, I discovered that I had a natural healing ability but I had no idea how I was doing so or what was going on!

When I saw the sign – literally and figuratively speaking – and signed up for the Reiki workshop it was to start the most incredible journey and align me with my purpose on this planet which I believe is to heal, promote positive energy and thinking, empower people with the ability to heal themselves and bring about change from the ground up – or should I say earth – Planet Earth - up!

When we start our Reiki journey it is with level 1 which is for self-healing and our enthusiasm bubbles over into wanting to heal our friends and family too. Everyone's Reiki journey is different as we are all leading individual lives and have different aspects of our being which require positive encouragement for our own greatest good.

When we're attuned, our journey involves the following four aspects:

Healing: The hands-on healing of yourself and others on a physical, emotional and spiritual level and so we take responsibility for our own wellbeing.

Personal Growth: Issues brought to the surface, healed and released thus stimulating personal growth and development.

Spiritual discipline: Heightened awareness and self-awareness as we naturally tune into our higher consciousness. This brings a sense of responsibility for all life.

Mystical Order : As knowledge and experience grows, Reiki brings increased insights into life and The Universe.

Reiki always works to the highest and greatest good for each individual although it's not always in the most obvious way. Just as the saying goes 'God works in mysterious ways', so too can Reiki and when we observe how the energy brings about change, it's quite phenomenal.

I have been practicing Reiki since 2002 and a Reiki Master since 2007. It's said that you become a Master, not when you've mastered Reiki, but when Reiki has mastered you and from my personal experience, I absolutely agree with this. One of my joys in life is introducing people to this energy healing and way of life so that they can start to rise and shine and empower others to do the same.

I, or your chosen Reiki Master should be there for you throughout your Reiki journey whether it is to answer questions, address any issues that you encounter or if just want to chat about your latest experience.

The more open we are to receiving Reiki, the more we will receive and the stronger our connection with this dynamic energy will become and when we live our life to the Reiki Ideals, the more it seems there is no other way to exist. You may find that you already do so, in which case you feel that you're "home" as you begin the Reiki journey and that's exactly how I felt. With my years of practice, I prefer to call the Reiki ideals an affirmation or mantra* because in reciting it daily it brings about that way of being and so it becomes your way of life.

The Reiki Affirmation *(Hatsurei-Ho)*
Just for today I won't be angry
Just for today I won't worry
Just for today I do my day's work honestly
Just for today I give thanks to my teachers, my parents and my elders
Just for today I will be kind to every living creature
Just for today I count my many blessings

* A "mantra" or "affirmation" is a phrase or word which is repeated over and over again when working with energy, meditating,

practising some martial arts, healing, etc. It focuses our mind and strengthens the intent of whatever we wish to achieve at that moment.

With this in mind, by reciting the Reiki Affirmation, we are reprogramming ourselves into a more peaceful existence. By resolving not to be angry or worry, etc, instead of giving energy to these emotions and the what if's in life, we can focus our energies on creating a positive outcome for ourselves and for others.

Words and thoughts are so powerful that as I've demonstrated throughout Wakey Wake-Up Rise & Shine, if we're angry, we manifest more of that and more reasons to be angry.

The mantras associated with the Reiki symbols that we are given during our Reiki attunement, activate the different energy associated with each symbol, empowering the intent. Dr Mikao Usui was given the Reiki ideals to balance the physical aspect of his healing work and give us the tools to manage ourselves, our emotions and our health on a daily basis.

One thing is guaranteed and that is that it is life changing in the most enlightening of ways and can lead us closer to our divine life's purpose which is a wonderful experience in itself.

What is Reiki?
The word "Reiki" is made up of two words:
"Rei" is the higher intelligence, the deity, the wisdom, the source that guides The Universe
"Ki" is the life force energy that flows through every living thing.

Therefore, the word Reiki can be simplified into "Universal life force energy", which encompasses Universal wisdom to balance, heal and harmonise all aspects of a person's body, mind, emotions and spirit. Reiki's healing energy does many things. It clears blockages in the body's energy meridians – the highways along which energy flows, bringing your body to life; it repairs on an emotional, cellular and spiritual level and balances our chakras (energy centres). It can heal the past, make way for the future and take day-to-day worries away as we trust that the energy is being sent to us for our own greatest good.

In explaining Reiki, I like to use the analogy of a microwave oven:
The metal case that we see sitting on our kitchen top is our body
The microchip controlling the temperature, timer, how fast the turntable goes, etc. is our brain.
But none of that will work until it's plugged into the mains electricity to bring it to "life". Reiki is our body's electricity i.e. "Universal Life Energy".

A frequently asked question I get is "doesn't it tire you out when you're giving your own energy to heal someone?" The answer is that when we are attuned to be a Reiki Healer, we become channels for the Reiki energy and so we learn how to draw the energy in from around us and then pass it out through our hands to turbo charge our or the healee's body into healing itself.

If we ever feel that Reiki has stopped flowing when we're trying to give someone else a Reiki treatment, it is likely that we need healing ourselves and so it's time to concentrate on ourselves. After my awakening, I instinctively knew that I couldn't send healing to anyone but myself for months.

Our emotions are a good guide to our physical state and in the chapter about The Balance Procedure there is an emotional balance scale which gives us a fabulously clear indication of how to identify when something in our life needs our attention.

It is not always obvious what Reiki is up to when we cannot feel it. But simply we have to put our trust in it, because Reiki works on so many different levels it may be working on a spiritual layer for a while rather than a physical one so don't panic and think that there is something terribly wrong with you. It could be that we need to remove something from our world as it's not doing us any good, or that our higher self has tuned into the Reiki energy flow and has decided that it's time to heal an aspect of our past for example

The Reiki Tradition

Dr Mikao Usui was challenged by his students at the Christian University where he was Principal, to give them proof of the healing miracles of the bible. When he could not do this, as an honourable Japanese, he resigned and dedicated his life to discovering how Jesus healed. Despite being awarded a doctorate in the USA his question remained unanswered so he returned to Japan and visited Buddhist monasteries. He met a Zen abbot who allowed him to study sacred writings where he discovered the Reiki symbols, though not how to activate them.

He set off on a spiritual pilgrimage to the holy mountain of Kurama where he fasted and meditated until, on the 21st day, as the sun rose he saw a strong beam of light coming towards him. He lost consciousness and was shown beautiful bubbles of light of the colours of the rainbow, containing the Reiki symbols. He was attuned to each symbol and given a mantra* for each one. Dr Usui returned to Kyoto where he began to do healing work with the beggars there. After several years he noticed that some of the beggars were returning to the streets in much the same condition he had found them. When he asked them why, they said that they had found the responsibility of leading a "normal" life too much.

Dr Usui realised that spiritual healing was more important than physical healing. In meditation he received further guidance about the healing of the spirit through a conscious decision to take responsibility for one's own health and wellbeing in order for the Reiki healing energies to have lasting results.

There are three levels of Reiki – level 1 is for self-healing and that of friends and family.   Level 2 is practitioner level and enables us to send distance healing across space and time.   Reiki Mastership enables us to attune and teach others how to practice Reiki and brings the responsibility of hosting Reiki shares and offering guidance to our students as a life-long commitment.

When receiving Reiki it puts us into a most beautiful peaceful, meditative-like state. We can achieve this for ourselves or for those we are working on.   Generally speaking, when we are doing a treatment for ourselves or anyone else, we place our hands on or close to the seven main Chakras as these are the most receptive zones to receive the Reiki energy. However, I've done treatments via the shoulders as Reiki is a higher intelligence and so it knows where to go for the person's own greatest and highest good.

When we invoke Reiki's healing energy, we and our client feel heat in our hands, sometimes a tingling sensation and the person receiving the healing energy drifts into a peaceful state where healing can begin. As the Healer, we gradually work along the Chakra points throughout the treatment. Often in the early days of someone becoming attuned to Reiki, the Healer is reluctant to touch the person and that's absolutely fine. The energy will find its way just as it does when we send healing across distance and time – the only limits are in our minds and if we lift our preconceived ideas, we begin to see that everything is limitless.

A session typically lasts about one hour and during this time you as the Practitioner receive Reiki's healing energy too. I've often performed quite a few treatments in one day and I feel fabulous at the end of the day and always sleep very well – as do my clients. The first things my clients generally say is "wow, that was beautiful. I feel so peaceful". I therefore highly recommend learning this fabulous energy treatment so that you can take it with you wherever you go, heal yourself and others without the need for any equipment.

Over the years of me practicing Reiki I have encountered so many weird and wonderful experiences, not least feeling my late Grandfather holding my hand whilst I was at death's door.

Because our spiritual and mystical connection heightens the more we practice reiki, the more wonderful insights we receive which and they prove to us that animals are indeed sentient beings and worthy of respect and appreciation.

Creatures give me the most intriguing insights and horses often connected with me when I was massaging them or even when mucking out their stable so that I could relay information to their owners about their pain or upset.

Some years ago, when my mother's cat went missing for three days, I tuned in and he told me where he was – trapped in a box in a man's kitchen. I relayed this information to my mum who went and knocked on the door of the house I'd described and she was met by a very rude man who slammed the door in her face but twenty minutes later her cat reappeared. His claws were all torn and after he'd recuperated, she asked if I could tune in again to see if he had anything else to say. I relayed a few messages but doubting myself I asked him to tell me something that only he and my mum would know. He sent me a vision of my mum dancing around her bedroom. She has had a seriously bad back for decades and is on very strong painkillers so I asked her about it …. she told me that very rarely, when all the painkillers work and she is feeling good, she dances around her bedroom and up and down the hallway! "your cat has just grassed you up!" was my reply!

A few years after I had completed my Reiki Mastership – when Reiki had truly mastered me - I saw the spirit of a little girl sit up out of my client and another spirit of a young but slightly older boy hold out his hand to her and say "come on, it's time to go" and as she took his hand they drifted upwards. I was so shocked by this that it took me a couple of months to tell my client and when I did pluck up the courage, it turned out that my client had had unsuccessful IVF and the children would have been the ages that I estimated the spirits to be. Not only that, but as it was all happening, I'd had a strong sense of this healing session preventing a very serious ailment from manifesting. I hedged around this as diplomatically as I could whilst also trying to explain but my client stopped me and said that she knew on exactly which Reiki session it had happened as the pain that she had felt was so immense that she had almost asked me to stop, but a knowing within her told her that the process had needed to complete. My client and her husband now regularly see and have conversations with their spirit children in the woodland of their garden and it has brought them peace and love instead of the pain and disappointment of unsuccessful IVF. It's this kind of event which makes me so incredibly grateful that I have the gift of Reiki and the ability to attune anyone else to enable this gift within them.

Because I ask Reiki when I start a healing session, I often get insights drop into my head so that I can kindly tell my clients what they need to hear in order to release what is causing their dis-ease or disease. Furthermore, I often feel the pain that the client is going through as I am clairsentient (I have a gift for feeling what others feel) and again this helps me to empower them on the road to recovery.

Reiki is a very personal journey and these occurrences are welcomed by me. Not everyone will and if you don't want to get them then you won't as it's for your own greatest and highest good and freaking you out won't achieve that.

Reiki is practiced in many hospitals in the UK by Nurses, and is readily available in many Maternity Units and Oncology Departments and indeed, MacMillan Nurses recommend Reiki as it helps patients to manage their situations with calm and to boost whatever is needed within themselves at that time.

For details of my workshops, please visit my website: www.LindaJaneW.me as I offer Reiki attunements in person as well as virtual online courses on a one-to-one basis or for groups.

Yoga

When I first told my private Cardiologist that I had managed my arrhythmia naturally, once the machines proved that it was true and that I wasn't deluding myself, she asked "how? Yoga?" at that point my body wasn't strong enough to have done much in the way of yoga but her two words were to inspire me to want to reconnect with my yoga practice as soon as I was able.

Not only that, but those two words also encouraged me to actually go to my weekly yoga class even if my heart was feeling a bit fluttery, instead of fearfully staying home in case it proved too much for me and I flaked out.

On the two fluttery occasions that I have had to-date, during these classes my body achieved a beautiful calm and the flutters disappeared half–an-hour into the hour-and-a-half long session which both delighted and amazed me.

In providing an overview of yoga, rather than piece together research from across the internet, I asked my inspirational friend and Yoga Instructor, Tanya, if I could interview her so I could get it straight from the horse's mouth so to speak. Tanya was one of my first friends and clients in Spain and we hit it off straight away and I continue to admire her perspective on life, yoga and The Universe.

The "physical" practice of yoga is called "Asana" which is the name for the body postures, each Asana having a name such as "tree" pose, "frog" pose, "child" pose, "downward dog" pose, etc.

These asanas don't just work on our physical body, they work on an energetic level too by encouraging the flow of energy through our body's energy channels which are known as "meridians" in Chinese medicine, or "nadis" in yoga terms.

In Yoga there are five bodies of energy which are called sheaths: Physical (food body), Prana (energy), mind (emotional), intellect (wisdom and knowledge) and Bliss (pure light).

With the exception of the Bliss body which is our pure love and light, each body affects the other - up and down the scale - and so if something is going on in your emotional body it affects your physical body and visa-versa; your emotional body affects your energy body and so on.

Therefore, when we practice asanas and move the physical body, it has a direct effect on our emotional body i.e. our emotions. Even our ethics, morals and our inner growth through acquisition of knowledge are affected by movement as our energy sheaths are freed up to receive information into the intellect body of energy.

To my mind, this really reinforces the old adage that "exercise is good for you" – not only for our physical body, but exercise actually releases those emotional blocks that are causing dis-ease and so disease, and indeed Louise Hay and Dr Bach have been crusaders of this belief in more recent years.

At various points in my yoga practice over the years, I have found myself crying softly during or after one of the heart opening asanas so I personally can understand this from a layperson's perspective and it is interesting that in the years running up to my heart attack, I obviously had no idea that this was going to happen but the yoga practice most certainly did release feelings of hurt and upset.

Prana is the life force energy that gives every living thing life. In Reiki terms it is the "ki", in Chinese medicine it is "chi" and it flows throughout the body via the lymphatic, circulatory and nervous systems.

Because our Prana body and our Physical body are very closely interlinked, this is why we practice asanas to prepare the body for the higher practices of yoga which is where we come into stillness.

"Pranayama" is practice of breath control in yoga. As we have explained, Prana is life force energy and so when we learn to control the breath, we are taking control over our very "life" "force" "energy".

We can influence our pranic body through our breath because this is the most physical way to access the pranic body and is something that we can regulate if we consciously decide to do so.

"Pratyahara" is the practice of drawing the senses inwards. When practicing asanas and pranayama, it prepares the physical body and prana body for being able to manage our yoga practice.

I can relate to this from my Reiki perspective as when I was becoming more enlightened and filling with love and light during my Reiki practices, any negativity from around me was physically painful. I had to stop reading newspapers and watching the news and even violent movies were toxic to me and upset me to the core and as Tanya said, the madness that we become aware of can in turn drive us crazy if we draw such negativity inwards.

Therefore, with yoga we start with our physical body and we learn how to control it with the movements and postures to make our body healthy. As the different poses work on different parts of our body, practicing these asanas shifts stagnant or negative energy and brings about good health.

The Asanas aid digestion, physical strength and mobility. It is important to note that flexibility is not as important to start with, but will come about from being healthily mobile in your body. Mobility is much more important than flexibility and working within our comfort zones rather than competing with the mat next door!

To me this is fascinating to hear because whilst writing this book, when recalling a particularly dark event which led up to my heart attack, my body tightened.

I was so engrossed in recounting the tale and when I snapped back into the present moment in my mountain *casa*, I felt an uncomfortable tightness from my solar plexus chakra (emotional chakra) all the way down to my root chakra (responsible for feeling safe) along with heart palpitations. My abdomen felt tender and as tight as a drum and so I tried several of my holistic practices which in the past had worked a treat but this particular episode felt different and I didn't understand why.

This is one of the two occasions I mentioned above when I did indeed go to my yoga class and it was resolved within half-an-hour. It probably helped that it was Valentine's day and so Tanya had focused the class around our heart – which was perfect for my moment!

This is a great example of what Tanya explained, in that as we are moving our physical body, it helps to release the baggage that we've stowed away. We can't release it from our Prana body or our emotional body until we move our physical body because it is literally stuck in the physical body.

We therefore must move our physical body as this then has the desired knock-on effect on our emotional body and helps to release those trapped dis-eases. We also have to release something emotionally to release something physical - it's a two-way street - and so my tears were the emotional release to facilitate the physical release!

It is really important that we work on all aspects of ourselves i.e. physically, emotionally and mentally. We start on our physical because it's the easiest thing to access because it is tangible and we are more in touch with it. We can see it, feel it, sense it, and then things start to happen as the synergy between four of our yoga bodies become more coherent.

If we feel physically ill it affects our mind too, so the healthier we keep our body, the healthier our mind and visa-versa.

In striving for a healthy body we reiterate that this is defined by mobility and not being underweight or overweight. The Asanas will bring you back into balance and what is the right weight for you as an individual and so yoga will not make you lose weight if you don't need to.

Yoga is not just a physical practice - it goes beyond that, but many people in the west only understand yoga as a physical form of exercise.

However, many of the practices I use also come under that heading and so when my Cardiologist said "yoga?" I actually was - I was meditating, channelling and rebalancing life force energy that gave the body known as Linda, life. I found and practiced self-love, drawing my senses inwards and being aware of myself and my inner self.

When we're not practicing pratyahara, our awareness is in the outside world, e.g. "I've got to go out partying and have fun" or "I have to go to work even though I don't feel well" but now my awareness is very much within my body. I have to listen to my heart, feel my heart, feel any anxiety or stresses in my body, notice how I'm feeling mentally or as Tanya so eloquently puts it 'internal landscape awareness'. I no longer cut them off by busying about forgetting to eat or having a coffee instead of resting. It is about being aware of what's going on within.

Meditation is part of yoga and is considered the last step before we reach the final step of yoga and what we practice is called "dharana" or focused concentration. During this practice, pick something to focus on such as a flower, a candle flame, or a rock (do you know that in Japan there are parks where people go to contemplate the rocks) and try not to take the mind elsewhere – this is also known as "mindfulness".

Mindfulness is achieved by focused concentration, and when we become that focused we become in communication with it - we are no longer aware of anything else other than our point of concentration - THEN we are in meditation. When we can sustain that and we are no longer aware of "self" as an individual because we have achieved an enlightened realisation of the whole. A knowing of what we are. In "Samadhi" – we are it, we feel it, on a completely different level and we have experienced it rather than knowing of it.

To use the analogy that you can know of the existence of a red rose but until you see it and smell it, touch it you haven't experienced it.

Once we have an understanding of ourselves, we can take a grounded way of looking at death and it no longer overtakes us with fear. We know that we are energy and so if a loved one is dying, it is only their physical body and so their energy continues to exist. When we understand life on that level, whilst it is painful to lose someone, it is easier to come to terms with as we understand that this is simply our loved one continuing out of their body.

I found exactly this scenario with both Penny-horse - my beloved beauty of a beasty of fifteen years - and more recently with my cat Princess Jade. By appreciating the circle of life, I was able to use Reiki to ease them into the spirit world and so help them both to move forwards in their journeys. As Tanya explained, if I'd held on to them too much, then their spirits could have found it difficult to leave and go where they needed to go.

With the heightened awareness from yoga practices we can understand that we are emotional beings and we are here for a reason, to experience things and to learn and to grow.

When people don't learn from experiences and continue round in the same pattern, it's a shame that they are still suffering rather than moving forwards but who is to say that we ourselves weren't in that place a couple of lifetimes ago? We need to go through these experiences to reach where we are in this lifetime. There needs to be people at different levels for us to observe and to show us the things that we need to know by providing a reflection of what is alive inside of us. If everything is white we don't see it - you can't see white on white - so we have to see colours, tones and shades, of everyone being different.

If someone is doing better than us, they are showing us the way because they have come into our awareness and showing us what we want to aspire to and so it is up to us to then work with that awareness and do what we can to achieve it.

It also shows us how far we have come when we no longer react, behave, etc. In that way and so we can appreciate ourselves rather than feeling that we are not good enough because we see those who we think are better than us. Or on the flip side of the coin, looking down on someone thinking 'get a grip!'

When practicing Asanas, don't put too much effort in to start with and try not to feel that you should be looking a certain way and avoid getting competitive with your poses. It is your own individual practice and so how it feels in your own body is the key.

Each Asana is a shape or form inspired by nature. When putting our body into that shape, there is no universal alignment because there is no universal body - we are all completely different and so although some yoga schools may dictate that you should, you don't have to achieve perfection.

Within the shape of the asana there are lots of different ways that we can adjust it to work for our body and we should always listen to that. The amount of effort that we put in, is not measured by how forcefully we are achieving the pose, it is measured by how steadily we can maintain the rhythm of our breath whilst holding the posture.

If we are putting in too much effort then our breathing can be laboured. However, If we are putting in the right amount of effort to hold ourselves nicely in the posture, and we are feeling expansion in our body, our breath is easy and we feel physically lighter, then that is the right level for us as an individual. We should feel light and at ease.

If we are not putting enough energy into the posture then our body will feel a bit floppy, maybe heavy and so we need to draw more Prana energy into our being through breathing to lighten ourselves.

When you first start doing yoga you might find that your body does feel heavy or that you huff and puff as chances are there is a lot of emotional, physical and mental debris to shift. Then as you continue your yoga practice, your body then starts to get use to the postures, strength and a knowing in the body like muscle memory "where did I feel good? Where was I struggling?" There is a transition period so go for ease in the body and the breath.

We don't have to practice for a whole hour a day, just do ten minutes here and there and it all adds up and then integrate it into your life.

I found this myself the other day when the backs of my legs tightened up and so I used some of the yoga practices that Tanya teaches and after just ten minutes they had loosened up. As you'll have read in my journal, the tightness in my legs was directly associated with my cardiovascular system having a bit of a struggle at that time. By loosening my leg muscles, the blood vessels loosened up, and my heart was at ease again.

Yoga postures can be incorporated into daily life in order to bring about health and well-being. Do check out my website for information on our Posture Awareness course.

My thanks to Tanya for her inspirational words. Namaste.

Printed in Great Britain
by Amazon

21974230R00175